Jesuit Studies

Contributions to the arts and sciences

by members of the Society of Jesus

JESUIT STUDIES

Bishop Lancelot Andrewes

JACOBEAN COURT PREACHER

A STUDY IN EARLY SEVENTEENTH-CENTURY

RELIGIOUS THOUGHT

Maurice F. Reidy, s.j.

LOYOLA UNIVERSITY PRESS

Chicago, 1955

IMPRIMI POTEST: William E. FitzGerald, S.J.
Provincial of the New England Province
August 1, 1955

IMPRIMATUR: ✠ Samuel Cardinal Stritch
Archbishop of Chicago
August 5, 1955

During the last thirteen or fourteen years of Elizabeth I and throughout the reign of James I, Lancelot Andrewes preached a constant invitation to the pursuit of a vigorous Christian life. He stepped into the vulgar Jacobean court, the outstanding preacher of his age, and taught an asceticism compounded of penance, fasting, abstinence, and personal devotion to Christ. Legitimate successor of Hooker, logical predecessor of Laud, he was a leader in the movement which finally determined that the English Church be Anglican, and not Calvinist as it might well have been; on the other hand, he was a most articulate defender of the new Church against the strong challenge of the Catholic champions Cardinals Bellarmine and Perron. English history still lacks a satisfactory appraisal of Lancelot Andrewes and his work. This study analyzes that part of his writings which Andrewes himself considered his chief work, and which, so far, has been examined principally for form rather than for content. Upon the composition and the delivery of his numerous sermons Andrewes expended most of his energy and his hours of labor, yet his controversial writings and particularly his devotional masterpiece, the *Preces Privatae*, a remarkable mirror of his intense interior life, have commanded far more attention than the sermons. Indeed, the *Preces Privatae*, which he apparently never intended for publication, have become his greatest title to fame and truly deserve the acclaim they continue to receive. In his excellent work, *The Preces Privatae of Lancelot Andrewes*, Canon Brightman produced a definitive study which eliminates need for specific treatment of the *Preces* here.[1] Through the efforts of Professor McIlwain, Father Brodrick, Bishop Frere, and Canon Ottley, Andrewes' controversial writings, the *Tortura Torti*, the *Responsio ad apologiam cardinalis Bellarmini*, and the *Two Answers to Cardinal Perron*, have been sufficiently examined to justify the omission of any direct consideration of them in the present study.[2]

By the peculiar quirks of history Lancelot Andrewes is better known through the accidents of his career than through those writings which in his own judgment were the essence of his labors. I have sought, therefore, to analyze the dogmatic content and the ascetical doctrine of the most authentic Andrean sermons by summarizing what might be called Andrewes' "public" thought and by trying to answer within reasonable limits the question: What did Lancelot Andrewes preach to his Elizabethan and Jacobean court audiences on the subject of Christian doctrine, Christian ascetical practice, and the relation that exists between the two?

Three further studies of Andrewes might still be made. First, his teaching should be submitted to a careful comparison with the writings of his contemporary Anglican theologians, Hooker, Laud, Cosin, Donne, and others, in order to determine more precisely where he belongs in this second generation of Anglican leaders; this study should afford a basis for such a comparison. Secondly, Andrewes deserves a biography. No completely satisfactory biography has yet appeared; in fact, one may not be possible, for only a limited amount of material is

---

[1] F. E. Brightman, translator, *The Preces Privatae of Lancelot Andrewes* . . . (London, 1903).

[2] See *infra*, 7-8.

available. However, a collation of the biographical miscellany in Volume XI of Andrewes' *Works*,[3] a search among the letters, diaries, and biographies of his numerous correspondents and friends, a study of his episcopal registers (where they are still extant), his *Libri detectorum,* and other sources might well bring to light new material which would make possible a more formal biographical study than anything we now have. Finally, a study of Andrewes' influence on the Oxford Movement might sharpen our understanding of that nineteenth-century Anglican revival.

The most valuable account of Andrewes' life, and the one on which nearly all others depend, is that of his amanuensis, Henry Isaacson, who lived with him and frequently attended him at court. Unfortunately, *An Exact Narration of the Life and Death of Lancelot Andrewes* is very brief.[4] An even shorter but still valuable contemporary notice is an extract reprinted in the *Works* from Sir John Harington's *A Briefe View of the State of the Church of England.*[5] A third account, also by a contemporary, is the sermon preached by John Buckeridge, bishop of

---

3 [J. P. Wilson and James Bliss, editors], *The Works of Lancelot Andrewes, Sometime Bishop of Winchester* (in *Library of Anglo-Catholic Theology*), 11 vols., Oxford, 1841-1854, herein referred to simply as *Works.* The *Works* were published with varying title pages from 1841 to 1854. In 1854 new title pages were issued for the separate volumes, each bearing the general title used above plus a subtitle for the individual volume. References to material from other authors reprinted in the *Works* will be introduced by the word *Works* and the volume number, followed by the author's name, the title of his work, and the page numbers as they appear in the *Works.* In handling Scripture I have kept throughout the texts and references as they appear in the *Works.* The references are accurate, but there are variations in the wording of some of the Scripture quotations. Since what appears in Andrewes' writings is the material on which he was working, I have kept the Scriptures in that form. For further comment on this problem, see *infra,* 32-33, and the editor's discussion, *Works,* I, v-viii.

4 *Works,* XI, Henry Isaacson, *An Exact Narration of the Life and Death of . . . Lancelot Andrewes, Late Bishop of Winchester . . . ,* i-xxxiii.

5 *Works,* XI, Sir John Harington, *A Memoir of Bishop Andrewes* (from his *A Briefe View of the State of the Church of England*), xxxv-xxxviii.

Ely, at Bishop Andrewes' funeral.[6] All three are sympathetic, firsthand reports, but are lacking in detail. In addition to the first two items the editor of Volume XI of the *Works* has published therein eight of Andrewes' letters, a table of the principal dates in his life, a chronological list of his writings, and his will, and has heavily annotated all the biographical material in the volume from numerous standard sources of information on Andrewes' period.[7]

Later authors who have written specifically on Andrewes have supplied very little new material. John Henry Overton's "Lancelot Andrewes" in the *Dictionary of National Biography* is an excellent notice with a fair bibliography.[8] A rather odd and loosely constructed work containing a mass of information not entirely relevant is Arthur T. Russell's *Memoirs of the Life and Works of Lancelot Andrewes,* which tries to capture Andrewes for the Low Church.[9] Throughout the *Memoirs* Andrewes frequently drops far from sight in the morass of biographical detail which crops up around almost every name appearing in the text. Quite superior is Robert L. Ottley's *Lancelot Andrewes,* which considers Andrewes under the natural headings of preacher, prelate, and theologian. But this, again, is not a definitive, full-length study.[10] The most recent approach to a serious biography, Douglas Macleane's *Lancelot Andrewes and the Reaction,* barely hints at the reaction in which

[6] *Works,* V, John Buckeridge, *A Sermon Preached at the Funeral of . . . Lancelot Late Lord Bishop of Winchester . . . Southwark . . . the Eleventh of November,* A.D. *MDCXXVI,* 257-98.

[7] See, for example, *State Trials,* Strype's *Whitgift,* Birch's *Court of James I,* Winwood's *Memorials,* and so forth.

[8] John Henry Overton, "Lancelot Andrewes." In Leslie Stephen and Sidney Lee, editors, *Dictionary of National Biography* (Oxford, 1921-1922), I, 401-05.

[9] Arthur T. Russell, *Memoirs of the Life and Works of the Right Honorable and Right Rev. Father in God Lancelot Andrewes, D.D., Lord Bishop of Winchester* (London, 1863).

[10] Robert L. Ottley, *Lancelot Andrewes* (Boston, 1894).

Andrewes played so prominent a part, and so fails to execute the promise of its title. Nevertheless it does contain numerous suggestions on his life, work, and historical significance.[11] Florence Higham has recently published a brief, sympathetic study, *Lancelot Andrewes*, which makes good use of the sparse bibliographical material available.[12]

Less pretentious than any of the preceding are a number of essays dealing with Andrewes from specific and limited points of view. A paper by Gerrard Thomas Andrewes, entitled *Bishop Lancelot Andrewes and His Influence on the Church*, contributes nothing new.[13] Walter Howard Frere's *Lancelot Andrewes as a Representative of Anglican Principles* depends too much on Andrewes' controversial writings against Cardinal Perron.[14] Hugh Ross Williamson's "Lancelot Andrewes" in his *Four Stuart Portraits* is a recent and very unfavorable appraisal.[15] Its hostile treatment vigorously challenges the traditional picture of the "good and gentle Andrewes" which S. R. Gardiner drew.[16] In passing judgment in his *Four Stuart Portraits*, Ross Williamson also places too great an emphasis on the controversial writings, a procedure that cannot be considered as completely fair, for Andrewes was not essentially a contro-

---

[11] Douglas Macleane, *Lancelot Andrewes and the Reaction* (London, 1910).

[12] Florence Higham, *Lancelot Andrewes* (New York, [1952]).

[13] Gerrard Thomas Andrewes, *Bishop Lancelot Andrewes and His Influence on the Church* (Winchester, 1906). Rev. Gerrard Thomas Andrewes was a collateral descendant of Bishop Andrewes. His son, Rev. Lancelot Andrewes of Oriel College, Oxford, assured me that he knows of no family papers which might contribute to our knowledge.

[14] Walter Howard Frere, *Lancelot Andrewes as a Representative of Anglican Principles* (London, 1899). It is clear that Andrewes is one of Frere's heroes. See Walter Howard Frere, *The English Church in the Reigns of Elizabeth and James I. (1558-1625)*, in W. R. W. Stephens and William Hunt, editors, *A History of the English Church* (London, 1904), V, *passim*.

[15] Hugh Ross Williamson, *Four Stuart Portraits* (London, 1949), 61-82.

[16] Samuel R. Gardiner, *History of England from the Accession of James I. to the Outbreak of the Civil War 1603-1642* (London, 1899), II, 120.

versialist.[17] A formal biography, however, must take account of Ross Williamson's attack.

Attention should be called to the various introductory and prefatory remarks which frequently accompany editions, translations, and studies of Andrewes' *Preces Privatae*. The most thorough of these brief notices is the biographical section of Brightman's *The Preces Privatae*.[18] The most provocative is Whyte's *Lancelot Andrewes and His Private Devotions*. Quite in the spirit of Williamson's appraisal is the following passage. With his appointment to the bench of bishops, Whyte writes,

> that sad drop and deterioration of Andrewes' character began which cannot be kept hid from any unprejudiced reader of his life, and which stands written out in a sea of tears the bitterness of which every reader of sensibility must surely taste on every page of his penitential *Devotions*.[19]

Very little of the manuscript material which the writer examined in England has been used, for most of it was irrelevant to the problem of this study.

Among the many scholars in England who generously aided the writer in his search for material on Andrewes were E. A. B. Barnard, keeper of the Ely Episcopal Archives; Canon Norman Sykes, of Emmanuel College, Cambridge; Sir Ellis H. Minns, president of Pembroke College, Cambridge; Canon Claude Jenkins of Christ Church, Oxford; the Reverend Lancelot Andrewes of Oriel College, Oxford, a collateral descendant of Bishop Andrewes; Professor J. E. Neale, of the Institute of Historical Research; and two American scholars then resident in England, Professor Wallace Notestein of Balliol College,

---

[17] Perhaps the same comment may be made respecting Brodrick's treatment of Andrewes. See James Brodrick, S.J., *The Life and Work of Blessed Robert Francis Cardinal Bellarmine, S.J. 1541-1621* (New York, 1928), II, 169-260.

[18] Brightman, *The Preces Privatae*, xxv-xxxviii.

[19] Alexander Whyte, *Lancelot Andrewes and His Private Devotions; a Biography, a Transcript, and an Interpretation* (Edinburgh, 1896), 8.

Oxford, and Leslie Hotson, who kindly sent the writer all the Andrewes references in his remarkable file. Their lordships, the bishops of Chichester, Ely, and Winchester, Andrewes' former sees, graciously aided the writer by extending permission to consult their respective archives, or by reporting thereon.

Reverend Philip J. Donnelly, S.J., of Weston College and the Gregorian University; Reverend John W. Moran, S.J., of Weston College; Reverend William L. Lucey, S.J., of the College of the Holy Cross; and Reverend John F. Shea, S.J., of St. Robert's Hall, kindly read the manuscript and made several useful suggestions for which the writer is most grateful. To the staffs of many libraries, particularly that of the Library of the Boston Athenaeum where he did his basic research, and the Dinand Library of the College of the Holy Cross the writer acknowledges his sincere thanks for patient assistance. To Dr. Wilbur K. Jordan, president of Radcliffe College and professor of history at Harvard University, the writer owes his deepest debt for generous and sympathetic guidance and encouragement during several years of pleasant association at Harvard. All errors, inaccuracies, and shortcomings are, of course, the author's responsibility.

M. F. R.

September 8, 1955
Feast of Our Lady's Nativity

CONTENTS

CHAPTER I

Lancelot Andrewes
and His Work

Lancelot Andrewes (1555-1626) led a life of profound routine which was broken principally by his frequent preaching before Elizabeth and James I and their respective courts. Indeed, its most exciting events seem to have been his escape from death through the miscarriage of the Gunpowder Plot, which he describes so vividly in his sermon on the seventh anniversary of that fateful day, and a second escape from death, or at least from serious injury, when he fell from his mount while riding one day in 1611 with his friend Isaac Casaubon, the scholarly Swiss theologian who had recently come to England.[1]

Oldest of thirteen children, Lancelot Andrewes was born in 1555 in the parish of All Hallows, whose badly blitzed church lies within sight and easy walking distance of Southwark Cathedral where he lies buried.[2] As a youth Andrewes manifested such talent and enthusiasm for study that two schoolmasters

---

[1] *Works*, IV, Gunpowder Sermon IV, 272-73; *Works*, XI, Appendix C (chiefly extracts from Casaubon's diary), lxxxiii.

[2] This biographical sketch follows Isaacson's *Exact Narration*. Material from other sources will be acknowledged. Dates, except where otherwise noted, are taken from *Works*, XI, Appendix A, "Table of the Principal Dates of Bishop Andrewes's Life, with Further Notices," li-lix, and Appendix B, "List of Works, with Biographical and Other Notices," lx-lxxii.

contended for the honor of educating him. Studying first at the Coopers' Free School in Ratcliff and then at the Merchant Taylors' Free School in London, he attained to an excellence in Greek and Hebrew, but became so engrossed in academic pursuits that his parents and masters had to force him to take recreation.[3] In 1571 his industry and promise won him a scholarship at Pembroke Hall, Cambridge, where he was to be associated for some thirty-five years. Following successful competition for a vacancy with Thomas Dove, afterwards bishop of Peterborough, Andrewes, who had obtained a bachelor of arts early in 1575, was chosen fellow of Pembroke in October 1576. Meanwhile, without his knowledge, he was nominated scholar at the new Jesus College, Oxford, by its founder Hugh Price.[4] He was admitted to the degree of master of arts at Cambridge in 1578; ordained deacon in 1580 and priest in 1581, in which year he was serving as senior treasurer of Pembroke.[5] He took his degree of bachelor of divinity in 1585, succeeded to the mastership of Pembroke four years later, and received his degree of doctor of divinity probably in the same year.[6]

In this academic prelude to his ecclesiastical career, then, Andrewes had climbed well toward the top; it was in fact through his work at Pembroke that his fame spread and the way to ecclesiastical preferment opened up to him. Shortly after receiving his degree of master of arts he was appointed catechist in Pembroke. His Saturday and Sunday afternoon lectures on the Ten Commandments in the college chapel drew hearers from many of the other colleges and from the countryside roundabout. These resulted in his *Pattern of Catechistical Doc-*

---

[3] *Works*, V, Buckeridge, *Funeral Sermon*, 289.

[4] Andrewes was also incorporated a master of arts of Oxford in 1581 (*Works*, XI, v, note p). His university life, however, was spent at Cambridge.

[5] See Macleane, *Andrewes and the Reaction*, 27, for the date of his ordination to the priesthood.

[6] *Works*, XI, viii, note h, and Appendix A, li.

trine, first published in 1630, a second edition following in 1641.[7] Quite naturally, it would seem, for a man engaged in such work, Andrewes developed into a sort of father-confessor and was "deeply seen in all cases of conscience, and in that respect was much sought unto by many, who ever received great satisfaction from him in clearing those doubts which did much perplex them."[8]

In 1586 his renown brought him to the attention of Henry Hastings, earl of Huntingdon and president of the North, who forthwith chose him chaplain. Accompanying the earl on a journey through the North, Andrewes preached frequently and held private conferences with recusants, many of whom, priests included, he is said to have won to the Protestant religion.[9] In 1589 he came into the favor of Sir Francis Walsingham, secretary of state to Queen Elizabeth, who procured for him positions as vicar of St. Giles without Cripplegate, prebend and residentiary of St. Paul's, and prebend of the collegiate church of

---

[7] *Works,* VI, *A Pattern of Catechistical Doctrine. Wherein Many Profitable Questions Touching Christian Religion Are Handled, and the Whole Decalogue Succinctly and Judiciously Expounded,* 1-286.

[8] *Works,* XI, Isaacson, *Exact Narration,* vii. Andrewes continued a like practice when he held the prebend in St. Paul's to which was attached the office of penitentiary. "While he held this place, his manner was, especially in Lent time, to walk duly at certain hours in one of the aisles of the church, that if any came to him for spiritual advice and comfort, (as some did, though not many,) he might impart it to them" (*Works,* XI, Harington, *Memoir,* xxxvi-xxxvii).

[9] This type of work was most congenial to Andrewes, and he was frequently assigned to it. In 1593, along with Alexander Nowell, dean of St. Paul's, he consulted with the Puritan John Udall (see *Works,* XI, viii-ix, note 1; Frere, *The English Church in the Reigns of Elizabeth and James I.,* 262-63, where reference is made to a conference with Henry Barrow). As bishop of Chichester Andrewes was called upon to confer with the Catholic Sir Toby Matthew; for an account of this interesting meeting see A. H. Mathew, editor, *A True Historical Relation of the Conversion of Sir Tobie Matthew to the Holy Catholic Faith; with the Antecedents and Consequences Thereof. Edited, and now published for the first time, with a preface, by his kinsman, A. H. Mathew* (London, 1904), 92-111.

Southwell. He so busied himself with preaching and lecturing at St. Giles and St. Paul's that he endangered his health and caused his friends no end of worry.[10] About the time that he became attached to the earl of Huntingdon, chaplaincies to Archbishop Whitgift and to Queen Elizabeth were bestowed on him.

During this stage in his career Andrewes had to take a stand on the issue of Puritanism. He had reached Cambridge the year that Whitgift, then vice-chancellor of the university, succeeded in driving Cartwright from his professorship and the pulpit.[11] A Puritan party remained active, however, and we are told that, recognizing Andrewes' ability, they tried to enroll him among their own. Apparently impressed at first with their pretensions to strictness and piety, the young scholar was suddenly disillusioned when he found some of them playing at bowls of a Sunday afternoon.[12] It is easy enough to understand the attraction Puritanism might have had for Andrewes. His own very decided inclination toward a strict personal asceticism, to which his sermons, his *Preces Privatae*, and contemporary notices attest, would naturally lead him to investigate the Puritan pattern for a holy life; but its rigidity and barrenness proved uncongenial to him, and he veered off into a more traditional position. If he turned his back on Puritanism, however, it was not through any indifference to a high degree of personal holiness, for this always remained his own ambition and the ideal he labored to see realized in a Church whose framework and spirit were them-

---

[10] *Works*, XI, viii, see notes e and f. Many of these lectures and sermons appear in 'Αποσπασμάτια Sacra; or a Collection of Posthumous and Orphan Lectures, Delivered at St. Paul's and St. Giles His Church (London, 1657). For their genuinity see *Works*, XI, Appendix B, lxxvii, where Bliss, one of the editors of the *Works*, comments: "There does not appear to be sufficient evidence to justify one in ascribing these sermons, at least in their present form, to Bishop Andrewes. Accordingly, they are not reprinted in this edition." These sermons were not used in the analysis of Andrewes' thought.

[11] Frere, *The English Church in the Reigns of Elizabeth and James I.*, 156.

[12] Macleane, *Andrewes and the Reaction*, 53.

selves far more traditional than the organization which the Puritans envisioned for England.[13]

Whatever youthful waverings he experienced, Andrewes came down clearly and forcefully against Calvinist doctrine when he penned his *Judgment* on the celebrated Lambeth Articles which Whitgift, then archbishop of Canterbury, sent to Cambridge in 1595 to be the norm for the university on the knotty problem of predestination.[14] Beyond this and a *Censura censurae D. Barreti de certitudine salutis,* written apparently before the *Judgment,* Andrewes seems to have taken little part in the dispute which raged over the Articles.[15] In any case, by this time he had definitely committed himself to the church party of which Hooker was at the moment the most able leader, and which Laud was soon to ruin. Andrewes had begun the move which was to win for him leadership in prestige and influence in High Church affairs.

---

[13] Harington related that Walsingham, hearing of Andrewes' fame "and meaning to make use thereof, sent for him . . . and dealt earnestly with him, to hold up a side that was even then falling, and to maintain certain state points of Puritanism. But he that had too much of the ἄνδρος [ἀνδρεῖος?] in him to be scared with a councillor's frown, or blown aside with his breath, answered him plainly, that they were not only against his learning, but his conscience" (*Works,* XI, Harington, *Memoir,* xxxvi).

[14] *Works,* VI, *Bishop Andrewes' Judgment of the Lambeth Articles,* 287-300. For the Articles see Walter Hook and W. R. W. Stephens, editors, *A Church Dictionary: a Practical Manual of Reference for Clergymen and Students,* fifteenth edition (London, 1896), 431. The *Judgment* is undated, but in it Andrewes writes: "Per hos sedecim annos ex quo presbyter sum factus, me neque publicè neque privatim vel disputâsse de eis, vel pro concione tractâsse; etiam nunc quoque malle de eis audire quàm dicere" (*Works,* VI, *Bishop Andrewes' Judgment of the Lambeth Articles,* 294). The date of his ordination was 1581; the *Judgment* would therefore have been written in 1596 or 1597, and would thus have been quite timely.

[15] *Works,* VI, *Censura censurae D. Barreti de certitudine salutis,* 301-05. William Barret had denied the certainty of assurance and final perseverance in a sermon preached for the bachelor of divinity degree in 1595 and was censured therefor. See Frere, *The English Church in the Reigns of Elizabeth and James I.,* 283.

For the ten years until 1605 Andrewes became increasingly involved in a threefold activity: he carried the responsibility of head of a university college, the burdens of an active London vicar, and began to sit on various ecclesiastical commissions, a function he had often to fulfill up to the year of his death. Impressed by his preaching, Elizabeth had him made prebend of Westminster in 1591, and finally dean in 1601. As dean Andrewes interested himself particularly in the abbey school and won himself numerous friends among the "young fry" who regularly accompanied him on the recreative walks that he took to Chiswick.[16]

When James I succeeded Elizabeth, Andrewes was nearly fifty years old, firmly established, and fairly well off in every respect, but he was to rise even higher under the new monarch at whose coronation he assisted in July of 1603. Appointed to the High Commission in August of the same year, he next participated in the Hampton Court Conference, January 14-16, 1604, where he defended the use of the cross in baptism.[17] In July he was named head of the committee which undertook the translation of the Pentateuch and the history from the Book of Joshua to the First Book of Chronicles exclusive.[18] Of the ele-

---

[16] *Works*, XI, xviii, note q, where the following is quoted from Bishop Hacket's *Life of Archbishop Williams:* "['Andrewes] never walked to Chiswick for his recreation without a brace of this young fry, and in that wayfaring leisure had a singular dexterity to fill those narrow vessels with a funnel. And, which was the greatest burden of his toil, sometimes thrice in a week, sometimes oftener, he sent for the uppermost scholars to his lodgings at night, and kept them with him from eight till eleven, unfolding to them the best rudiments of the Greek tongue, and the elements of the Hebrew grammar; and all this he did to boys without any compulsion of correction.' "

[17] Macleane, *Andrewes and the Reaction*, 98. James asked about the antiquity of the signature with the sign of the cross in baptism. Andrewes answered that out of Tertullian, Cyprian, and Origen it appeared that it was used. In British Museum, Additional MSS., 28, 571, f. 201, are found extracts from these three fathers with an attribution in a different hand to Dr. Andrewes and the date 1605. Neither hand appears to be Andrewes'.

[18] *Works*, XI, Appendix A, lii.

vation of Lancelot Andrewes to the episcopacy, which took place in 1605, Bishop Mathew writes:

> Into this body there was now to enter a spiritual force of fine strength and lasting influence. It was the succession to the See of Chichester in 1605, which was to mark the moving of the waters. For in that year there came to the episcopate Lancelot Andrewes with his scholarly piety and his keen grave zeal; his attachment to the words of Scripture; his heavy oaken eloquence.[19]

At the same time he was made lord high almoner, and re-signed the mastership of Pembroke, the vicarage of St. Giles, and the deanship of Westminster; and "because of the exility" of Chichester he received *in commendam* the parsonage of Cheam in Surrey.[20] Chichester's "exility" was not to make possible for him the quiet life he always preferred, for he was soon called upon to assist James in the latter's controversy with Bellarmine over the Oath of Allegiance.[21] Under the name of Matthaeus Tortus, Bellarmine had answered the king's *Triplici nodo, triplex cuneus,* which had been published anonymously in London in the year 1607.[22]

Reluctantly but obediently Andrewes addressed himself to the work, and after months of furious labor published his *Tortura Torti* in 1609.[23] Late in 1609 Bellarmine subsumed in

---

[19] David Mathew, *The Jacobean Age* (London, 1938), 10.

[20] *Works*, XI, Isaacson, *Exact Narration*, x, and note p. See also *Works*, XI, Appendix A, lii.

[21] For an excellent discussion of the use James I made of various assistants in his theological controversies, see David Harris Willson, "James I and His Literary Assistants," *Huntington Library Quarterly*, VIII (1944-1945), 35-37.

[22] *Triplici nodo, triplex cuneus. Or an Apologie for the Oath of Allegiance* (London, 1607), reprinted in *The Political Works of James I. Reprinted from the Edition of 1616 with an Introduction by Charles Howard McIlwain, Harvard Political Classics, I* (Cambridge, Massachusetts, 1918), 71-109. For good summaries of the controversy see McIlwain's "Introduction," lix-lxxix; and Brodrick, *Blessed Robert Bellarmine*, II, 169-260.

[23] *Works*, VII, *Tortura Torti: sive; ad Matthaei Torti librum responsio, qui nuper editus contra apologiam . . . Jacobi . . . regis, pro iuramento fidelitatis* (Londini, 1609).

an *Apologia*.[24] As a reward for the *Tortura Torti* Andrewes had been translated to Ely in September of 1609, but he was not yet done with the uncongenial business of literary polemic, for James enjoined upon him the further task of replying to Bellarmine's *Apologia*.[25] Andrewes dutifully complied and published a *Responsio ad Bellarminum* in 1610.[26] And still the controversy dragged on, for we find him some ten years later writing against a new Catholic champion in his *Two Answers to Cardinal Perron*.[27] Throughout the *Tortura Torti* and the *Responsio ad Bellarminum* Andrewes labors in a heavy turgid Latin over practically the whole field of disagreement between Rome and the Established Church. Showing at every turn his remarkable knowledge of the Scriptures, the fathers, and ecclesiastical history, he violently disrupts the picture one forms of him in reading the sermons or the *Preces Privatae* by descending to personalities and by overindulging his propensity for the pun. In all of this, of course, he was but the child of his day, for religious controversy in the seventeenth century was often bitter and frequently even vulgar. Still it is a little startling to find him contrasting John Fisher and Thomas More with John the Baptist in this fashion: the Baptist was killed because he said to Herod, "You may not have your brother's wife"; Fisher and More,

---

[24] *Apologia Roberti S.R.E. cardinalis Bellarmini, pro responsione sua ad librum Iacobi . . . regis. . . . Accedit eadem ipsa responsio iterum recusa, quae sub nomine Matthaei Torti anno superiore prodierat* (Romae, 1609).

[25] *Works*, XI, Appendix A, lii.

[26] *Works*, VIII, *Responsio ad apologiam cardinalis Bellarmini, quam nuper edidit contra praefationem monitoriam . . . Iacobi . . . regis . . . omnibus Christianis monarchis, principibus, atque ordinibus inscriptam* (Londini, 1610).

[27] *Works*, XI, *Two Answers to Cardinall Perron* . . . (London, 1629), 1-105. The involved background for the *Two Answers* is described in *Works*, XI, Preface, 5-6. For brief summaries of the *Tortura Torti* and the *Responsio ad Bellarminum* see Ottley, *Lancelot Andrewes*, 59-71 and 154-76; for the matter contained in the *Two Answers* see Frere, *Andrewes as a Representative of Anglican Principles*, which draws heavily throughout on the *Two Answers* for its analysis of Andrewes' teaching.

quite the contrary, opposed Henry VIII's divorce from Catherine of Aragon, and so were put to death for saying, "You must keep your brother's wife."[28] Andrewes was out of character in controversy, and he knew it, for he once wrote to the French Protestant theologian Du Moulin:

> I never could learn this trick of sawing, or (which is all one) of tossing replys. No, not, when my years were fitter for it. But now old age, which of it self is a diseas, and yet never cometh without diseases attending it, plucks me by the ear, and bids me get me out of this cockpit, and rank myself with them, whose whole business is *Prayer*.[29]

From 1609 to 1618 Andrewes held the see of Ely in the fen country of Cambridgeshire. But, as in the case of his work as bishop of Chichester and Winchester, little has been uncovered to enable us to form a judgment of his ability as an episcopal administrator. On Bancroft's death in 1612 it was generally expected that Andrewes, whose reputation was now European as a result of the controversy with Bellarmine, would succeed to Canterbury; but Abbot, bishop of London, passed over the Thames to Lambeth.[30] Disappointed or not, Andrewes soon

---

28 *Works*, VII, *Tortura Torti*, 442: "Annon haec Baptistae vox vita sua constitit, *Non licet tibi habere uxorem fratris tui?* Quae vero Mori causa atque Roffensis? Annon ex tota diametro contraria? *Non licet tibi non habere uxorem fratris tui; Licet vero habere, Non licet dimittere.*"

29 *Of Episcopacy. Three Epistles of Peter Moulin Doctor and Professor of Divinity. Answered by . . . Lancelot Andrews, Late Lord Bishop of Winchester. Translated for the Benefit of the Publike* (no place, 1647), 43.

30 Bishop Mathew thinks "it was the Bishop of Ely's very assets, his piety and defined theological erudition, and perhaps most of all a certain delicate and permanent seriousness of approach, which made his sovereign hesitate. Possibly, since the relations with Lambeth were so important to him, the King felt that he must have there a prelate who, like Abbot, would be companionable" (Mathew, *Jacobean Age*, 96). Macleane doubts that Andrewes possessed the grip and the statesmanship required for piloting the Church through the dangers that lay ahead. "His three episcopates were uneventful and scarce put his mettle to the proof" (Macleane, *Andrewes and the Reaction*, 116).

showed himself ready to serve the king without question, for he voted for nullity in the famous Essex case, possibly the most controversial step he ever took.[31] If we take into account his extreme exaltation of kingship and the saccharine adulation he lavished on James in many a sermon, we need not, perhaps, be entirely surprised; but it is difficult not to suppose that he might have regretted his action. The controversy with Bellarmine over, and the Essex affair a painful memory, the next notable events in Andrewes' career were his appointments as privy councilor of England in 1616 and of Scotland in 1617; his translation to Winchester in 1618; and his appointment as dean of the Royal Chapel on January 1, 1619. Of his character and virtues we shall have something to say when we discuss his ideal of the clerical state and his ascetical teaching.

To trace Andrewes' life in greater detail would merely delay the main work of this essay. Enough has been said to serve as a background for a study of his thought. One must remember, of course, that over the years from his catechetical instruction at Pembroke to his death in 1626 he delivered hundreds of lectures and sermons, served in numerous official capacities, acted as spiritual guide and counselor to all who sought his advice, consulted with recusants, attended the king at court and on his progresses through the realm, administered his successive dioceses, and, withal, managed to lead a life of prayer and study. That he contrived to hold on to this latter style of living argues a certain withdrawnness and shyness in the man which

---

[31] For an account of Andrewes' part in the affair see *Works*, XI, Appendix A, lii-liii. Of Andrewes' obvious change of sentiment, once the king's mind was known, Gardiner writes: "All that can be said is, that against such a man it is impossible to receive anything short of direct evidence, and that it is better to suppose that he was, by some process of reasoning with which we are unacquainted, satisfied with the evidence adduced, though he must have felt that there was that in the conduct of Lady Essex which prevented him from regarding the result of the trial with any degree of satisfaction" (Gardiner, *History of England*, II, 173-74). That judgment is too favorable.

every picture of him the writer has seen strongly confirms. His
eyes, set in a face of delicately fine features, are always averted
or cast down; his cap is usually drawn down full to the ruff
about his neck, as though to shut out the clamor of the world.[32]
Apparently he did not like to be painted or sketched, for we
find on the back of a painting at Pembroke a legend which explains that the original sketch was made without Andrewes'
knowledge as he sat at table.[33] He seems even to have stood off
from his episcopal brethren, whether from his own choice for
love of quiet and retirement, or through theirs, for the reverence and awe in which they generally seem to have held him.[34]
But to scholars, men of accomplishment or aspirants to great-
ness, he was ever accessible, and among his scholarly friends
he numbered Cluverius, Heinsius, Erpenius, Vossius, Grotius,
Du Moulin, Isaac (and his son Meric) Casaubon, John Harington, Francis Bacon, George Herbert, Hooker, and Laud.[35]

---

[32] Mathew, *Jacobean Age*, 77-78.

[33] AD EXEMPLAR QUOD INSCIO EPŌ SAMUEL WRIGHT À CHARTIS
TAM CALAMO QUAM PENICILLO PERITUS PRANDII TEMPORE
FURTIVIS DEPINXIT COLORIBUS BOXHORNE EX HAGA FECIT. Sir
Ellis H. Minns, president of Pembroke College, Cambridge, kindly made this
transcription. See Aubrey Attwater, *Pembroke College, Cambridge: A Short
History*. Edited by S. C. Roberts (Cambridge, 1936), 58. Samuel Wright was
Andrewes' secretary at one time.

[34] See *Works*, XI, xxviii, note y, where the following eulogy from Hacket's *Life
of Archbishop Williams* is quoted: " 'This is that Andrewes, the ointment of
whose name is sweeter than all spices. . . . This is that celebrated Bishop of
Winton, whose learning King James admired above all his chaplains; and that
King, being of most excellent parts himself, could the better discover what
was eminent in another. Indeed, he was the most apostolical and primitive-
like divine, in my opinion, that wore a rochet, in his age.' "

[35] *Works*, V, Buckeridge, *Funeral Sermon*, 292; *Works*, IX, Andrewes' correspondence with Du Moulin concerning episcopacy, 173-216; *Works*, XI,
Appendices, *passim*, for references to many of these. In the British Museum,
Sloane MSS., 118, are found letters received by Andrewes from both the
Casaubons and from Herbert, Du Moulin, Grotius, and several lesser lights,
most of whom were thanking Andrewes for favors received or begging assistance of one sort or another.

Beyond the works of Andrewes already mentioned there are few, but a quick survey of the material contained in the *Works* will help to round out a judgment of his thought. Simply to enumerate the volumes given to his various writings will show the predominance of his sermons and will help in estimating what portion of his time and labor he devoted to them. It should be clear, in consequence, that an analysis of Andrewes' thought based on the sermons will fairly reflect his mind.

Of the eleven volumes of the *Works* the first five contain his English sermons to the number of one hundred and twenty-two. These will be broken down into their various categories when we come to examine Andrewes as a preacher. The sixth volume contains five different works, chief of which is *A Pattern of Catechistical Doctrine*, whose origins have been explained above.[36] It does not adhere strictly to the accepted form of a catechism, but develops as a course in moral theology on the Ten Commandments, which indeed it was. Andrewes' treatment is traditional, orthodox, well-balanced, neither oversevere nor lax. As in the case of most of the nonsermon works, we shall have occasion to refer to it for purposes of cross reference and confirmation. It is not in the precise form in which Andrewes framed it, for it was very probably published from the notes of his hearers.

The second item, the *Judgment of the Lambeth Articles*, and the third, the *Censura censurae D. Barreti*, have been introduced.[37] In brief they are critical of the Articles and of the reasons for which Barret was condemned, and reveal Andrewes as non-Calvinist in his attitude toward predestination and the certainty of salvation. His *Form of Consecration of a Church and Churchyard*, the fourth item, is a delightful piece of local coloring which reports in detail the procedure through which

---

[36] See *supra*, 2-3.
[37] See *supra*, 5.

he went in an actual consecration on September 17, 1620.[38]
Andrewes' love for a dignified and richly ritualistic liturgy
stands forth on every page. The fifth piece, *A Summary View
of Government*, a pretentious schematic treatise on church government, is calculated to establish episcopacy (without the
papacy) against the Puritans.[39] The last entry, *A Discourse of
Ceremonies*, written with an obvious anti-Puritan slant, defends
current Anglican liturgical practice, even to the inclusion of
some Roman remnants.[40]

Volumes VII and VIII, the *Tortura Torti* and the *Responsio
ad Bellarminum*, respectively, have been sufficiently discussed
for our purposes, for any further analysis would lead us astray
and into the tedious business of controversy.[41] They are, of
course, important Andrean productions, and must be carefully
considered in any complete study.

Three years after Bishop Andrewes' death, Laud and Buckeridge, bishops of London and Ely, edited several of his Latin
works which are reprinted as Volume IX of the *Works*.[42] In
their dedication to Charles I, who had commissioned them to
see to the publication of Andrewes' writings, they acknowledge
that the items in this volume were not as carefully polished as
were the English sermons they had recently edited. Andrewes,
they tell us, would undoubtedly have made changes before publishing them himself, especially since some of the writings are

---

[38] *Works*, VI, *Bishop Andrewes' Form of Consecration of a Church and Churchyard*, 307-33.
[39] *Works*, VI, *A Summarie View of the Government Both of the Old and New
Testament: Whereby the Episcopall Government of Christ's Church Is Vindicated: Out of the Rude Draughts of Lancelot Andrewes . . .* (Oxford, 1641),
335-62.
[40] *Works*, VI, *A Learned Discourse of Ceremonies Retained and Used in Christian
Churches*. Edward Leigh, editor (London, 1653), 363-92.
[41] See *supra*, 7-8.
[42] *Works*, IX, *Reverendi in Christo patris, Lanceloti, episcopi Wintoniensis, opuscula quaedam posthuma* (Londini, 1629).

from his earlier days; they have presumed to omit certain articles concerning topics on which Andrewes later changed his opinion.[43] The editors then take note of an important fact: Andrewes wrote very little. This, they hasten to explain, was not because he could not write, but rather because he would not; not for any lack of talent, but because of his great deliberation and caution.[44]

On the occasion of candidacy for the doctorate in theology Andrewes delivered the undated *Concio ad clerum pro gradu doctoris*, a learned and tedious lecture on sacrilege.[45] Four general classes of things are sacred, he declared: holy living, the means thereto (the Word, prayer, symbols or signs, censures), persons, and titles. The violation of any of these is sacrilege, and bitter is its punishment. Loaded with similar display, but a happier effort in many ways, is the *Concio ad clerum in synodo provinciali*.[46] The clergy must give good example, he urges; our estate and order has its importance and its strength not so much from political laws as from the consciences of men to which we must address ourselves, else no law whatsoever will help.[47]

---

[43] *Works*, IX, *Opuscula posthuma*, 3.

[44] *Works*, IX, *Opuscula posthuma*, 4. See also *Works*, XI, Harington, *Memoir*, xxxviii. Harington writes: "And whereas I know some that have not known him so long as I have, yet have heard and believe no less of his learning than I speak, find fault that he is not so apt to deliver his resolution upon every question moved, as they could wish, who if they be not quickly resolved of that they ask, will quickly resolve not to care for it: I say this cunctation is the mean between precipitation and procrastination, and is specially commended by the Apostle St. James, as I have heard him allege it, *Sit omnis homo βραδὺς εἰς τὸ λαλῆσαι, tardus ad loquendum, tardus ad iram.*"

[45] *Works*, IX, *Concio ad clerum pro gradu doctoris, &c.*, 7-28.

[46] *Works*, IX, *Concio ad clerum in synodo provinciali Cantuariensis provinciae ad D. Pauli. Die XX° Februarij.* A.D. *MDXCIII* (Londini, 1629), 29-51.

[47] *Works*, IX, *Concio ad clerum*, 39. He writes: "Scio ego vos advertisse Statum hunc atque Ordinem nostrum, non tam a politicis legibus, quam ab hominum conscientiis momentum habere atque vim suam: quibus nisi nos commendare in conspectu Dei, et in quibus nisi venerationem internam lucrari detur . . . frustra nobis faverit, frustra caverit lex ulla."

A Latin oration delivered before James I and Christian of
Denmark on August 5, 1606, has been translated and appears
among the English sermons, and will be considered when those
are examined.[48] The next of Andrewes' Latin works is a
Concio Latine habita, coram regia maiestate, XIII° Aprilis,
A.D. *MDCXIII.* Principally adulation of King James, this sermon takes on a value for us at its close when Andrewes suddenly
makes a definite statement of the Anglican rule of faith and an
equally clear declaration of what Anglicanism rejects in Catholicism and Puritanism.[49]

There follow in this volume of Latin writings three *Determinationes theologicae: De jurejurando* ἐπάκτῳ, *De usuris,* and
De decimis.[50] The *De jurejurando* is Andrewes' opinion of the
ex officio oath around which controversy raged for a number
of years in the late sixteenth century.[51] He pronounces the oath
illicit in capital cases, and licit in others only for the establishment of a basis for the case or of the truth of the proofs advanced.[52] The *De usuris* argues that usury is permitted by civil
law not because it is licit, but because the law tries to circum-

---

[48] *Works,* IX, *Concio Latine habita, coram regia maiestate, V°. Augusti, MDCVI*
. . . (Londini, 1629), 53-74. The English translation is in *Works,* V, 235-56.

[49] *Works,* IX, *Concio Latine habita, coram regia maiestate, XIII° Aprilis,* A.D.
MDCXIII, 91-93. We shall have to return to this later.

[50] *Works,* IX, *Quaestionis, nunquid per ius divinum, magistratui liceat a reo
iusiurandum exigere? Et id, quatenus ac quousque liceat? Theologica determinatio* . . . (Londini, 1629), 95-115; *Works,* IX, *De usuris, theologica
determinatio* . . . (Londini, 1629), 117-50; *Works,* IX, *De decimis, theologica
determinatio* . . . (Londini, 1629), 151-71.

[51] This was the "oath to answer interrogatories administered by the judge merely
in virtue of his office, apart from formal accusation or presentment" (Frere,
The English Church in the Reigns of Elizabeth and James I., 229-30) ; see
also 279, 356.

[52] *Works,* IX, *De jurejurando,* 115; "Si . . . disponatur judicium hoc (quo
utimur) ad lineam; et justitia haec ad perpendiculum verbi divini; nusquam
in iis peccari: exigere posse magistratum, idque a Reo, (praesertim dum ne
capitalis causa sit, aut sanguinaria) jusjurandum suum: idque eousque posse,
sive ut lis basin suam obtineat, dum status quaeritur: sive ut probationum
veritas elucescat, dum quaestio habetur."

scribe and moderate what it cannot prevent, and concludes by declaring "usuras legitimas esse illicitas."[53] The thesis of the *De decimis* is simply that tithes are not to be abrogated.[54] Throughout these three *Determinationes* Andrewes relies on a method with which we will become familiar as we study his sermons; he argues from Scripture, the fathers, the councils, and history, and constantly reveals an intimate knowledge of all four theological sources.

The concluding entry in Volume IX is a series of Latin letters exchanged between Andrewes and Pierre du Moulin, a French Protestant theologian, on the question of episcopacy.[55] The debate concerns the structure of the English Church; Andrewes holds for the *de jure divino* institution of episcopacy and for the formal distinction between the episcopal and the sacerdotal orders.

The *Preces Privatae* occupy Volume X of the *Works*.[56] We shall refer to these occasionally as explanatory of some of the features of the sermons, for as one reads the sermons he is forced to conclude that Andrewes led a life of intense prayer, a conclusion the *Preces Privatae* abundantly confirm.

In the final volume, XI, the editors have set several biographical notices along with the rest of Andrewes' work which they considered authentic. The *Two Answers to Cardinal Perron* have been mentioned.[57] *A Speech against Traske* was a star-

---

[53] *Works*, IX, *De usuris*, 134; quotation from 150.

[54] *Works*, IX, *De decimis*, 155.

[55] *Works*, IX, *Reverendi in Christo patris Lanceloti episcopi Wintoniensis responsiones ad Petri Molinaei epistolas tres, una cum Molinaei epistolis* (Londini, 1629), 173-216.

[56] *Works*, X, *Rev. patris Lanc. Andrews episc. Winton, preces privatae Graecè & Latinè* (Oxonii, 1675). The long and varied history of these devotions and the story of various MSS. and editions thereof are fully treated in Brightman, *The Preces Privatae*. There have been several editions and translations since Brightman's study, the most recent in 1950.

[57] See *supra*, 8.

chamber argument against one Traske, a "Judaizer," who was
attempting to introduce certain Jewish customs into the English
Church.[58] Andrewes strongly criticized the attempts and declared, "It is a good work to make a Jew a Christian: but to
make Christian men Jews, hath ever been holden a foul act, and
severely to be punished."[59] A second star-chamber speech, *Concerning Vows*, declares that a vow the countess of Shrewsbury
had taken to conceal knowledge of the marriage of her niece,
Lady Arabella Stuart, was invalid because it worked against the
administration of justice.[60] *A Discourse against Second Marriage*
answers negatively to the question, "Whether upon adultery
proved, or sentence recorded, a man be set at liberty, that he
may proceed to contract with another."[61] The Visitation Articles
used by Andrewes in his first visitation of the diocese of Winchester are an interesting revelation of the things he considered important in diocesan affairs; their general tone is "High
Church."[62] A second set of Articles differs little from the first,
but one of the questions included reveals Andrewes' interest in
oral confession. It asks if any minister has revealed anything
told him by a penitent.[63] Three brief succeeding pieces, *Notes on
the Book of Common Prayer, Form of Consecrating Church
Plate*, and a *Form of Induction*, are of no particular interest

[58] *Works*, XI, *A Speech Delivered in the Starr-Chamber against the Two Iudaicall
Opinions of Mr. Traske* . . . (London, 1629), 81-94.
[59] *Works*, XI, *Speech against Traske*, 84.
[60] *Works*, XI, *A Speech Delivered in the Starr-Chamber, Concerning Vowes, in
the Countesse of Shrewsburies Case* . . . (London, 1629), 95-105.
[61] *Works*, XI, *A Discourse Written* . . . *against Second Marriage, after Sentence
of Divorce with a Former Match, the Party Then Living. In Anno 1601*,
106-10.
[62] *Works*, XI, *Articles To Be Enquired of by the Church-Wardens and Sworne-Men
in the Primary Visitation of* . . . *Lancelot, Lord Bishop of Winton* . . .
Anno 1619 (London, 1619), 111-23.
[63] *Works*, XI, *Articles To Be Enquired of by the Churchwardens and Sworne-Men,
in the Triennial Visitation of* . . . *Lancelot Lord Bishop of Winton* . . .
Anno 1625 (London, 1625), 125-40. See Article 16, 131.

here.[64] *A Manual of Directions for the Sick,* apparently the manual used by Andrewes himself in his visits to the sick and dying when he was vicar of St. Giles, Cripplegate, reveals him at his pastoral best.[65] The last entry in this final volume of the *Works* is the *Private Devotions,* a translation based on the *Preces Privatae.*[66]

Despite the varied character of Andrewes' nonsermon writings, it is clear that the largest single type of work he produced, the writing which represented his own chief interest and reflected the various stages of his thinking over a long stretch of years, is the sermons. Lancelot Andrewes was essentially and primarily a preacher.

---

[64] *Works,* XI, *Notes on the Book of Common Prayer,* 141-58; *Works,* XI, *A Coppie of the Forme Used by the Lo: Bishop of Elye in Consecrating the Newe Church Plate of the Cathedrall Church of Worc*r*.,* 159-63; *Works,* XI, *The Manner of Induction Prescribed by . . . Lancelot Andrewes . . . ,* 164.

[65] *Works,* XI, *A Manual of Directions for the Sick. With Many Sweet Meditations and Devotions of . . . Lancelot Andrewes . . . To Which Are Added Praiers for the Morning, Evening, and H. Communion.* R[ichard] D[rake], translator (London, 1648), 165-222.

[66] *Works,* XI, *A Manual of the Private Devotions and Meditations of . . . Lancelot Andrews . . .* R[ichard] D[rake], translator (London, 1648), 223-338.

CHAPTER II

Andrewes
as Preacher

The theologically and politically tumultuous seventeenth century in England was eminently an age of the sermon. Its preachers voiced the varied and contradictory ideas and emotions of the day before a citizenry which looked to them for the articulate expression of public opinion and for leadership. They fulfilled a function beyond the purely religious as they preached to their adherents in cathedral, church, or court, before the public cross or furtively in conventicles, for they largely framed public opinion. Their influence equaled that of the modern press and radio broadcast.[1] In an age when every issue was liable to burn, whether it concerned the wearing of a vestment, the position of a table in a church, a rubric for the reception of the Eucharist, or the power of the monarch in things ecclesiastical, the origin of the episcopal order, the authority of Sacred Scripture in doctrine, ritual, and discipline, battles were fought not only on the civil podium but in the pulpit, whence the direction of attack and counterattack usually proceeded.

Deep as was its involvement in public affairs—and these were then inextricably interwoven with religious questions—the

---

[1] W. Fraser Mitchell, *English Pulpit Oratory from Andrewes to Tillotson, a Study of Its Literary Aspects* (London, 1932), 3.

pulpit was in no sense limited to the vulgar regions of controversy and agitation, for it also served as the platform for
high and noble theological discourse, and none so used it to
greater effect than Lancelot Andrewes. Defending the doctrinal,
the liturgical, and the disciplinary where he saw a need for
defense, Andrewes rather emphasized the moral content and
consequences of the doctrine he preached. Generally assuming
as proved and accepted the fundamental teachings of Christianity, he concentrated on unfolding their ascetical implications
for the practical business of daily living, and labored to breathe
life and spirit into a Church whose members had known little
but confusion in thought and practice for the years since the
break from Rome. In his sermons, then, we must look for an
assertion and exposition of Christian doctrine, for an unfolding
of the beauties of the Christian mysteries, for exhortation to a
Christian asceticism based on the truth discussed, rather than
for theological proof.

The collection of sermons on which our appraisal of Andrewes' thought largely depends was published in 1629 by Laud
and Buckeridge at the express command of King Charles I.[2]
The particular value of this edition rests on the fact that it
supplies us with the sermons in the very form in which Andrewes
preached them.[3] In addition they represent, though they do not

---

[2] *XCVI. Sermons by the Right Honorable and Reverend Father in God, Lancelot
Andrewes, Late Lord Bishop of Winchester* (London, 1629). These were reprinted in 1631, 1635, 1641, and 1661. See *Works*, XI, lxxii. The sermons were
reprinted in the Anglo-Catholic edition from the edition of 1631, and occupy
four and a half volumes.

[3] Mitchell writes: "The written sermon, printed after delivery in the author's lifetime or after his death as was the case with Andrewes' 'XCVI Sermons,'
from the student's viewpoint is certainly the most satisfactory. We feel that
we know all about it, as we cannot feel that we know about the other forms
of sermons. Thus Andrewes wrote, thus Andrewes spoke, thus his editors
published his sermons; and whether delivered to the court at Greenwich or
Whitehall, or read in the studies of the clergy or by the pious in their
closets, it was thus that his style impressed his generation, stimulating in

exhaust, his pulpit activity during the whole span of his mature and public life from 1588 to 1624.[4] In the *Works* the sermons are grouped according to occasion and topic rather than in strict chronological order, but are chronologically arranged within each series.

The first group of sermons, seventeen in number, were preached on Christmas Days before James I in Whitehall, and their subject matter was, of course, the Nativity.[5] Frequent preaching before the same congregation and on the same topic was often enough Andrewes' lot, but nowhere does he better reveal versatility and ability in handling the same subject with great freshness each time he approached it than in this series. Of a truly lofty tone, these sermons penetrate deeply into the mystery of the Incarnation and into the nature of the virtue he considered most peculiar to it, humility. Free of querulousness, they are positive, restrained, heavily exegetical, and follow a rough pattern which is characteristically Andrean. An introductory section briefly reviews the chosen Scripture text, the division follows the natural divisions of the text, and the body of the sermon, adhering strictly to the division, discourses on the mystery. The mystery is considered in the light of a gift to man, while his reciprocal duty to God, specified to some extent according to a particular sermon's treatment of the Nativity, is ultimately, and in all but one instance, reduced to the reception of the Eucharist. Andrewes had a firm conviction of the importance of this central liturgical function.

---

aspirants to pulpit fame immediate imitation or provoking criticism and antagonism" (Mitchell, *English Pulpit Oratory*, 16). "There came to our hands," say Laud and Buckeridge in their dedicatory epistle, "a world of Sermon-notes, but these came perfect. . . . As the Sermons were preached, so are they published" (*Works*, I, xiii, xiv).

[4] As previously noted (p. 4, note 10), we are not including the 'Αποσπασμάτια *Sacra* in this analysis; for while they represent a great deal of his sermon output, their authenticity, at least as to form, is not satisfactory.

[5] *Works*, I, *Sermons of the Nativity*, 1-302.

Quite different in tone and purpose from the Nativity sermons is a brief series of eight preached on Ash Wednesdays before either Elizabeth or James.[6] Whereas in the former group the emphasis was heavily doctrinal, in this we find Andrewes bearing strongly on practice. Suiting the season, these are "moral" sermons on repentance and fasting, and aim at the specific action of self-denial. How unpopular his subject and how neglected the practice, he well knew; hence it is with great deliberation that he fashions his very direct attack on unwilling human nature.

A second set of sermons preached in Lent are the six placed first in Volume II of the *Works*.[7] These have no consistent theme. The first two are on government, the third on giving to the Church, the remaining three are homilies on Lot's wife, Dives and Lazarus, and St. Paul's zeal for souls. Since the last of these was delivered in 1596, they afford interesting instances of his earlier work. They are noticeably free of the ruggedness characteristic of many a later sermon. Practices which afterwards became faults are here engaged in with control, so that these read more easily than, for example, do the Nativity sermons, the earliest of which was preached in 1605. Though they lack a topical unity, the lenten sermons have in common a mellowness and unction which stamp Andrewes as an utterly earnest preacher. With courage he faced a court and a queen riding the wave of material success, and without demagogic ranting urged them to mind their souls and the life hereafter and laid before them the example of Paul's high dedication to the salvation of souls. Herein, too—and it is very generally true of him—he reveals himself as a positive preacher: positive doctrine, pursuit of virtue and the good, these he

---

[6] *Works*, I, *Sermons of Repentance and Fasting, Preached upon Ash-Wednesday*, 303-454.

[7] *Works*, II, *Sermons Preached in Lent*, 1-116.

preaches consistently. To errors he points, to sin, penance, death, and the pains of hell; but when he finishes the gesture, his arm is swung toward virtue, toward heaven, toward Christ. If Lancelot Andrewes unsettled the consciences of his hearers— and he certainly tried to stir them—he might have left his congregation concerned, but never bitter. A preacher cannot but have his words measured by what his audience knows him to be; from such examination of Andrewes without doubt there emerged convincing argument for exactly what he preached.

Following Andrewes' lead through the cycle of the Christian year, we find the next group of sermons dealing with the Passion.[8] Unfortunately only three in number, these, if they were all we had of Andrewes, would suffice to prove his excellence as a preacher. The Passion easily lends itself to an emotional exaggeration which he completely avoids. With a real sense of its implications, a fine emotional and imaginative restraint, he manages in these treatments a vivid picture of the sufferings of Christ. His hearers could hardly have gone away unimpressed.

The longest series among the authentic "XCVI" is the Easter group of eighteen sermons dating from 1606 to 1624. There is no sermon for Easter of 1619, and the one for 1624 was not delivered, though it was prepared.[9] This constitutes a complete treatise on the Resurrection, and contains several thoroughly touching homilies on the human-interest aspects of this central Christian mystery. If one were to read only a few and not all of this series, he might get a very unbalanced idea of Andrewes' ability as a preacher, for they are quite uneven in quality. The same may be said of the Whitsunday group of fifteen, which roughly parallel the Easter sermons.[10] As a group these are average Andrean sermons, quite doctrinal; probably because of

---

[8] *Works*, II, *Sermons Preached upon Good-Friday*, 117-84.
[9] *Works*, II, *Sermons of the Resurrection*, 185-428, and *Works*, III, 1-103.
[10] *Works*, III, *Sermons of the Sending of the Holy Ghost*, 105-401.

the difficulties inherent in talking about a spirit and Andrewes'
penchant for playing with the term, and because of his fondness
for drawing analogies and discovering symbolical meanings,
these lack sharp definition and clarity.

Volume IV of the *Works* contains two sets of sermons quite
different in character from all previous groups. Each commem-
orates an attempt on the king's life and was preached on the
appropriate anniversary.[11] Andrewes accepted the familiar official story of the Gunpowder Plot, with which one deals; but of
the Gowry Conspiracy, which occasioned the first of these
commemorative series, he had his doubts.[12] The father of two
brothers Gowry " 'had been taken away by form of justice in
the year 1584, whilst the King was yet a minor, and forced he
was unto it as unto many other things that agreed not with his
mind.' "[13] In 1600 the brothers made an attempt on James's life
at Perth in Scotland. By a great show of courage, the story relates, James successfully resisted the treacherous assault until
rescued by his companions. Both brothers died in the attempt,
and their posterity was disinherited.

These sermons represent Andrewes' major pronouncements
on political questions, for they examine the origin of kingly
power, the sacredness of the royal person, the wretchedness of

---

[11] *Works,* IV, *Sermons of the Conspiracy of the Gowries,* 1-200; *Works,* IV, *Sermons of the Gunpowder Treason,* 201-405.

[12] Quoting from Plume's *Life of Hackett,* Macleane offers the following story:
" 'Though some people have denied the Treason, yet our good Bishop
[Hackett] was assured that the most religious Bishop Andrewes once fell
down upon his knees before King James and besought his Majesty to spare
his customary pains upon that day, that he might not mock God unless the
thing were true. The King replied: Those were much to blame who would
never believe a treason unless their Prince were actually murdered; but did
assure him, upon the faith of a Christian and upon the word of a King, their
treasonable attempt against him was too true' " (Macleane, *Andrewes and the
Reaction,* 101).

[13] *Works,* IV, 4, note a, where a description of the attempt is quoted from Spottiswoode's *History of the Church of Scotland.*

treason, the divine protection afforded royalty, and so forth. They also reveal the very close tie which he considered binding the altar to the throne.[14] Andrewes' utter submission to the royal power and his complete conviction of the theory of the divine right of kings is clearly manifest in his disgustingly adulatory addresses to James with which these sermons usually close.

The Gowry series was preached in various places on the fifth of August as part of the celebration annually held in honor of and thanksgiving for James's escape from death. Probably because of the nature of the topic and the narrational character of the treatment, its sermons are generally smoother in style, and longer than those of previous groups. The pattern to which most of them conform involves an analysis of an appropriate Scripture text (which has to do with the sacredness of kingship, or an unsuccessful attempt against a scriptural ruler) and a comparison of the scriptural incident with the Gowry Conspiracy. James invariably comes out a greater king than the scriptural monarch and more favored in his escape. Andrewes reserved to the Gowry sermons the greater part of his teaching on kingship, for in the Gunpowder sermons he rather exalts the day of the deliverance, urges the joy proper to it, inveighs against the heinousness of the plot, and extolls God's mercies. Throughout these runs a strong emphasis on acknowledging God's favor in preserving the king and Parliament from death; but this acknowledgment must be manifest, he urges, in acts: holiness, righteousness, and a proper divine service. In both groups Andrewes' whipping boys are the Catholics with their "regicides," Suarez and Mariana, Bellarmine with his "people," and the Puritans with their "presbytery"—all enemies of the king.

---

[14] Father Pollen reminds us that Catholics also erred in this regard, particularly under Mary. See John Hungerford Pollen, S.J., *The English Catholics in the Reign of Queen Elizabeth: A Study of Their Politics, Civil Life and Government* . . . (London, 1920), 5-6, 362.

Nothing need be said here of the *Occasional Sermons,* for we shall refer to them individually in their proper places.[15] Twelve in number, they have no unity of subject; the twelfth is a translation of a Latin sermon.[16] Chiefly the products of the earlier part of Andrewes' maturity, they are sweeter in tone, smoother in style, fresher and more filled with optimism than many later sermons, the result perhaps of the enthusiasm of a younger man whose vision still had something of the roseate, whose style had not yet crystallized.

To the well-authenticated sermons which were published by Laud and Buckeridge the editors of Andrewes' *Works* have added two series whose fragmentary and uncertain character do not deprive them of some value for our purposes.[17] The first, a group of nineteen sermons on prayer, together with the *Preces Privatae,* will form the basis for an appraisal of Andrewes' teaching on prayer; while the second set, the sermons on the temptation of Christ, affords numerous instances of his insights into human nature and the struggle between good and evil within the soul.

From this enumeration of Andrewes' authentic sermons it will be seen how much store he set by preaching. He had definite ideas on its value, on its place in the liturgy, and on its limitations. In the first place, he asks,

> let us see how we serve His word, that part of His service which in this age—I might say in the error of this age—carries away all. For what is it to "serve God in holiness?" Why, to go to a sermon;

---

[15] *Works,* V, *Certain Sermons Preached at Sundry Times, upon Several Occasions,* 1-256.

[16] See *supra,* 15.

[17] *Works,* V, *Nineteen Sermons upon Prayer in General, and the Lord's Prayer in Particular,* 299-476; *Works,* V, *Seven Sermons upon the Temptation of Christ in the Wilderness,* 477-558. The history of their appearance in print, in one form or another, may be found in *Works,* V, v-viii, where also the editor assays their genuinity as Andrean remains.

all our holiday "holiness," yea and our working-day too, both are come to this, to hear—nay, I dare not say that, I cannot prove it— but to be at a sermon.[18]

The sermon is by no means the center nor the whole of our liturgy, for there is no fullness "of our Liturgy or public solemn Service, without the Sacrament. Some part, yea the chief part is wanting, if that be wanting."[19] And even when we falsely make it the center, how do we treat it?

We come to it if we will, we go our ways when we will; stay no longer than we will, and listen to it while we will; and sleep out, or turn us and talk out, or sit still and let our minds rove the rest whither they will; take stitch at a phrase or word, and censure it how we will.[20]

It is nothing but a stratagem of Satan to shrink up our service of God into one part, and that a part

where we may be or not be: being, hear or not hear; hearing, mind or not mind; minding, either remember or forget; give no account to any what we do or not do; only stay out the hour, if that, and then go our way, many of us as wise as we came; but all in a manner hearing . . . a sermon preached, no otherwise than we do a ballad sung. . . . Eye-service God likes not, I am sure, no more should I think doth He ear-service.[21]

It is entirely wrong to compare the parts of divine service, "to set them at odds together these two ways, as the fond fashion now-a-days is, whether is better, Prayer or Preaching; the Word or the Sacraments."[22] Sermons are important; do not give up attending them:

For, benefacitis attendentes. Yet not to be carried away with the common error, that sermon-hearing is the consummatum est of all

---

18 Works, IV, Gunpowder Sermon IX, 376-77.
19 Works, I, Nativity Sermon I, 62.
20 Works, IV, Gunpowder Sermon IX, 377.
21 Works, IV, Gunpowder Sermon IX, 377-78.
22 Works, III, Easter Sermon XIV, 22.

Christianity; and so we hear our sermons duly, all is safe, more needs not. But to resolve with ourselves that only will not do it, somewhat there must be besides. And when all is done, it must be *factores verbi.*[23]

With this last recommendation that we be "factores verbi" Andrewes reveals the essence of his asceticism. Christianity demands action. "There is no article of faith or mystery of religion at all, but is as a key to open, and as a hand to lead us to some operative virtue."[24] Too often with us, he complains, the word "turneth to nothing but wind."[25] After we hear the word of God we should

> get us a little out of the noise about us, and withdraw ourselves some whither, where we might be by ourselves, that when we have heard Him speak to us, we might hear what He would speak in us. When we have heard the voice before us, we might hear the other behind us, *Haec est via.*[26]

All preaching "is but to this end," to get us to pray;[27] and "the only true praise of a sermon is, some evil left, or some good done upon the hearing of it."[28] As things are, men either do not come to sermons, "or if they do it is to make jests. Or, at the best it is but as 'they hear a song of one that hath a pleasing voice,' and no more comes of the sermon than of the song."[29] Time and time again Andrewes chided his hearers for their inattention at a sermon, and for their failure to turn what they heard to practical use:

> The hearing we will give Him [Christ]; but soft, no law, by your leave. Our case is this: so long as it is but *praedicabo,* but

23 *Works,* V, Occasional Sermon IX, 202.
24 *Works,* V, Occasional Sermon IX, 196.
25 *Works,* I, Nativity Sermon VI, 99.
26 *Works,* III, Pentecost Sermon V, 199.
27 *Works,* III, Pentecost Sermon XI, 318.
28 *Works,* I, Ash Wednesday Sermon VII, 423.
29 *Works,* I, Ash Wednesday Sermon VI, 407.

preaching, we care not greatly though we hear it; but if it once come to *legem*, to be pressed upon us as "a law," farewell our parts; we give Him over, for law binds, and we will not be bound. . . . Leave Christ His book to preach by, but keep the law in our own hands.[30]

Andrewes had both advice and criticism to offer for the preacher as well as for the laity, whose patience in the face of some specimens of pulpit oratory is a thing to be marveled at in any age. Let the preacher not seek the praise of men, he advises, for if the

> fruit of our labors be but the fruit of men's lips, we are like to make but a cold reckoning of it, "to inherit the wind." . . . And sure it is, on whom a sermon works aright, it leaves him not leisure to say much, to use many words, but makes him rather full of thoughts.[31]

We preachers, he says in another place, are the "Lord's remembrancers; as to God for the people by the office of prayers, so from God to the people by the office of preaching."[32] The preacher's duty is to preach to men *"non quae volunt audire, sed quae volunt audisse,* 'not what for the present they would hear, but what another day they would wish they had heard.' "[33] Let the preacher not worry so much about "volubility of utterance, earnestness of action, straining the voice in a passionate delivery"; let him rather concentrate on the soundness of his doctrine, for "it is the evidence of the Spirit in the soundness of sense that leaves the true impression." All these other things have their place, but they "come in passion; move for the present, make us a little sermon-warm for the while; but after, they flit and vanish, and go their way—true mark leave they none."

---

[30] *Works,* I, Nativity Sermon XVII, 300.
[31] *Works,* I, Lenten Sermon VII, 423.
[32] *Works,* II, Lenten Sermon IV, 64.
[33] *Works,* I, Ash Wednesday Sermon IV, 358.

It is the wisdom of speech that is " 'the nail,' the nail red-hot, that leaveth a mark behind, that will never be got out."[34] Let the preacher use a text, for this will keep him to his point.[35] Let him draw on that "storehouse" and "very life of memory" the "history of time," as Scripture so constantly recommends, for this is but to turn the wheel and set "before us some case of antiquity which may sample ours, and either remembering to follow it if it fell out well, or eschew it if the success were thereafter."[36] As early as the days of his catechetical lectures at Pembroke, Andrewes drew up a pattern for the preacher in which he urges him to "deliver the word . . . with authority, gravity, and majesty; as knowing that it is not his own word, but the everlasting truth of God." And he should beware those among his hearers who have "*pruritum aurium,* 'itching ears' . . . a desire to hear an eloquent declamation out of a pulpit; to have a period fall roundly, pleasing the ear, and doing the soul no good."[37]

I have quoted at great length in recording Andrewes' ideas on preaching, partly to introduce the reader to the flavor of his writing and partly because it would otherwise have been difficult to convey the sharpness of his convictions on an activity very dear to his heart. The preceding selections, of course, are not exhaustive of the instances wherein he took occasion to express himself on the place of the sermon in the liturgy, on the reverence due it, and on its limitations as a tool for the forwarding of the work of the Church; but these selections should be sufficient to make clear one important point—that Lancelot An-

---

[34] *Works,* III, Pentecost Sermon II, 141-42.

[35] *Works,* III, Pentecost Sermon X, 280; where Andrewes says of Christ's first sermon (Luke 4:18-19) : "There was no fear Christ would have ranged far from His matter, if He had taken none; yet He took a text, to teach us thereby to do the like."

[36] *Works,* II, Lenten Sermon IV, 64-65.

[37] *Works,* VI, *Catechism,* 197, 196.

drewes was essentially a practical preacher.[38] This aspect of his sermons in particular, almost completely neglected hitherto, will demand a considerable amount of attention in the present study, for the practical nature of his preaching forms one of the major characteristics of all his work and proves in a most conclusive way that he was neither principally Lutheran nor Calvinist in his theology. Andrewes was constant in his insistence on the effort of the individual himself,[39] as Sir John Harington has noted quite aptly in his *Memoir:*

> Two special things I have observed in his preaching, that I may not omit to speak of. One, to raise a joint reverence to God and the Prince, to the spiritual and civil Magistrate, by uniting and not severing them. The other, to lead to amendment of life, and good works, the fruits of true repentance. . . . Of the second kind I might say all his sermons are.[40]

A reading of even a few of the sermons will show that Andrewes made use of the whole Christian heritage, albeit eclectically, as the source of thought and argument. He was outstandingly one of those seventeenth-century divines who "desired to gather up all that was best in the Church's past, and to adapt it for English use."[41] As early as the days of Hooker "men had been gradually unlearning some of those opinions, which intimacy with foreign Protestants had tended to foster, and had adopted a tone and way of thinking more like that of

---

38 Macleane, *Andrewes and the Reaction,* 171, insists on this.

39 See, for example, *Works,* V, Occasional Sermon IX, 186, on the text "And be ye doers of the word, and not hearers only, deceiving your own selves" (James 1:22).

40 *Works,* XI, Harington, *Memoir,* xxxvii.

41 Felix R. Arnott, "Anglicanism in the Seventeenth Century." This is the second of two introductory essays in Paul Elmer More and Frank Leslie Cross, editors, *Anglicanism, the Thought and Practice of the Church of England, Illustrated from the Religious Literature of the Seventeenth Century* (London, 1935). See lxxii. Arnott's essay is a very satisfactory summary of seventeenth-century Anglicanism. This work of More and Cross is most helpful for a study of things Anglican.

the early Church."[42] The whole cast of Andrewes' mind, in fact, was toward the past. What Brightman observes of the *Preces Privatae*—namely, that in them little use was made of sixteenth-century materials—may equally be affirmed of his sermons, and indeed of most of his extant works, for we find Andrewes referring very seldom to contemporary or recent writers except when in controversy he takes issue with them.[43] He drew rather on the rich tradition of the Christian past. The Scriptures, patristic writings, the first four councils, the scholastics, and the writers of ecclesiastical history—these were his favorite fonts whether he was trying to illustrate or prove a theological position or urging a course of conduct; and while he never hesitated to appeal to the probative force of reason, it was always as to a confirmatory and supplementary source and not as to a final arbiter. In the use of these rich repositories of ideas Andrewes was apt to be heavy, pedantic, tiresomely detailed, and yet more haphazard in some respects than his modern counterpart would ever dare to be; and thus in all he showed himself very much the child of his age.[44] One of his editors remarks:

> With respect to the quotations generally, and particularly those from Scripture, it will be found that they are scarcely ever given

---

[42] *The Works of That Learned and Judicious Divine, Mr. Richard Hooker: with an Account of His Life and Death, by Isaac Walton.* Arranged by the Rev. John Keble, second edition (Oxford, 1841), I, lxx. Says Brightman a little more rhetorically in his introduction to *The Preces Privatae*, xlvii: "They [the *Preces*] represent for the individual what it was the mission of Andrewes and his fellows to vindicate for the English Church—the inheritance of all the past, criticized by the best spirit of the Renaissance, adjusted to the proportion of Holy Scripture, and adapted to the needs of the present."

[43] Brightman, *The Preces Privatae*, xliii ff.

[44] Arnott, "Anglicanism in the Seventeenth Century," in More and Cross, *Anglicanism*, lvi: "The Seventeenth Century was an age of vast erudition. The number of marginal references to the Scriptures and the writings of the Fathers is amazing to one reading the folio editions for the first time. It is true that as yet the historical and critical faculties of scholars were not highly developed. . . . Scholarship was ponderous rather than brilliant, and with a few notable exceptions used mainly in order to lay low theological opponents."

in the exact words of the author referred to, but that the sense or substance of a passage is for the most part rather quoted from memory, than given with that exactness which is usual in the present day. This remark will be found to apply not merely to English, but to Latin and Greek quotations, and it would perhaps be difficult to point out many instances to the contrary.[45]

He was the child of his day in another and a better sense. Reliance on Scripture was characteristic of the period; and whether Andrewes was preaching a sermon, deciding a moral issue, or seeking to confound his opponents in controversy, he turned most effectively and most consistently to the Holy Scriptures.[46] No page of his sermons lacks at least an allusion to Scripture, and his mind was so impregnated with it "that its expressions became the natural vehicle of his own thoughts."[47] He was, of course, a recognized Scripture scholar, as his appointment to head the company of translators who sat at Westminster indicates.[48] A purely mechanical indication of his familiarity with the Scriptures is the index of texts appended to the last volume of the *Works*.[49] It occupies forty-nine pages of double-column entries, many of which are multiple. Andrewes, as befitting a non-Puritan, seems not to have succumbed to excessive devotion to the Old Testament, for the references in the index are roughly half for the Old and half for the New. The Old Testament, of course, containing as it does many more books than the New, offers a great deal more matter. Andrewes'

---

[45] *Works*, I, vii.

[46] John Hunt, *Religious Thought in England from the Reformation to the End of Last Century. A Contribution to the History of Theology* (London, 1870), I, 191. Hunt calls Milton's reliance on Scripture "characteristic of that age."

[47] James Russell, Preface to Edmund Venables, editor, *The Private Devotions of Lancelot Andrewes, D.D., Successively Lord Bishop of Chichester, Ely, and Winchester,* revised and new edition (London, 1883), vii.

[48] See *supra,* 6.

[49] *Works*, XI, "Index of Texts to Sermons," 339-90. The title is a little misleading, for the index actually includes references to Scripture and distinguishes with an asterisk the text of sermons.

use of it is broader; for example, he builds his theory of kingship and the divine right of kings on the Old Testament, while
his treatment of the New Testament is generally more allusive.
In any case, he was a master of the Scriptures and had a rare
ability to put them to lively use. He knew all the major versions
of the Bible then current: the Genevan Bible of 1560, from
which most of his sermon texts are taken; the Bishops' Bible
of 1568 and 1572, the official version until the King James
version supplanted it; the Rheims version of the New Testament,
1582 (and presumably the Rheims version of the Old Testament, 1610); and the Vulgate.[50] Naturally accepting the Anglican canon of the Scriptures, he rates the apocrypha as next
in authority.[51]

In one of his earlier sermons Andrewes proposed this estimate of the value of Scripture:

> The commendation of the word of God is, that "Every Scrip-
> ture is profitable for our instruction." "Every Scripture is profit-
> able;" yet not "every Scripture," in every place alike. For the
> place and auditory have great interest in some Scripture, and a fit
> Scripture hath a greater and fuller force in his own auditory. And
> God in so excellent a manner hath sorted His Scriptures, as there
> lie dispersed in them several texts seasonable for each time, and
> pertinent to each place and degree; for Prince, for people, for rich,
> for poor, for each his peculiar Scripture in due time and place to
> be reached them.[52]

---

[50] Russell, *Memoirs of the Life and Works of Lancelot Andrewes*, 272; *Works*, I,
vii-viii. See Mitchell, *English Pulpit Oratory*, 135 and 160, for the influence
of the Vulgate on the Anglo-Catholic preachers. Andrewes generally used the
Genevan Bible for his sermon texts.

[51] *Works*, VIII, *Responsio ad Bellarminum*, 209-10, where he contends that the
Anglican canon and that of the Jews is the same for the Old Testament; "All
the ancient writers are full of allegations from them [the *Apocrypha*]; ever
to these writings yielding the next place after the Canon of the Scriptures,
and preferring them before all foreign writers whatsoever" (*Works*, V, Occasional Sermon II, 61).

[52] *Works*, V, Occasional Sermon I, 3-4. This was preached in 1588.

This might well be taken as his cardinal principle on Holy Scripture. All the Scriptures are profitable, for in them "whatsoever the heathen have spoken wisely, we have far more wisely uttered by the Holy Ghost in one place or other."[53] They are the source of our comfort and hope, they contain the books of the law which serve as precepts for our direction and the history which yields examples for our imitation, and reverent should be our attention to them: "A man may hear a story, and never wash his hands, but a mystery requireth both the hands and heart to be clean that shall deal with it."[54] The real basis of their value and of the reverence due them, of course, is the fact of their inspiration, to which Andrewes recurs with frequency. Inspiration was in his day an accepted fact, and he seems to have held for verbal inspiration: "But sure to purpose it is, the Holy Ghost useth no waste words, nor ever speaks but to the point we may be sure."[55]

Andrewes' teaching on the interpretation of Scripture seems to have gone through a certain evolution. In a sketchy section of the *Catechism* entitled "Of our religion as different from the Papists' " he specifies as critical the difference in the means used by each for the interpretation of Scripture.[56] "They have

---

[53] *Works*, V, Sermon on the Temptation of Christ III, 508.

[54] *Works*, II, Easter Sermon V, 266; *Works*, IV, Gunpowder Sermon X, 401; the quotation is from *Works*, I, Nativity Sermon III, 32.

[55] *Works*, III, Easter Sermon XVIII, 84. See also *Works*, I, Nativity Sermon V, 64, and 72: "By which word [*hodie*] the Holy Ghost may seem to have marked it out, and made it the peculiar text of the day"; and "Now upon all these He setteth an *ecce*, and well He may; and that is never set by the Holy Ghost but *super res magnae entitatis*, 'upon matters of great moment.' " Andrewes is referring to the text of his sermon in both instances; see Luke 2:10-11. Of another sermon text (Joel 2:12-13) he says: "But it is not Joel, God it is that speaketh Who best knoweth what turning it is that pleaseth Him best; and Whom we must needs leave to prescribe the manner how He would have us to turn unto Him" (*Works*, I, Ash Wednesday Sermon IV, 366).

[56] *Works*, VI, *Catechism*, 57-61.

the Fathers, Councils, the Church and the Pope," he says; "we have not so." The Scripture, however, is not for private interpretation. There must be a certain and infallible interpretation of Scripture, otherwise we would always be uncertain; to determine it we need an authoritative interpreter. Private interpretation seeks to devise a sense for Scripture, but the real business of interpretation is to give Scripture its proper sense. The ability to interpret correctly is a gift, given to those in the Church, not "to the common sort of every private man, but to the learned." Nor is this gift restricted to some one bishop, as the papists claim. It is not the letter which is the word of God, but the meaning of a passage, and that is what we seek. Thomas Aquinas advises, continues Andrewes, that we must take the literal sense in a matter of faith or morals, that in others we may take the tropological sense; and further that each place in Scripture has its one true sense, the one the construction will give if no absurdity follows.[57] Having laid down these general principles, Andrewes then enumerates six means of interpretation "as we allege them": prayer, comparison of places ("the less plain must be referred to the more plain"), an examination of the original ("inspectio fontium"), a knowledge of the dialect in which the Scriptures are written, a consideration of the scope of the sacred writer, and lastly a study of the antecedents, consequences, and circumstances involved.[58] These are admirable criterions indeed, and Andrewes remained faithful to them. What interests us particularly here in view of his later opinions and practice is his rejection of the fathers as interpreters of the Scripture. "We shall not find one place of a hundred which they all expound alike, so that few of their expositions should be received."[59] Of both fathers and the councils, which the papists

---

[57] *Works*, VI, *Catechism*, 57-58.
[58] *Works*, VI, *Catechism*, 58-59.
[59] *Works*, VI, *Catechism*, 60.

allege as interpreters, he says, "if there be doubt in the scriptures, there is much more in the exposition" which they attempt
to give.[60] Councils too have contradicted one another.[61] So
neither of these means of interpretation which the Catholics
postulate is sound. Nor is the pope any better guide, for popes
have subscribed to heresy in the past, and the Church, fourth
of the Roman Catholic means of interpretation, is just as bad,
for it too is liable to error.

How accurately this section in the *Catechism* represents
Andrewes' teaching at the time of his catechetical lectures at
Pembroke (*c.* 1580) is a difficult question, for the lectures were
published, as far as can be determined, from the notes of his
hearers.[62] The norms of interpretation here recommended, insofar as they reject the fathers and the councils, have a definite
Puritan tinge, and differ to that extent from those scattered
throughout the sermons. It seems fair, however, to conclude that
Andrewes once held and taught a doctrine on interpretation
more or less as indicated in this section of the *Catechism*. It will
be remembered that he was subject in his early academic career
to Puritan influence; the Puritans at Cambridge thought they
saw in him a likely candidate for their party. Henry Hastings,
earl of Huntingdon, whose chaplain he was, had definite Puritan leanings, and Walsingham exerted pressure on Andrewes in
the same direction. Is it likely that, unless Andrewes had shown
some sympathy with Puritan teaching, these approaches would
have been made to him?[63] The publishing of an edition of the

---

[60] *Works*, VI, *Catechism*, 59.
[61] *Works*, VI, *Catechism*, 60.
[62] See *supra*, 2, *Works*, VI, *Catechism*, iii-iv. Of the section we have been discussing above Macleane says that it "consists of a few fragmentary notes
only. . . . It is impossible to believe that Andrewes would have allowed this
part of the Catechistical Doctrine to see the light in its present unripe and
almost absurd form" (Macleane, *Andrewes and the Reaction*, 33, 34).
[63] See *supra*, 4-5, note 13.

Catechism under Puritan auspices in 1642 may indicate that Andrewes' early teaching was actually more acceptable to that party than were his later and more mature efforts.[64] This interesting problem is one of the rare instances where a change in Andrewes' teaching is discernible.[65]

As often happens in the changes which maturity brings, Andrewes' position on the interpretation of Scripture broadened; so considerably in fact that, whereas once he had rejected the fathers as a means of interpretation, he later relied on them very heavily. He was to treat the councils with more respect; and both these sources were to become essential parts of his rule of faith for the English Church. A similar broadening of approach manifests itself in his handling of Scripture, which developed greater freedom of movement and confidence as time went on. He distinguished, for example, four senses that the Scripture would bear, and he did not hesitate to develop now one, now another, with his sure and steady touch. Beyond the literal sense are the analogical, the moral, and the prophetical. All four are exemplified, he says, in the text for his Pentecost sermon of 1614: "Thou hast led captivity captive, and received gifts for men; yea, even the rebellious hast Thou led, that the Lord God might dwell there." In this passage the literal sense refers to Moses when he ascended Mount Sinai on the way from Israel's long captivity and received the Law, the priesthood, and the Ark of the Covenant; the analogical sense refers to King David and his carrying of the Ark up to Mount Sion—

---

[64] The publisher was Michael Sparke, who published for William Prynne. The *Catechism* in Sparke's edition was entitled *The Morall Law Expounded. 1. Largely, 2. Learnedly, 3. Orthodoxly, That Is the Long Expected and Much Desired Work of Bishop Andrewes upon the Ten Commandments* . . . (London, 1642). Macleane calls attention to this apparent anomaly (*Andrewes and the Reaction*, 40, note 1).

[65] For another, see his teaching on the origin of government discussed *infra*, 186-88.

"As Moses to Sinai, so David to Sion"; while the moral sense
arises from the two previous:

> That, as whensoever God's people are carried captive and made
> thrall to their enemies; as then God seemeth to be put down, and
> lie foiled for a time, that one may well say, *Exsurgat Deus*, to
> Him: so when He takes their cause in hand and works their deliver-
> ance, it may well be said, *Ascendit in altum*, "He is gone up," as
> it were, to His high throne or judgment-seat, there to give sentence
> for them. Ever the Church's depressing is, as it were, God's own
> humiliation; and their deliverance, after a sort His exaltation. For
> then He hath the upper hand. And this is the moral.[66]

The fourth and highest sense is the prophetical. If God may be
said to be "down" in any captivity, such as of Egypt or of
Babylon, and then in any deliverance "to be got up on high: in
this of Christ, of all other, it is most pregnantly verified."[67] It
is this sense which Andrewes develops in his sermon.[68]

This freedom and breadth in his use of Scripture, this will-
ingness to depart from the literal and to deal with the riches
of a more extended sense, are well illustrated in a remarkable
sermon delivered in 1616 on the text "Mercy and Truth shall
meet; Righteousness and Peace shall kiss one another. Truth
shall bud out of the earth; and Righteousness shall look down
from Heaven" (Psalm 85:10-11). We can do no better than to
quote directly from an introductory paragraph:

> As his manner is, the Psalmist in it under one compriseth the
> type and the truth both; by those things which befell the people of
> the Jews, the Church typical, shadowing out those things which

---

[66] *Works*, III, Pentecost Sermon VII, 222.
[67] *Works*, III, Pentecost Sermon VII, 223.
[68] Three years earlier Andrewes made similar distinctions of sense in his sermon
text. Of the verse "The Stone Which the builders refused, the same Stone is
become . . . the Head of the corner" (Psalm 118:22), he says that the Holy
Ghost applies it through St. Peter's mouth to Christ (the prophetic sense),
that historically it applies to David (the literal sense). See *Works*, II, Easter
Sermon VI, 270, 271.

were to befall the Antitype of it, Christ and His Church. For, *primâ et propriâ intentione*, it cannot be denied but the Psalm was first set according to the letter upon the turning back of the captivity of Babel. But the Prophet knew well that was not their worst captivity, nor should be their best delivery. There was another yet behind concerned them more, if they understood their own state aright, which was reserved to the Messias to free them from. To that he points.[69]

Here we find Andrewes introducing the notions of type and antitype. The basis of the typical sense, he says in another place, is the correspondence existing between Christ and patriarchs, prophets, and people before Christ, "of whom the Apostle's rule is, *omnia in figurâ contingebant illis;* 'that they were themselves types,' and their sufferings forerunning figures of the great suffering of the Son of God."[70] When the Holy Ghost speaks in the New Testament, He opens unto us the meaning of the types and prophecies of the Old.[71] Whereas prophesying in the Old Testament meant foretelling the future, in the New it means speaking "magnalia Dei," applying the Old Testament prophecies, explaining them, lifting the "veil of Moses' face," and not foretelling the future.[72] It is necessary, of course, to have prophecies explained to us, for the "Prophets use to speak of things to come as if they saw them present before their eyes." They speak to their people in their own language; to express the enemies of their souls, for example, the prophets use the titles and terms of those nations and cities which were known to be the sworn enemies of the commonwealth of Israel.[73]

These quotations from Andrewes' principles for the interpretation and use of Scripture have been drawn, it will be

---

[69] *Works*, I, Nativity Sermon XI, 175-76.
[70] *Works*, II, Passion Sermon II, 139.
[71] *Works*, II, Passion Sermon I, 119.
[72] *Works*, III, Pentecost Sermon XI, 312-13.
[73] *Works*, III, Easter Sermon XVII, 62, 63.

noticed, from a wide variety of his sermons. Without doubt they reflect far more faithfully than do the notes of the *Catechism* his method for determining and expounding the sense of Scripture. Since we have been discussing his treatment and understanding of prophecy, the following long but very striking quotation from his first sermon on the Passion may serve as a conclusion to this section. It illustrates his knowledge of Scripture, as well as his method of arguing from it, and offers a good example of his abrupt, syncopated style.

> 1. First, the better to specify and particularize the Person of Christ, by the kind, and most peculiar circumstance, of His death. Esay had said, *Morietur*, "Die He shall, and lay down His soul an offering for sin." 2. Die—but what death? a natural or a violent? Daniel tells us, *Occidetur;* He shall die, not a natural, but a violent death. 3. But many are slain after many sorts, and divers kinds there be of violent deaths. The Psalmist, the more particularly to set it down, describeth it thus: "They pierced My hands and My feet;" which is only proper to the death of the Cross. 4. Die, and be slain, and be crucified. But sundry else were crucified; and therefore the Prophet here, to make up all, addeth, that He should not only be *crucifixus*, but *transfixus;* not only have His hands and His feet, but even His heart pierced too. Which very note severs Him from all the rest, with as great particularity as may be; for that, though many besides at other times, and some at the same time with Him were crucified, yet the side and the heart of none was opened, but His, and His only.[74]

To one of the principles laid down in the *Catechism* in particular Andrewes remained faithful: he detested private interpretation. This business of trusting every man "upon his own single bond . . . to deliver the meaning of any Scripture, which is many times nought else but his own imagination," is "the disease of our age."[75] He will have no "ἰδίᾳ ἐπιλύσει,

---

[74] *Works*, II, Passion Sermon I, 121.
[75] *Works*, V, Occasional Sermon II, 57.

'private interpretation' of our own head; but Micah by Matthew, the Prophet by the Evangelist—ever the best."[76] When a difficulty arises, he rules, the text may not be tampered with: "*non potest solvi Scriptura.*"[77] Look to the occasion, for the occasion "of the speaking is ever the best key to every speech."[78] Compare the texts by way of harmony and exposition, that the one may make plain the meaning of the other, even as Christ did in resisting the temptations of the devil. This conference of Scripture with Scripture is a wise course."[79] We should always "expound the lesser number [of texts concerning a given point] by the greater, and not contrary . . . the former writer . . . by the latter."[80]

Scripture should never be forced to deliver a meaning which it does not have. We must not put more into a speech of Christ, for example, than is there naturally, for that is all we have received from the Lord and all we are to deliver to our hearers.[81] "We do but make ourselves to be pitied otherwhile, when we stand wringing the Scriptures, to strain that out of them that is not in them, and so can never come *liquide* from them, when yet we have for the same point the Churches' custom clear enough," he tells his hearers on Easter of 1618.[82] In fact, he says in another place, "to destroy a text is not so evil as to make a text destroy itself."[83] Andrewes used the Scriptures with great assurance, logic, and good sense; if he strains them a little on occasion, it is usually for a devotional rather than for a dogmatic point, and one is rarely inclined to retort to him that even

---

76 *Works*, I, Nativity Sermon X, 154.
77 *Works*, I, Nativity Sermon VI, 92.
78 *Works*, II, Passion Sermon III, 159.
79 *Works*, V, Sermon on the Temptation of Christ V, 526.
80 *Works*, XI, *Discourse against Second Marriage*, 109.
81 *Works*, I, Ash Wednesday Sermon VI, 399.
82 *Works*, II, Easter Sermon XIII, 406.
83 *Works*, I, Ash Wednesday Sermon V, 384.

the devil quotes Scripture to his purpose.[84] He even has a word for translators, so meticulous is his care for accuracy in handling the sacred texts: "I wish no word ever narrowed by a translation, but as much as might be left in the latitude of the original tongue."[85] His own translations, it might be remarked, follow this norm even to the sacrifice of strict literalness, but they are rarely forced.[86] Finally, despite his caution against the fathers as interpreters of the Scriptures in the *Catechism*, Andrewes made full use of their authority, and this significant change represents his greatest departure from the earlier norms of the *Catechism*.[87] But it is entirely consonant with the general development of his theology and his theological method, for the two main sources of his thought and arguments are the Scriptures and the fathers of the first five centuries.

To sense the full flavor of Bishop Andrewes' masterly use of Holy Scripture there is no substitute for reading his sermons, for, as has been suggested, the Scriptures grew to be the natural vehicle for the expression of his thought.[88] If we attempt to specify the outstanding characteristics of his handling of the sacred writings, we might safely list four: thorough acquaintance, sympathetic understanding, penetrating insight into the complex interrelationships of the sacred books, and, finally, control. It will not do to try to exemplify each, but a few instances of Andrewes at work with the Scriptures will, perhaps,

---

[84] See *Works*, IV, Gunpowder Sermon II, 224, where he advises his hearers that he is taking the liberty of changing one word of a text that it might better suit his purpose.

[85] *Works*, I, Nativity Sermon III, 228.

[86] See *supra*, 41, note 74, for an example of the fullness Andrewes gives his translations.

[87] *Works*, II, Easter Sermon V, 259-60, where he appeals to Augustine, Gregory, and Jerome to guide him. See also *Works*, II, Passion Sermon II, 140: "And this rule, and the steps of the Fathers proceeding by this rule, are to me a warrant to expound and apply this verse, as they have done before." For the rule see *supra*, 40 ("*ômnia in figurâ contingebant illis. . . .*").

[88] *Supra*, 33.

enable the reader to appreciate how eminently he possessed these qualities. Notice, for example, how in the following sentence he refers effectively to eleven minor figures (or groups thereof) in the Scriptures. In one of his rare references to the poor he writes:

> The tidings of the Gospel are as well for "Lydia the purple seller" as for "Simon the tanner;" for "the Areopagite," the judge at Athens, as for the "jailor" at Philippi; for "the elect lady" as for widow "Dorcas;" for the "Lord Treasurer of Ethiopia" as for "the beggar at the beautiful gate of the temple;" for "the household of Caesar" as for "the household of Stephanas;" yea and, if he will, for "king Agrippa" too.[89]

Lancelot Andrewes' delicate appreciation of the real and the human in Scripture runs through every line of this very delightful characterization of Mary Magdalen. No one, he tells us, ever had to suffer more unfavorable interpretation of his best deeds than those she had more than once to sustain.

> Three special virtues of hers the Gospels record, and in every one of the three she was repined at. 1. When, in the bitterness of her soul she shewed her repentance with tears, Simon the Pharisee did what he could to disgrace her. 2. When, in a hungry desire to receive comfort by the word of grace, she shewed her devotion in sitting at Christ's feet, Martha, her own sister, made complaint of her. 3. And now here again the third time; when, in an honest regard of her duty she sheweth her thankfulness for comfort received, Christ's own Disciples both grudge and speak against her. So that, if she washeth His feet with tears, it contents not; if she anoint His head with balm, it is a matter of mislike; if she sit still and say nothing, it is all one; still Mary is found fault with, ever her doings stand awry.[90]

Who has not felt at some time in his life quite as Andrewes describes Mary here?

------

[89] *Works*, III, Pentecost Sermon X, 290.
[90] *Works*, II, Lenten Sermon III, 58.

It is not unusual to meet in Andrewes a neat, novel treatment and arrangement of disparate facts whose inner relationship he is quick to see. In one of the Nativity sermons, for
instance, he makes the point that Christ came to the Gentile as
well as to the Jew; even this was foreshadowed in the Old Testament history: "the heathen were never wholly out." Where was
the Law given? he asks; was it not on Sinai, a mountain in a
heathen land? And by whom was it given? was it not by Moses,
and he married to a heathen woman so that his children were
heathen by "half blood"? And were not the silk and gold and
the riches of the Tabernacle the very spoils of Egypt, "and so
heathen stuff"? What of the Temple? It was founded on the
threshing floor of Ornan the Jebusite, a heathen, and so on
heathen soil. The materials of which it was built came from the
land of a heathen king (Hiram) and the chief workman on it
was the son of a man of Tyre and so a heathen also.[91] This is
not superficial rhetoric; it is the outpouring of a man who knew
his Scripture and who penetrated to its deepest unities.

We might multiply examples of Andrewes' use of the Scriptures by the hundreds, but we must pass on. Perhaps, however,
the retailing of an incident or two may be pardoned. Andrewes'
interest in Scripture did not limit itself to his own work. He was
concerned to see scriptural studies advanced, and such seems to
have been his reputation. Amongst the Sloane manuscripts in
the British Museum are two Latin letters to him from one John
Boys, a learned canon of Ely.[92] The first expresses gratitude to
Andrewes for favors shown and professes friendship and indebt-
edness. The second strives very gently to stir Andrewes to return
to Boys "schedulas illas, in quibus veterem interpretem cum

---

[91] *Works*, I, Nativity Sermon XIV, 239-40.
[92] British Museum, Sloane MSS., 118, f. 24, John Boys to the Bishop of Winchester
[Andrewes], October 28, 1619; f. 30, John Boys to the Bishop of Winchester,
"postridie animarum [November 3]," 1624.

recentioribus aliquot in quattuor Evangeliis compono." Boys
had sent them to Andrewes for examination three years before
and is anxious to complete the work that he might send it on
again to the bishop for further criticism.[93] The "schedulas" seem
to have been Boys's comparision of the Vulgate with modern
versions of the New Testament mentioned by Russell in his
Memoirs of Andrewes.[94] When Nicholas Fuller felt his death
approaching, he sent the bishop a Hebrew lexicon on which he
had been working, along with some other unfinished papers.
From Allington he wrote on August 17, 1622:

> I have here sent unto your Lordship an Hebrew Lexicon, con-
> taining the several significations of the Hebrew and Chaldee roots
> gathered by me out of all the translations both Greek and Vul-
> gar Latin, that were ever used in the Church of Christ. And to
> the Lexicon pertaineth a little book of short observations upon
> very many words of the Bible, together with certain small papers
> therein. The Lexicon was gathered for this purpose, that out of
> it . . . there might be framed 2 artificial Lexicons: the one,
> wonderful large: which, having proceeded therein by the space of
> some 24 sheets (as is here to be seen, though never perused by me)
> I gave clean over, perceiving evidently, that it was not possible for
> me, being already an aged man, ever to finish one quarter thereof.
> The other an abridgment of the former, which, because I was in
> good hope within the space of 2 or 3 years at most to have ended,
> I was beginning to undertake. But at the very instant my sickness
> seizing upon me, overthrew all. Now therefore let all be as it shall
> please God and your Lordship to dispose of. It may be my singular
> friend Mr. Erpenius might use it to some good intent.[95]

Andrewes felt himself the heir of all the Christian past, and
it was largely in his appeal to it that he departs from the Puritan

---

[93] British Museum, Sloane MSS., 118, f. 30.

[94] Russell, *Memoirs of the Life and Works of Lancelot Andrewes*, 410.

[95] Bodleian Library, Additional MSS., C, 279, f. 95 (spelling and punctuation
modernized). Erpenius was a Dutch scholar who had introduced Andrewes
to Fuller, as is delightfully related in an undated and unsigned MS. in the
Bodleian. See *infra*, 90-91.

principle of regarding the Scriptures as the sole and exclusive source of Christian teaching. He ranges through the fathers, the early Christian writers, and the scholastics with a sense of possession and familiarity. Augustine, Chrysostom, Basil, Gregory, Eusebius, Aquinas, Bernard—these as well as the sacred writers were his to use, and use them he did. It is as if he should say: These men are Christians, and so are a part of my heritage; they are not Roman Catholics, or Puritans, and therefore of an opposing camp; they are Christians. Christianity is the great fact in history, and for Andrewes Anglicanism (though he would not have used the term) is but the English expression of it. Harington writes of him that he "gathered before he did spend, reading both new writers and old writers, not as tasting, but as digesting them and finding according to our Saviour's saying, ὁ παλαιὸς χρηστότερος, the old to be more profitable."[96] In his first letter to Du Moulin, Andrewes compliments the French theologian on his respect for the authority of antiquity: "Amo te de hoc verbo," he writes, and adds, "Ego quidem sic sensi, sic semper affectus fui."[97]

Patristic study in the sixteenth and seventeenth centuries had not attained a very high level of criticism, of course, and Andrewes suffered from the deficiencies of his day.[98] He did, however, have a nascent sense of criticism.[99] What engages and interests us here is precisely the fact that he appealed to the fathers as authorities. "Quicquid enim quadringentis post Christum annis, unanimi consensu, Patres ad aeternam salutem esse necessarium statuerunt, aut cum iis ita esse sentiam, aut modesto saltem silentio obmutescam, reprehendere certe non

---

[96] *Works*, XI, Harington, *Memoir*, xxxvi.

[97] *Works*, IX, *Responsiones ad Petri Molinaei epistolas*, I, 184.

[98] Dom Gregory Dix, *The Shape of the Liturgy*, second edition (Westminster, 1947), 626-27. Dom Dix mentions particularly the lack of critical texts and poor knowledge of context.

[99] See *infra*, 212-13.

audeo," King James had written in his *Monitory Preface*. When Andrewes came to consider this passage in his *Responsio ad Bellarminum*, he accepted it without distinction.[100] The fathers were to form a part of his rule of faith;[101] and throughout the sermons one constantly meets expressions such as, "The rule of the Fathers is," "So say the Fathers with uniform consent," "There is not one of the Fathers that I have read, but interpret it" thus and so, "As the Fathers read the third of Habbakuk," and so forth.[102]

In sermon after sermon one will find some father quoted or alluded to: Justin Martyr, Chrysostom, Gregory of Nyssa, Gregory the Great, and above all Augustine, who was undoubtedly Andrewes' favorite.[103] For dogma, exegesis, and practice Andrewes turns with confidence and decision to Augustine: "Take that from Augustine," he says, for example, in concluding a paragraph of exegesis in the Christmas sermon delivered in 1616.[104] Linked very often with the fathers in Andrewes' writings are the councils of the Church, the first four of which, in common with Anglicans generally, he accepted as authentic sources of true Christian teaching: "I conclude," he says in one place, "with the style of the Councils: *Sequentes igitur et nos per omnia Sanctorum Patrum vestigia;* 'we herein do but tread in the steps of our Holy Fathers', and follow them who were

---

[100] *Works*, VIII, *Responsio ad Bellarminum*, 207-08. For the quotation from James see 207, note k. James used *quingentis* and *quadringentis* indiscriminately, says Andrewes, 207.

[101] See *infra*, 78-79.

[102] *Works*, III, Pentecost Sermon II, 135; *Works*, I, Nativity Sermon XI, 175; *Works*, II, Easter Sermon VI, 270; *Works*, I, Nativity Sermon XII, 204.

[103] There is about a column and a quarter of references to Augustine in the "Index to Sermons, Etc.," *Works*, XI, 397; there are two columns in the *Index generalis* to the Latin works, *Works*, IX, 8.

[104] *Works*, I, Nativity Sermon XI, 192. Augustine is appealed to as advocating the practice of fasting in *Works*, I, Ash Wednesday Sermon V, 379, and in support of the dogmatic belief in the actuality of hell fire, *Works*, I, Ash Wednesday Sermon VII, 426.

followers therein of God Himself."[105] In another place he takes as authoritative a definition of the Fourth General Council.[106] Among the ecclesiastical writers we meet, *passim*, Origen, Theodoret, Tertullian, Eusebius, to whom, however, he does not assign authority as high as that of the fathers and the councils.

That Andrewes should have been familiar with the scholastics was most natural. Scholastic influences still made themselves felt in the universities during the days of his matriculation at Pembroke; there had hardly been time, even where the Puritan influence was strong, to drive them from the lecture halls and the libraries, and the normal divinity curriculum in Andrewes' day still relied heavily on the works of the schoolmen.[107] The libraries were full of scholastic writings; Andrewes' own, given by him to Pembroke College, contains such stalwart scholastics as Aquinas, Suarez, Cajetan, Canisius, Stapleton, Richard Middleton, Albertus Magnus, among many others.[108]

In the sermons the schoolmen are not so often referred to by name, nor used anywhere near as frequently, as the fathers. Their opinions are adduced largely in a subordinate and confirmatory position; for their authority, Andrewes says, is not good for ancient times.[109] Scattered throughout are a few common scholastic expressions for which Andrewes offers a quasi

---

105 *Works*, IV, Gunpowder Sermon X, 401.

106 *Works*, I, Nativity Sermon VI, 91.

107 James Bass Mullinger, *The University of Cambridge from the Royal Injunctions of 1535 to the Accession of Charles the First* (Cambridge, 1884), 350.

108 *Works*, XI, "The Will of Bishop Andrewes," (codicil) cxiv-cxviii. This list does not correspond exactly with the list in Christopher Wren's MS. Catalogue of the Benefactors of the Library at Pembroke College, 1617. Andrewes' library is not kept separately in the Pembroke Library. The writer examined some of these books in the hope of finding *marginalia*, and so forth. He found none, but in Stapleton's voluminous *Principiorum fidei* of 1587 nearly every page has sentences or phrases neatly underlined—the mark of an intent reader. Andrewes usually signed his name on the title page; a progression in the style of his signature is clearly discernible.

109 *Works*, VII, *Tortura Torti*, 246.

apology by saying, "as the schoolmen call it," or "as the schoolmen term us," and so forth[110] Among the scholastics he seems not to have any particular favorite, though he accords Aquinas the respect which both Catholics and Protestants were wont to allow him as the greatest of the schoolmen.[111]

Let it be enough here to say that Andrewes also used the materials of ecclesiastical history as sources for his arguments. We must note, however, that he did not restrict himself to Christian (and scriptural) sources, for many are the allusions to, or quotations from, the writers of classical antiquity. Though he was not particularly an enthusiast for the classics, except perhaps during his days as a university don, they formed a part of his broad literary and historical knowledge, and one comes across the names of Terence, Juvenal, Virgil, Pliny, Thucydides, Horace, Ovid, as he reads the sermons.[112] Such writers are called in, of course, more for purposes of illustration than as witnesses to religious truth. Quite in keeping with a practice common among the Anglo-Catholic writers, Andrewes, who knew Hebrew well, drew also on later Semitic writings.[113] Within four sermons of the lenten group we find him referring to writers as varied as Pliny, Juvenal, St. Bernard, St. Gregory,

---

[110] *Works*, I, Nativity Sermon X, 164, 165; *Works*, II, Passion Sermon I, 128, and so forth.

[111] John K. Ryan, *The Reputation of St. Thomas Aquinas among English Protestant Thinkers of the Seventeenth Century* (Washington, 1948). The second chapter, "King James I and Lancelot Andrewes," 23-29, studies Andrewes' use of St. Thomas in the works of the Bellarmine controversy. Father Ryan's major conclusions are that the works of Aquinas were well known and widely used during the century, that he was acknowledged the greatest of the schoolmen, that the knowledge and use of Aquinas diminished as the century went on (118-19). Andrewes, he writes, "was decidedly scholastic in his cast of mind" (25). I do not agree with his further judgment that Andrewes' *Catechism* reveals him "a decadent scholastic in the most literal sense of that abused term" (25).

[112] Mitchell, *English Pulpit Oratory*, 183, 214.

[113] Mitchell, *English Pulpit Oratory*, 184.

St. Augustine, St. John Chrysostom, Theophylact, Josephus,
Virgil, Ovid, and Seneca, quite without any attempt at ostenta-
tious display.[114]

Plato and Aristotle, too, are laid under contribution.[115]
There was no contradiction between reason and revelation for
Andrewes; even St. Paul, he tells us, seems to have drawn ideas
from Plato.[116] "Religion and reason both teach us" is an expression frequently on his lips.[117] "If it be lawful," he says, "to
reason from that which 'nature teacheth,' as St. Paul doth
against men's wearing long hair, it is not unlawful neither to
reason from the wisest and most pithy sayings of natural
men."[118] The systematic use of reason, therefore, which is philosophy, is a legitimate source of argument. Anyone at all
familiar with scholasticism feels very much at home, then, when
he meets in Andrewes such scholastic commonplaces as "Unumquodque propter operationem suam" (the principle of finality),
"Unumquodque propter quid, et illud magis" (the principle of
causality), or the definition of person, "Naturae rationalis indi-
vidua substantia" (nicely translated by him as "a single or
determinate substance of a nature endued with reason"), and
an application of the familiar distinction between substance
and accidents.[119]

The length of the foregoing section must find its justification
in the necessity imposed on us by the character of this study of
determining the fonts of Andrewes' ideas. Had he chosen Scripture alone, he would have been a Puritan. Choose it he did, and

---

114 *Works*, II, Lenten Sermons II, IV, V, VI.
115 *Works*, I, Nativity Sermons, III, 33; XII, 207, and so forth, for Aristotle;
    Works, I, Nativity Sermon VIII, 128, for Plato.
116 See note 115.
117 *Works*, II, Lenten Sermon III, 40.
118 *Works*, V, Occasional Sermon II, 62.
119 *Works*, III, Easter Sermon XVIII, 93; *Works*, V, Occasional Sermon IX, 194;
    Works, IV, Gunpowder Sermon V, 280; *Works*, III, Pentecost Sermon VI, 205.

it is clearly the supreme source of his thought; but since he also chose to join to it the rich treasures of the Christian past, he was Catholic to that extent. He repudiated the prime Reformation principle of private interpretation, and so was no Lutheran, no Calvinist. The power and right of interpretation he placed as a gift, in the bosom of the Church; the learned—the fathers, for example—possessed it, but it was not the exclusive prerogative of one specific office or of a council under the presidency and jurisdiction of the holder of that office, and so he was not a Roman Catholic. Given all these, there was but one thing left—Andrewes was an Anglican, and the last thing he would have called that position is a compromise.

CHAPTER III

Andrewes'
Sermon Style

Whether or not the badly worn aphorism that "the style is the man" can really be said to express the relationship that exists between an author and his writing—or between a preacher and his sermon—the statement nevertheless has this pertinence to Bishop Lancelot Andrewes: his mode of expression seems first to have made, and then to have ruined, his reputation. I do not mean to say that there was no substance to his preaching, or that his manner alone accounted for the fame he won among his contemporaries; but rather that his style, at least as it appears in the written sermon, seals off from us of the present nearly the whole of Andrewes' fine theological thought. It was largely his style which drew to him the light of contemporary popularity; it is his style which has since pulled over him a blanket of neglect. His collected sermons were published five times in the seventeenth century, only once since; and that nineteenth-century edition was, of course, a very calculated effort, and not a response to popular demand.[1] But for his *Preces Privatae*, which continue to be published in one form or another, An-

---

[1] 1629, 1631, 1635, 1641, 1661; 1841-1843; the 'Αποσπασμάτια *Sacra* were published in 1657. Occasionally a single sermon or a selected group appeared in the nineteenth century.

drewes would be consigned to nearly total oblivion.[2] T. S. Eliot considers his own short essay on Andrewes hardly more than a preliminary to the removal of "the remains of his reputation to a last resting place in the dreary cemetery of literature."[3] I am not here concerned to promote a vogue for the reading of Lancelot Andrewes. I am examining him as an historical figure whose importance in the development of Anglicanism commands our attention. However, because of the real bearing his stylistic qualities had on his influence in his own day, and because one cannot read his sermons without being extremely conscious of his style, a few observations on it will not be out of place at this point.

Sermons are written to be preached. Their effectiveness depends very greatly on delivery. How much of the preacher's *pectus* escapes us in a reading we cannot tell, yet the cold printed word may yield enough of the spirit and the form to allow us at least to classify the sermons Bishop Andrewes has left us. Of him particularly it has been said that his delivery "must have possessed a force which we cannot recapture, since it fascinated Elizabeth and James, both of them astute critics."[4] Certain it is that he was the court preacher of his day, and that his style set a pattern many tried to imitate. Among the Anglican divines of the seventeenth century John Hacket (1592-1670), bishop of Coventry and Lichfield; Henry King (1592-1669), bishop of Chichester; Richard Cosin (1594-1672), bishop of Durham; Mark Frank (1613-1664), master of Pembroke Hall; Ralph Brownrig (1592-1659), bishop of Exeter; and William

---

[2] A French adaptation appeared in 1946; a new edition of A. E. Burn's selections from the translation of F. E. Brightman in 1949; a photographic reproduction of the 1897 edition of Newman's translation in 1950.

[3] T. S. Eliot, *For Lancelot Andrewes, Essays on Style and Order* (New York, 1929), 3-4.

[4] Arnott, "Anglicanism in the Seventeenth Century," in More and Cross, *Anglicanism*, lxiii.

Laud took Andrewes as their model and guide in preaching.[5]
But Andrewes' style made little permanent impression on English literature.[6] It was too artificial, too precious, too rough.[7]
Indeed, Andrewes has even been blamed for the decay of pulpit
oratory: " 'The great corruption of the oratory of the pulpit
may be ascribed to Dr. Andrewes, whose high reputation on
other accounts gave a sanction to that vicious taste introduced
by him.' "[8]

One exasperated reader of the bishop's sermons reminds us
that Shakespeare had little Latin and less Greek—but what
marvelous English! Andrewes, on the other hand, he continues,
"had all the Latin and all the Greek and everything else that
his great contemporary had so little of," but made pretty
poor work of English.[9] The modern reader plodding steadfastly
through the sermons will no doubt incline to agree with, even
to applaud, a description of Andrewes which refers to him
as a writer of " 'a singular, abrupt, jagged, tangled style, in

---

5 Mitchell, *English Pulpit Oratory*, 154, 164-76, 323.

6 Mitchell, *English Pulpit Oratory*, 175: "By striving after effects which gratified
the demand of the moment, 'metaphysical' or 'witty' preaching forfeited for
practically all its leading preachers a permanent place in English literature,
and the men who won the applause of their contemporaries are consequently
forgotten by posterity."

7 " 'I had almost marred my own natural trot, by endeavouring to imitate his
artificial amble,' " one disillusioned disciple confessed (*Works*, XI, xxv, note
p, Bishop Felton quoted from Fuller's *Worthies*). Trevor-Roper accuses Andrewes of preaching "sermons of unreadable preciosity" (H. R. Trevor-
Roper, *Archbishop Laud 1573-1645* [London, 1940], 30). "This jerkiness
or abruptness—the inability to achieve the λέξις εἰρομένη on which literary
grace so largely depends—is not only noticeable in Andrewes' own work, but
is a characteristic of all preaching which aimed at close imitation of his
style" (Mitchell, *English Pulpit Oratory*, 163).

8 Birch, *Life of Archbishop Tillotson*, quoted in J. H. North, *The Classic Preachers
of the English Church* (London, 1878), 172.

9 Whyte, *Andrewes and His Private Devotions*, 3. The same writer's later lament
betrays a singular lack of appreciation of the sermons: "What a pity it is,
I have sometimes exclaimed to myself, that anything of Andrewes's has been
preserved besides his *Devotions!*" (19).

reading whom one seems to be walking through a thicket crammed with thoughts and thoughtlets, and is caught at every tenth step by some out-jutting briar.' "[10]

Even in the days of his popularity Andrewes had his hostile critics, among them, naturally, the Puritans:

> The earlier Puritans had recoiled from the extraneous learning and the 'metaphysical' ingenuities of men like Andrewes with their thrice-varied MS. sermons, because they felt that such preaching did not speak to men's condition as their own plainer, more purely Scriptural discourses were likely to do.[11]

On one occasion, possibly when Andrewes preached in Edinburgh (June 1617), James asked a Scottish lord how he liked the sermon. Probably to the king's surprise, the good Scot answered that Andrewes " 'was learned, but he did play with his text as a jackanapes does, who takes up a thing, and tosses and plays with it. . . . Here's a pretty thing, and there's a pretty thing.' "[12] Late in the seventeenth century John Evelyn remembered Andrewes' characteristics as he attended a sermon on April 4, 1679, as revealed by the comments he records in his diary: "The Bp. of Gloucester preach'd, in a manner very like Bishop Andrews, full of divisions, and scholastical, and that with much quicknesse." Again, four years later, on July 15, 1683, he writes in his diary:

> A stranger, an old man, preach'd on 6 Jerem. 8 . . . much after Bp. Andrews's method, full of logical divisions, in short and broken periods, and Latine sentences, now quite out of fashion in

---

[10] Archdeacon Hare, as quoted in North, *Classic Preachers*, 173. Commenting on Hilaire Belloc's rhythmic style, a reviewer has recently observed that Belloc's "rhythm is as plain to read as the notes on a musical score. The antithesis of Belloc's prose would be the prose of Launcelot [sic] Andrewes" ("The European Mind. Hilaire Belloc's Thought and Writings," *Times Literary Supplement*, May 21, 1954, 322).

[11] Mitchell, *English Pulpit Oratory*, 21.

[12] *Works*, XI, lxix. The passage is taken from Aubrey's *Lives of Eminent Men* as quoted in Nichols' *Progresses*.

the pulpit, which is grown into a far more profitable way, of plaine and practical discourses.[13]

Since we are not primarily concerned with literary criticism, these few passages may suffice to indicate how Andrewes stood with the critics of his own and later generations. His hostile critics have been the more numerous; their judgment is borne out, in the main, by the fate his sermons have suffered. It is certainly true "that the value of Bishop Andrewes' Sermons is to be found in his matter rather than in his manner, and that it is for his thoughts rather than for the style in which they are clothed that the study of them is recommended."[14]

What in general were the characteristics of the style which Andrewes' affected? His preaching is called interchangeably "metaphysical" or "witty." Its characteristic notes had a vogue, not only among preachers, but among literateurs as well. John Donne was of course most prominent among the literary "metaphysicals," while Andrewes was "the greatest of the 'metaphysicals'" among the preachers.[15] "Wit" involved insights into the nature of things, their relations and consequences; quickness in fancy, farfetched simile, antithesis, puns, conceits, and passion; while a "facility in discovering resemblances between the most disparate things, especially where one of these happened to be of a religious character, was of the

---

[13] William Bray, editor, *Memoirs Illustrative of the Life and Writings of John Evelyn. . . . Comprising His Diary, from the Year 1641 to 1705-6* . . . (New York, 1870), 407, 446. Mitchell notices these entries, *English Pulpit Oratory*, 308.

[14] North, *Classic Preachers*, 172. It is somewhat difficult to reconcile T. S. Eliot's claim that Andrewes' "prose is not inferior to that of any sermons in the language, unless it be some of Newman's" with his previous concession that "the sermons of Andrewes are not easy reading. They are only for the reader who can elevate himself to the subject" (Eliot, *For Lancelot Andrewes*, 24, 8-9). Mr. Eliot makes several sharp and sympathetic observations on Andrewes' style.

[15] Hunt, *Religious Thought in England*, I, 466; Mitchell, *English Pulpit Oratory*, 398.

very nature of 'witty' preaching as understood by the Jacobean court." "Metaphysical" merely defines the form which "witty" preaching took in early seventeenth-century England.[16] In speaking of a style of preaching as "metaphysical,"

> we mean that it is quaint and fantastic, not because it employs unusual or whimsical expressions or images, but that when it does employ such it derives them from a background of remote learning, and adapts them to use by a curious transmutation effected by means of the peculiar temperament or deliberate endeavour of the preacher.[17]

It was not the material so much as the use to which it was put which distinguished the "metaphysical" preacher. The greater the ingenuity with which he adapted his examples, the more unexpected the parallels he drew, the more subtle, psychological, and learned the images he employed, the more characteristically was he a "metaphysical." It was not the mere use of quotation, but its application to an unexpected "point" which, while essentially verbal, conveyed something of greater import; it was not punning and quibbling for their own sakes, but the "accents of the divine" contained in the "jingle of human phrases" which counted.[18] As an example of the "metaphysical" part of a sermon, we might note the following passage from the second Nativity sermon. Andrewes is discussing the Incarnation; having established the need for the Incarnation of a Divine Person, he asks:

> But why this Person the Son? Behold, "Adam would" have "become one of Us"—the fault; behold, one of Us will become Adam, is the satisfaction. Which of Us would he have become? *Sicut Dii scientes*, 'the Person of knowledge.' He therefore shall become Adam; a Son shall be given. Desire of knowledge, our

---

[16] Mitchell, *English Pulpit Oratory*, 6, 7.
[17] Mitchell, *English Pulpit Oratory*, 7.
[18] Mitchell, *English Pulpit Oratory*, 149.

attainder; He in "Whom all the treasures of knowledge," our
restoring. Flesh would have been the Word, as wise as the Word—
the cause of our ruin; meet then the "Word become flesh", that so
our ruin repaired.[19]

Such writing makes wretched reading today; as for preaching,
we can wonder that men once could take it. One who knows thoroughly the seventeenth-century English pulpit has written of
this style that it is

> the verdict of contemporaries and posterity alike, that the compo-
> nents of 'metaphysical' preaching were not such as were in them-
> selves intrinsecally valuable, that the use to which they were put
> by the 'witty' preachers was not consonant with the great ends of
> Christian oratory, and, that both the material and methods em-
> ployed rendered impossible the cultivation of a prose style suited
> either to delivery in the pulpit or to give to religious discourses in
> their printed form the dignity of literature.
>
> On two counts, therefore, both for what it was, and for what
> it could not become, 'witty' preaching stands condemned.[20]

Perhaps it will not be too great a digression to investigate
a little more closely the specific form these qualities take in
the sermons written and preached by Andrewes. To begin with,
no reader of the sermons will fail to recognize that he was a
meticulous workman. The studied and very neat articulation of
sermons within a series, of parts within a sermon, paragraphs
within parts, sentences within paragraphs, and particularly, as
in the Nativity sermon quoted above, of words within sentences,
makes entirely credible this observation of one of the original
editors of Andrewes' works:

> He was always a diligent and painful preacher. Most of his
> solemn Sermons he was most careful of, and exact; I dare say few
> of them but they passed his hand and were thrice revised, before
> they were preached; and he ever misliked often and loose preach-

---

[19] *Works,* I, Nativity Sermon II, 22.
[20] Mitchell, *English Pulpit Oratory,* 194.

ing without study of antiquity, and he would be bold with himself
and say, when he preached twice a day at St. Giles', he prated
once.[21]

In the longer unified series of sermons—the Nativity, Easter,
and Pentecost groups, for example—Andrewes seems to have
made it a principle never to repeat his treatment; rarely does
he repeat even his text. Strict adherence to this rule did not
allow him to take up again the narrative of a mystery when once
he had handled it, and resulted occasionally in his straining to
find a novel and pertinent frame for his sermon.[22]

With noticeable frequency Andrewes relates a sermon to a
previous one or postpones a point until the next time he is called
on to preach the same mystery. On Christmas Day of 1620, for
example, he refers to a sermon preached five years previous:
"Of the place, of Bethlehem, out of Micah, it hath formerly
been treated. I but touch it and pass it now."[23] In a Pentecost
sermon he notes: "Upon Him the Spirit was; 'the Spirit of God
upon Me,' last year. Upon us, not the Spirit; but *de Spiritu*,
'of My Spirit' only, this year."[24] In his Ash Wednesday sermon
of 1623 he speaks of "three points yet behind [he means
ahead], which will ask more time than is left, nay more than
hath been already spent, and so the work of some other time."
Precisely the three points mentioned form the burden of his
sermon which he delivered on Ash Wednesday of the following
year.[25] Since he failed to develop all the points of his division
in the Nativity sermon preached in 1620, these points were

---

[21] *Works*, V, Buckeridge, *Funeral Sermon*, 295.
[22] *Works*, II, Easter Sermon XIII, 404-28, for example, which is nothing but a
    learned lecture on the custom of keeping Easter; and *Works*, III, Pentecost
    Sermon XI, 301-22, a rather uninspired effort, but important for showing
    Andrewes' theological methodology.
[23] *Works*, I, Nativity Sermon XIV, 237.
[24] *Works*, III, Pentecost Sermon XI, 305.
[25] *Works*, I, Ash Wednesday Sermon VII, 429; *Works*, I, Ash Wednesday Sermon
    VIII, 435.

carried on in his next Christmas sermon, which was not delivered until the year 1622.[26]

Attention should be directed momentarily to his sentences
and to the great emphasis he set on the use of words. His
failure, except rarely, to write in long, flowing periods of balance, subordination, and contrast results in a hectically jagged
style. He was totally addicted to the short sentence; yet no one,
says T. S. Eliot, "is more master of the short sentence than Andrewes."[27] Andrewes himself tells us "those that in fewest words
comprise most matter, are most praised."[28] We find him, then,
exercising an extreme economy in the structure of the sentence,
as in the following, wherein he restricts himself, be it noted, to
monosyllables: "These are all well and true all, but all short."[29]
And again, in a similar sentence he manages to combine brevity,
movement, and climax: "Here is joy, joy at a sight, at the sight
of a day, and that day Christ's."[30] A classicist will be reminded
of the Demosthenic whip! He could rapidly sketch a sharp picture with a very few words, as in this reference to the coming of
the Magi:

> It was no summer progress. A cold coming they had of it at
> this time of the year, just the worst time of the year to take a jour-
> ney, and specially a long journey in. The ways deep, the weather
> sharp, the days short, the sun farthest off, *in solstitio brumali*, 'the
> very dead of winter.'[31]

---

26 *Works*, I, Nativity Sermon XIV, 235 (where the division appears); *Works*, I,
Nativity Sermon XV, 249.

27 Eliot, *For Lancelot Andrewes*, 17.

28 *Works*, II, Lenten Sermon IV, 61.

29 *Works*, I, Nativity Sermon VI, 87.

30 *Works*, I, Nativity Sermon VIII, 118.

31 *Works*, I, Nativity Sermon XV, 257. See the opening lines of Eliot's "Journey
of the Magi": "'A cold coming we had of it,/ Just the worst time of the
year/ For a journey, and such a long journey:/ The ways deep and the
weather sharp,/ The very dead of winter'" (T. S. Eliot, *Collected Poems,
1909-1935* [London, 1936], 107).

Or as in his description of a "stage-fast":

> It skills not a whit for any of these [the qualities of a genuine
> fast] in the stage-fast; so he can set his countenance well, have the
> clouds in his forehead, his eyes somewhat hollow, certain wrinkles
> in his cheek, carry his head like a bull-rush, and look like leaven,
> all is well.[32]

Words fascinated Andrewes. When he applies himself to a
Scripture text, says one author, "he rolls his text like a sweet
morsel under his tongue, until he has extracted from it not only
all its nourishment but the last vestige of its flavour."[33] His habit
of taking up every word in a text became a characteristic vice
of the Anglo-Catholic preachers.[34] In discussing his text for Ash
Wednesday in 1623 Andrewes insists:

> Of which words there is not any one waste or to spare. Every
> one of them is *verbum vigilans*, as St. Augustine speaks, 'awake
> all;' never an one asleep among them. Each hath his weight. Nor
> never an one out of his place, but, as Solomon speaks, "upon his
> right wheel," standing just where it should. We will take them as
> they lie.[35]

But, Andrewes tells us, "there is for the most part in each text
some one predominant word."[36] In the Nativity sermon of 1618
on the text "And this shall be a sign unto you, etc." (Luke
2:12-14), he hammers unmercifully on the "predominant"
word until a reader wants to cry for relief. "Sign," or the plural
thereof, occurs one hundred and thirty-nine times; the Latin
"signum," or the oblique cases, appears forty-three times; vari-

---

[32] *Works*, I, Ash Wednesday Sermon VI, 409.

[33] North, *Classic Preachers*, 176.

[34] Mitchell, *English Pulpit Oratory*, 97.

[35] *Works*, I, Ash Wednesday Sermon VII, 420. The text is from Matthew 3:8:
"Bring forth therefore fruit worthy amendment of life." The first three points
of the division are: "I. 'Bring forth.' II. 'Bring forth fruit.' III. 'Bring forth
fruit therefore'"—hardly a promising beginning!

[36] *Works*, I, Nativity Sermon XVI, 265.

ous derivatives, Latin or English, number twenty-two![37] This, it must be admitted, is a most outlandish example, and it would be unfair indeed to leave the impression that such lapses were particularly frequent.

When in another sermon Andrewes mentions three senses of a given word and comments: "They be all true, all tend to edify," he gives us the key to his devotion to words; this, undoubtedly, is the reason why he so constantly rings the changes on a single word or phrase.[38] He wants to drain it of everything which the fertility of his imagination and devotion suggest to him as present—"All tend to edify."[39] He loves to toy and play with words and terms; dividing and picking out detail, he leaps at his idea, snatches it up, fondles it, points an indicative finger at it, whirls it about, until the sheer weight of words forces home the point he wants to make. He had a peculiar habit of "letting off words like squibs so that they break into a number of dazzling images," which leaves his reader exhausted, confused, and entirely too conscious of artificial striving.[40]

Most outrageous of his verbal faults are his puns: "He that cometh here in clouts, He will come in the clouds one day"; "And now to that *cum* let us come"; "Never care for *benedicentur* no more than Esau, but for *bene vescentur;* and if *bene vestientur* too, then all is well"; and the classic example: "If it be not *Immanu-el*, it will be *Immanu-hell;* and that and no other place will fall, I fear me, to our share. Without Him this we

---

[37] *Works*, I, Nativity Sermon XII, 196 ff. The words used are: sign, and the plural; *signum*, in the nominative or some other case; *signatus*, signed, signified, assigned, signature, ensign, countersign, and signal. The count is approximately accurate. The total is 204. The sermon itself contains about ten thousand words.

[38] *Works*, I, Nativity Sermon XVI, 266.

[39] Mitchell speaks of this "curious economy in wringing the utmost meaning from words, and even grammatical constructions" as deriving from the fathers (*English Pulpit Oratory*, 54).

[40] Mitchell, *English Pulpit Oratory*, 162.

are. What with Him? Why, if we have Him, and God by Him, we need no more; *Immanu-el* and *Immanu-all*."[41] Of the same pattern, and even more characteristic, is Andrewes' habit of peppering his pages with Latin, Greek, and (though not so frequently) Hebrew words. All this results in a preciosity which makes for very difficult reading, and it is with relief indeed that one meets occasional passages of whimsy touched with a trace of genuine humor such as the following. Andrewes is speaking of the text "Your father Abraham rejoiced to see My day, etc." (John 8:56); the word that intrigues him is "exultavit":

> To give a spring, and not once but often; this was much, if all be well considered. For one to do it, one in years, fast upon an hundred as Abraham then was, for such an one to do it, it was very much.

Andrewes cannot leave the scene:

> It must needs be he was greatly, yea strangely affected with it, that it made him forget his gravity, and put a kind of indecorum upon his age, at those years to fall on springing.

And yet more:

> Judge then how great a good is the good of this day that not in the enjoying, but even in the desiring and that against the nature of desire, did put old father Abraham into this passion; and brought from him this act, the act of exultation, and made him even young again.[42]

There is no call to undertake a defense of Andrewes' style. Shall we blame him for casting his thought in a mold which suited his own generation and alienates ours? He was so utterly intent on getting across to his hearers the great truths of Christianity as he understood them and on urging men to their prac-

---

[41] *Works*, I, Nativity Sermon XII, 200; *Works*, I, Ash Wednesday Sermon V, 383; *Works*, I, Nativity Sermon VIII, 133; *Works*, I, Nativity Sermon IX, 145.
[42] *Works*, I, Nativity Sermon VIII, 125.

tical consequences that he would undoubtedly have adopted another way had he known a better. The substance is there behind the façade of his composition, but one must dig to reach it. Since the business of prayer—meditative prayer—is precisely to dig, it comes to pass that Andrewes' sermons afford good material for meditation. What is enormously difficult in the reading—and presumably in the hearing—is at the same time a treasury of ideas for prayerful reflection, and this enduring quality of the sermons has been recognized by at least one modern admirer.[43] T. S. Eliot deems the *Preces Privatae* worthy of association with the *Spiritual Exercises* of St. Ignatius.[44] Had he chosen to do so, he might well have said the same of the sermons. Compare the development of almost any sermon picked at random from among the "XCVI" with the Ignatian method of contemplation, application of the senses, or the second method of prayer, which bids the exercitant ponder each word of a text or a prayer as long as he finds fruit therein, and the similarity is striking. We need not suppose that Andrewes knew the *Exercises*, though his acquaintance with contemporary Catholic writings makes the supposition entirely plausible.

So much, then, for the several qualities of Andrewes' style: its "witty" or "metaphysical" nature, the care he exercised in seeking fresh treatment and avoiding repetition, the character of his sentences and paragraphs, and the peculiarly Andrean worship of the word.[45] Many other factors must be passed over: his

---

[43] North, *Classic Preachers*, 176: "Often his sermons, or portions of them, are meditations rather than sermons: meditations shaping themselves into sermons, in which the thought seems to have wholly occupied him to the exclusion of care for language. And this is the source of some of the defects of his style."

[44] Eliot, *For Lancelot Andrewes*, 12-13.

[45] Eliot, *For Lancelot Andrewes*, 15: "We find his examination of words terminating in the ecstasy of assent. Andrewes takes a word and derives the world from it; squeezing and squeezing the word until it yields a full juice of meaning which we should never have supposed any word to possess."

emotional power, his graciousness, his imagination and his fancy, and all the standard rhetorical practices he knew and used, and explained on occasion to his Elizabethan and Jacobean audience. It now remains to trace the pattern of a typical Andrean sermon and so conclude consideration of the dress in which Andrewes clothed his thought. The following, from a manuscript in the British Museum, may serve as a good introductory analysis:

> The method which Bishop Andrews observes in his sermons.
>
> Generally his sermons are at solemnities, and so his first work is to bring his text close to the season. Then he proceeds either with a certain descant upon the text, coming by degrees to the full sense of it, after which he divides, or sometimes he carries the context along. In his division he is most accurate, and commonly witty; using some similitude or figurative expression, he divides by single terms, and subdivides, dispatching all commonly in one sermon. He handles each part in its own order, rejecting the opposite first. Towards the conclusion he ever applies all, by instruction, reprehension, consolation, etc. He is generally very acute and witty, yet very grave and serious, often ironical in his reprehensions. He dives to the very bottom of the text, fetches out all the bowels of it, quotes fathers but sparingly, brief and concise in everything, the least tedious of any. He treads a path merely his own, and is inimitable till another comes along that has his parts: his judgment, learning, discretion, wit, piety and gravity. There is no hope to see another such volume of sermons.[46]

For his Christmas sermon of 1606, which was preached before James I in Whitehall, Andrewes chose the very appropriate text: "For unto us a child is born, and unto us a Son is

---

[46] British Museum, Lansdowne MSS., ccxxiii, f. 4 (spelling and punctuation modernized). This volume is listed in the Catalogue of Lansdowne MSS. as: "A volume of miscellaneous historical collections, written for the most part, during the reigns of James I., Charles I. and II." The MS. is undated and has no indication of authorship. It seems probable that it is of the seventeenth century. Andrewes quoted the fathers more than "sparingly."

given; and the government is upon His shoulder; and He shall call His Name Wonderful, Counsellor, the Mighty God, the Everlasting Father, the Prince of Peace" (Isaias 9:6). It was to be too much for him in that he had not time to explore all the possibilities that the text offered, but the sermon he managed to build on but a part of his text is worthy of examination, not because it is his best, or even one of his best, but because it is typical.[47]

This text, Andrewes begins, sounds more like a history of the Nativity than a prophecy, but we recognize it as from Isaias and therefore as the foretelling of a future event. Nothing so strengthens our faith as to find that the things we believe were plainly foretold many years before they actually occurred. Only God " 'Who calleth things that are not as if they were,' " can cause prophecies to be written of Himself. Prophecies are more persuasive even than miracles which may "move much," of course; but there have been " 'lying miracles.' " Mahomet and all the false prophets of whom we have read were never mentioned until they were born. This prophecy in our text applies to a child, but not to Ezekias as the Jews have claimed, for it was in no way true of him that " 'His throne should be established from thenceforth for ever,' " as the next verse goes on to say; and for us the application of this text to Christ by the evangelist Matthew is conclusive. Having next explained the occasion of the prophecy, Andrewes proceeds to his division:

> The parts, *ad oculum*, 'evidently,' are two; I. a Child-birth, and II. a Baptism. I. The Child-birth in these, "For unto you," &c. II. The Baptism in these, "His Name," &c.
>
> In the former; I. First of the main points, the Natures, Person, and Office; 1. Natures in these, "Child" and "Son." 2. Person in these, "His shoulders," "His name." 3. Office in these, "His government." II. Then of the deriving of an interest to us in these,—

---

[47] *Works*, I, Nativity Sermon II, 18-31.

"to us," two times. And that is of two sorts: 1. By being "born;" a right by His birth. 2. By being "given;" a right by a deed of gift.

In the latter, of His Baptism, is set down His style, consisting of five pieces, containing five uses, for which He was thus given; each to be considered in his order.[48]

Addressing himself to his first point and relying on the Council of Seville for his exegesis, Andrewes argues that "Child" imports Christ's human nature; "Son" His divine nature. All through His life you see these two:

> At His birth; a cratch for the Child, a star for the Son; a company of shepherds viewing the Child, a choir of Angels celebrating the Son. In His life; hungry Himself, to shew the nature of the Child; yet "feeding five thousand," to show the power of the Son. At His death; dying on the cross, as the "Son of Adam;" at the same time disposing of Paradise, as the "Son of God."[49]

But why was it necessary that there be two natures? The nature that sinned, he replies, must bear its punishment, therefore the Child—there must be a human nature. But our human nature could not have borne what in justice it must needs suffer, the Son could; therefore there must be here a divine nature. "The one ought but could not, the other could but ought not." And so, "that He might be liable He was a Child, that He might be able He was the Son; that He might be both, He was both." The striking explanation of why it was the Second Person who must become incarnate in the plan of Redemption has already been quoted.[50] "Flesh would have been the Word . . . meet then the 'Word become flesh,' that so our ruin repaired."

The person of the Child and the Son is but one, for both have but one name, " 'His Name shall be called,' " and both these have but one pair of shoulders, " 'Upon His shoulders.' "

---

[48] *Works*, I, Nativity Sermon II, 18-21.
[49] *Works*, I, Nativity Sermon II, 22.
[50] See *supra*, 58-59.

This one person in two natures was eminently fitted to be mediator of God and man, for here is division—the two natures, and unity—the one Person. In this one Person are joined the chief nature of heaven and the chief nature of earth, and so we find the two supporters of all—justice and power. God lacked a shoulder on which justice might be exercised, man lacked the shoulder of power needed to repair the damage of sin.

> A meet Person to cease hostility, as having taken pledges of both Heaven and earth—the chief nature in Heaven, and the chief on earth; to set forward commerce between Heaven and earth by Jacob's ladder, "one end touching earth, the other reaching to Heaven;" to incorporate either to other, Himself by His birth being become the "Son of man," by our new birth giving us a capacity to become the "sons of God."[51]

Now God saw that the Child should be "poorly" born; but, that we might not think of Him "too meanly," God makes "amends for the manger," and tells us that the Child, the Son, is also a prince. His principality is not of this world, else

> his officers, as they would have seen Him better defended at His death, so would they have seen Him better lodged at His birth, than in a stable with beasts; for if the inn were full, the stable we may be sure was not empty.[52]

And Christ is come to establish a government "that none imagine they shall live like libertines under Him, every man believe and live as he list." They that be Christ's "must live in subjection under a government." Andrewes then seizes the opportunity to remind his hearers (and so to flatter James) that this government is a principality "wherein neither the popular confusion of many, nor the factious ambition of a few, bear all the sway, but where One is Sovereign."

---

[51] *Works,* I, Nativity Sermon II, 23.
[52] *Works,* I, Nativity Sermon II, 24.

But why should the government be on His *shoulders*—
wisdom governs, and wisdom is in the head?

> Belike, governments have their weight—be heavy; and so they
> be; they need not only a good head, but good shoulders, that sustain
> them. But that not so much while they be in good tune and temper,
> then they need no great carriage; but when they grow unwieldly
> [*sic*], be it weakness or waywardness of the governed, in that case
> they need; and in that case, there is no governor but, at one time
> or other, he bears his government upon his shoulders.[53]

It is indeed to be wished that governors might always "bear
their people only in their arms by love, and in their breasts by
care," but sometimes they must "not only bear with them, but
even bear them also." Christ did this and much more, for there
are two differences between Him and other governors: others
bear and suffer the faults and errors of their government, but
they do not suffer for them. Christ did both; He endured them
and endured for them, and all this quite willingly:

> "Come," saith He, "you that are heavy laden, and I will refresh
> you," by loading Myself; take it from your necks, and lay it on
> Mine own. Which His suffering, though it grew so heavy as it
> wrung from Him plenty of tears, a strong cry, a sweat of blood,—
> such was the weight of it;—yet would He not cast it off, but there
> held it still, till it made Him "bow down His head and give up the
> ghost." If He had discharged it, it must have light upon us; it was
> the yoke of our burden, as in the fourth verse He termeth it: if
> it had light upon us, it had pressed us down to hell, so insupport-
> able was it. Rather than so, He held it still and bare it; and did
> that which never Prince did—died for His government.[54]

And the second difference is that He did all of this alone:
"Upon His only shoulders did the burden only rest."

From these two facts, says Andrewes, the prophet argues to
a third, "the point here of principal intendment":

---

[53] *Works*, I, Nativity Sermon II, 24-25.
[54] *Works*, I, Nativity Sermon II, 26.

If, for His government sake, He will bear so great things; bear
their weaknesses as the lost sheep, bear their sins as the scape-goat;
He will over the government itself, as in Deut. 32. He maketh the
simile, stretch forth His wings, "as the eagle over her young ones,"
and take them, and bear them between His pinions—bear them, and
bear them through. They need take no thought; "No man shall take
them out of His hands," no man reach them off His shoulders. He
had begun so to carry them, and through He would still carry
them; at least-wise, till this Child Immanuel were born. Till then
He would; and not wax weary, nor cast them off. And, like the
scape-goat, bear their sins; and like the eagle, bear up their estate,
"till the fulness of time came," and He in it, with the fulness of all
grace and blessing. And this point I hold so material as *Puer natus*,
nothing, and *Filius datus*, as much, without *Princeps oneratus;* for
that is all in all, and of the three the chief.[55]

Andrewes then works over the word "nobis" and reads into
it several ideas. "Nobis" is *acquisitive positus;* we are the
gainers by all this great mystery. It profited Christ nothing. He
had a far nobler nativity before creation—certainly to be thus
basely born He had no gain. "Nobis" is "in bar of Himself,"
and of the angels too, for "not an Angel in Heaven can say
nobis. Vobis they can, the Angels said it twice." This is also
"nobis" *inclusive:* Isaias includes "himself as having need
though a saint, and excludeth not Ahaz from having part though
a sinner"; Simeon the just, Paul the sinner, Jew and Gentile—
all in "nobis." But only those who include themselves by believing are in here, and so it is "nobis" *exclusive* as well. *"Facit
multorum infidelitas ut non omnibus nasceretur qui omnibus
natus est;* 'Want of faith makes that He, That is born to all, is
not born to all though,' "* he avers, quoting St. Ambrose.

We have a double interest in Christ. Since His humanity is
clearly ours, we have a good right to that, none to His deity. But
by deed of gift God has passed over to us even that, so that

---

[55] *Works*, I, Nativity Sermon II, 26-27.

"what by participation of our nature, what by good conveyance, both are ours." No time is left, Andrewes regrets, to tell of the harvest or the "booty of His Nativity," but in a word it is this:

> If the tree be ours, the fruit is; if He be ours, His birth is ours, His life is ours, His death is ours; His satisfaction, His merit, all He did, all He suffered, is ours. Farther, all that the Father hath is His, He is Heir of all; then, all that is ours too. St. Paul hath cast up our account, Having given Him, there is nothing but He will give us with Him; so that by this deed we have title to all that His Father or He is worth.[56]

"Quid retribuam—what return shall we make?" Andrewes asks in his peroration. By way of thanks let us "sing to the Father, with Zachary, *Benedictus;* and to the Son, with the blessed Virgin, *Magnificat;* and with the Angels, *Gloria in excelsis,* to the Prince with His 'government on His shoulders.' " By way of duty let us "render unto the Child, confidence; *Puer est, ne metuas:* to the Son, reverence; *Filius est, ne spernas:* to the Prince, obedience; *Princeps est, ne offendas."*[57] And St. Bernard advises us to look to our own interest—good practical counsel: *"De nobis nato et dato faciamus id ad quod natus est et datus; utamur nostro in utilitatem nostram, de Servatore nostro salutem operemur."*[58] Christ is given to us as an example to follow: *"Fieri voluit in vitâ primum, quod exhibuit in ortu vitae,"* says Cyprian. He is given *in pretium,* for a price "either of ransom, to bring us out *de loco caliginoso;* or a price of purchase of that, where without it we have no interest—the Kingdom of Heaven." He is given as " 'the living Bread from Heaven,' which is His 'flesh' born this day, and after 'given for the life

---

56 *Works,* I, Nativity Sermon II, 28.
57 *Works,* I, Nativity Sermon II, 29.
58 Andrewes translates: " 'With this born and given Child, let us then do that for which He was born and given us; seeing He is ours, let us use that that is ours to our best behoof, and even work out our salvation out of this our Saviour' " (*Works,* I, Nativity Sermon II, 29).

of the world.' " And He is given *in praemium* to be our final reward. Augustine put all four together, "so will I, and conclude," says Andrewes:

> *Sequamur* 1. *exemplum; offeramus* 2. *pretium; sumamus* 3. *viaticum; expectemus* 4. *praemium;* 'let us follow Him for our pattern, offer Him for our price, receive Him for our sacramental food, and wait for Him as our endless and exceeding great reward,' &c.[59]

This sermon, so typical of Andrewes' development of a theme, will acquaint the reader with the rhetorical and logical devices and the stylistic peculiarities which have deprived the bishop of lasting literary fame. His ideas do not sift readily from his taut, concentrated writing; one must, in fact, practically pry his thought from the brittle dress in which he clothed it. Neither the examination of the sources of Andrewes' ideas, nor the consideration of his style, is sheerly preliminary, for each must constantly be kept in mind in a study of the broad outlines of his thought. As the sources are chiefly traditional, so too is the theology. The difficult, tangled, almost tortured style renders very hazardous the task of reporting his ideas fairly and precisely.

---

[59] *Works*, I, Nativity Sermon II, 31.

CHAPTER IV

Andrewes
on the Church

The reader will quickly realize as we proceed that Andrewes' thought is utterly theological. That such should be the case is entirely natural, of course, for one whose sole interest was religion and whatsoever bore upon it. Two things we must notice at the outset: a lack of precision in his thought and a lack of originality. His thought was not always precise, not because he was a hazy thinker, but rather because of the exigencies imposed on him of walking a line which veered neither into Calvinism, which he rejected, nor into Roman Catholicism, which, albeit mildly, he hated and so rejected as well. Thus we find him spurning the Calvinistic teaching of mere virtual presence in the Holy Eucharist on the one hand, and as vigorously denying transubstantiation on the other; but it is impossible to decide with finality exactly what he does teach. He was torn by the necessity of remaining non-Roman and by his own inclination to adopt the ascetical implications of the orthodox Roman Catholic teaching on the real presence. Again, Andrewes lacked originality. He was not one to blaze new trails in the realm of theological speculation. He relied heavily on traditional sources, borrowed from them extensively, and allowed them to shape the general pattern of his thought. He was not daring by nature; hence after surveying the confusion and unrest which had followed in the wake of the several Reformation changes in England, he sought to steady and shape the Church's course along the lines Christianity had traveled since time immemorial—always remembering, however, to hold several points off the path of Rome.[1] Finally, in studying his theology we must try to appreciate not only his sheer doctrinal position, but his unctuous conviction and his insistence on the practical implications of doctrine as well, for these are peculiarly characteristic of Lancelot Andrewes.

Religion and the concerns of the Church were always his foremost interest. We are told that, when he was a privy councilor, he would inquire before a meeting whether or not the business of the day involved the Church and that, if it did not, he would say: " 'I will be gone.' "[2] The state of religion in England deeply distressed him:

> The stream of our times tends all to this. To make religion nothing but an auricular profession, a matter of ease, a mere sedentary thing, and ourselves merely passive in it; sit still, and hear a Sermon and two Anthems, and be saved.[3]

But religion as Andrewes conceived it was "outward as well as inward,"[4] and it consisted of three vital parts, preaching, prayer, and the sacraments; its highest end, he tells us, *"Summa religionis est, assimilari Ei quem colis,* 'to become like to Him we worship is the pitch of all religion.' "[5] It is no *"res precaria* . . . a matter of fair entreaty, gentle persuasion; neither *jura,* nor *leges,* but only *consulta patrum,* 'good fatherly counsel,' and

---

[1] Canon Brightman observes: "Originality was scarcely the chief note of his mind. He is marked rather by great, solid and readily-available learning than by great original ideas. He was scholarly, historical, inductive, rather than speculative and creative" (Brightman, *The Preces Privatae*, xxix).

[2] *Works*, XI, xi, note u, quoted from Lloyd, *State Worthies*. See also *Works*, V, Buckeridge, *Funeral Sermon*, 292-93.

[3] *Works*, III, Pentecost Sermon XI, 319.

[4] *Works*, V, Sermon on the Temptation of Christ VII, 554.

[5] *Works*, II, Easter Sermon XIII, 407; *Works*, I, Nativity Sermon XIII, 230.

nothing else."[6] The fostering of a genuine religious spirit in the Church of England was a tremendously serious business for Andrewes—in fact, the work of his life. He would have been terribly shocked had he ever suspected that Anglicanism might one day be defined as "churches built by Wren, devotions composed by Andrewes, the poetry of Donne and Crashaw, the superb organ prose of Barrow."[7] Shocked, indeed, because he labored to make it real, effective, permanent, substantial; and the sincerity of his endeavor has earned him a place "second to none in the history of the formation of the English Church."[8] If it is impossible for us to determine within the limits of this study the precise degree of influence that he exerted on the development of Anglicanism, we can at least assay the quality of his work considered in itself.

Andrewes did not create. Having decided what was the true path for Anglican development, he undertook to concretize the forms and the patterns which should prevail in what he considered the English expression of the great fact of Christianity. He had refused to go along with the Puritans; unlike Donne, he seems never to have had to make any decision with regard to Roman Catholicism, but it was his fate to be called to the defense of the new thing which Anglicanism undoubtedly was, against the old religion, even as his great predecessor, Hooker, had been its champion against Puritanism.[9] His action, however,

---

[6] *Works*, I, Nativity Sermon XVII, 289.

[7] Shane Leslie, *The Oxford Movement 1833 to 1933* (London, 1933), 19.

[8] Eliot, *For Lancelot Andrewes*, 24.

[9] Sir Toby Matthew quotes Andrewes as saying in a conference with him: " 'For my part, I am an old man, and I have been a lover of books, ever since I was born; and I understand so much of God's goodness that I desire so to believe in him, and so to serve him here, as that I may enjoy him hereafter. And certainly if in all this time I had been able to find just cause why I should hold myself to be unsafe where I am, I should not have failed to choose the best way to the next world, whatsoever it might have cost me in this.' " Andrewes was conferring with Sir Toby on the latter's conversion to Roman Catholicism (Mathew, *Conversion of Sir Tobie Matthew*, 93-94).

was not limited merely to buttressing the new Church's bulwarks against the onslaughts of a reinvigorated Roman Catholicism, for Andrewes also brought his weight to bear against the Calvinistic tendencies within the Church itself as early as his Cambridge days.[10] His main problem, as far as the specific character of the new Church was concerned, consisted in propagating the idea of the continuity of a Catholic tradition in the Church despite the organizational break occasioned by Henry and later Elizabeth; he had to sell, against a mounting resistance, the idea of a Catholicism that was episcopal, but not papal, in its constitution.[11] Andrewes was a leader in reducing the Calvinistic tone of earlier Elizabethan Anglicanism. That temper was never wholly driven from the English Church, as the sequel of three centuries has shown in the violent triumph of Calvinism in the Great Rebellion and in its persistence in the modern Low Church; but it is not too much to claim for Andrewes that, had it not been for him, there might never have endured a High Church—at least one which would have fostered within its bosom in the nineteenth century so nearly Catholic a phenomenon as the Oxford Movement. Though Andrewes cannot formally be classified as an Arminian, we may fairly conclude he was truly one in spirit; and a spiritual succession from Andrewes, through the Caroline divines and the nonjurors, to the nineteenth-century Tractarians is a most legitimate descent.[12] Intriguing as this relationship may be, it is too distracting a digression to pursue at this time.

---

10 See his *Judgment of the Lambeth Articles, supra*, 5.

11 See Mitchell, *English Pulpit Oratory*, 180, and Frere, *The English Church in the Reigns of Elizabeth and James I.*, 384.

12 Gina Harwood and Arthur W. Hopkinson, editors, *The Mantle of Prayer, A Book of English Devotions*, new edition (London, 1931), viii; and see Leslie, *The Oxford Movement*, Appendix VIII, "A Map of the Oxford Movement," 167. Andrewes' name is not included (he was not an Oxonian), but his influence on Laud, particularly, indicates that he was one of the patriarchs of the Movement.

Nor will it be possible to review Andrewes' every last theological position. One may legitimately assume that a preacher who found such favor with Elizabeth and James followed a line appropriately orthodox; that he did not deviate, for example, from the standard Anglican teaching of the Thirty-nine Articles. On one or two occasions, it is true, he was called to account for expressing opinions too Roman for Elizabeth and her court; generally, however, he exercised due caution with regard to doctrinal matters.[13] In things liturgical, where he was quite advanced, he avoided difficulty by proceeding slowly and by refraining from forcing his own liturgical practices upon the Church. Andrewes' great work was his attempt to restore life and vigor to the Church through the preaching of a practical and quite traditional theology.[14]

It was not Andrewes' manner to lay down a formal statement of a theological doctrine as it was contained, for example, in any one of the Thirty-nine Articles, and then expound it by parts. Generally speaking, his sermons must be sifted for the doctrinal basis which will be found quite orthodox in the Anglican sense. On one occasion, however, he made a very clear statement of a fundamental position which underlay the whole of Anglicanism and the structure of his own theological thought. In a Latin sermon preached at Greenwich on April 13, 1613, Andrewes summed up the Anglican rule of faith: we have one

---

[13] *Works*, XI, Appendix B, lxii, Rowland White to Sir Robert Sydney, quoted from the *Sydney Letters:* " 'Dr. Andrews made a strange sermon at court Sunday [the Sunday after Easter, 1600]; his text was the xx. chapter of the Gospel St. John, the 23d verse, touching the forgiveness of sins upon earth. That contrition without confession and absolution, and deeds worthy of repentance, was not sufficient. That the ministers had the two keys of power and knowledge delivered unto them; that whose sins soever they remitted upon earth, should be remitted in heaven. The court is full of it, for such doctrine was not usually taught there. I hear he was with Mr. Secretary about it, it may be to satisfy him.' "

[14] It would be extremely interesting and worth while to compare Andrewes point by point with the leading Anglican divines of his day.

canon of the Scriptures given us by God, he tells his hearers, two Testaments, three creeds, the first four councils, and the fathers of the first five centuries for our rule of religion.[15] The canon, of course, is that contained in the sixth of the Thirty-nine Articles, the two testaments are the Old and the New, the creeds the familiar Apostles', Athanasian, and Nicene creeds, and the councils, Nicaea I (325), Constantinople I (381), Ephesus (431), and Chalcedon (451). James I had made a fuller statement of the same in his *Premonition to All Most Mighty Monarchs,* so that Andrewes was here propounding the accepted Anglican rule of faith.[16] From what has been said previously of the sources of Bishop Andrewes' thought, it will be seen how completely he worked these fonts into his preaching. Through adherence to this rule of faith Anglicanism set itself off from the continental reformed churches, attempted to maintain its historical connection with the old Church, and at the same time, through the limitations contained in the norms, separated itself from Rome. In a sense the critical point is the sufficiency of Scripture. For the Puritan (the English counterpart of the continental Calvinist) Scripture and Scripture alone constituted the rule of faith; for the Catholic it was the Scripture, tradition, and the living *magisterium* of the Church; for the Anglican it was Scripture and the primitive Church. Anglicanism appealed to the Bible as the test of essential doctrine, to antiquity, to Catholic tradition, and to the authority of the Church "as arbiter in matters of faith and mistress in matters of discipline."[17]

---

[15] *Works,* IX, *Concio in discessu Palatini,* 91: "Nobis *Canon* unus in Scripta relatus a Deo, *Duo Testamenta, Tria Symbola, Quatuor Priora Concilia, Quinque saecula, Patrumque* per ea series, trecentos ante Constantinum annos, ducentos a Constantino, regulam nobis *Religionis* figunt."

[16] More and Cross, *Anglicanism,* 3-4.

[17] Frere, *Andrewes as a Representative of Anglican Principles,* 7; and Frere, *The English Church in the Reigns of Elizabeth and James I.,* 86, where Jewel's rule of faith is briefly summarized.

This problem of an objective rule of faith demanded some sort of definition. Having broken with Rome, the English had no one theologian to whom appeal could be made for final sentence in a dispute as the Germans could appeal to Luther or the Calvinists to Calvin, nor did they have any ultimate court of authority such as the Catholics had in the Council of Trent.[18] Some are far from Rome, complained Andrewes, "yet with their new perspective they think they perceive all God's secret decrees, the number and order of them clearly. . . . Luther said well that every one of us hath by nature a Pope in his belly, and thinks he perceives great matters. Even they that believe it not of Rome, are easily brought to believe it of themselves."[19] In the *Preces Privatae* he prays to be delivered from "privati spiritus interpretatione, innovatione in rebus sacris,"[20] and in the *Responsio ad Bellarminum* he writes: *"Ego in rebus fidei Judex non sum."*[21] Rejecting Rome and the Catholic position on one hand, Andrewes was on the other equally removed from the Puritan position, for he was in complete agreement with John Selden, who blamed the Puritan for saying he wanted to be judged by the word of God, but really meaning by himself— " 'he would have me believe him before a whole church, that has read the word of God as well as he.' "[22]

In the same *Concio in discessu Palatini* which contains Andrewes' rule of faith he cites the chief points in Roman Catholicism which the reformed English Church rejects: tradition *(fides non scripta)*, relics, the use of Latin in the liturgy, invocation of saints, images, communion under one species *("Eucharistiam* media parte *mutilent")*, transubstantiation *("Adorent*

---

[18] More, "The Spirit of Anglicanism," in More and Cross, *Anglicanism*, xx.

[19] *Works*, III, Pentecost Sermon XII, 328.

[20] *Works*, X, *Preces Privatae*, 203.

[21] *Works*, VIII, *Responsio ad Bellarminum*, 455.

[22] Quoted from John Selden's *Table Talk*, in G. N. Clark, editor, *The Oxford History of England* (Oxford, 1937), 72, note 1.

ibi sub *speciebus delitescens Numen,* de pistrino factum"*),* the papacy, and papal infallibility.[23] In the same place he then proclaims against the Puritans the apostolicity of episcopacy, the clerical nature of presbyters and deacons, and their subordination to bishops; all, he says, must render account "Deo primum, post et Regi."[24] Fortunately, this section summarizes for us, in a manner as clear as it is concise, contentions which Andrewes makes in numerous places in the sermons; it may be relied on as an exact statement of his teaching on enormously important points of doctrine, which happily excuses us from casting a wider net.[25]

Turning from the normative to the structural, we find Andrewes again quite articulate in speaking of the Church and its government. A conference with Sir Toby Matthew, held while Andrewes was bishop of Chichester, centered largely on the key question of the perpetual visibility of the Church. Catholics taught visibility as one of the distinguishing marks of the Church of Christ, while the embarrassment of trying to prove the authenticity of their own respective churches led Luther and Calvin to speak of the church as invisible—a perpetual visibility, obviously, worked against their pretensions. Andrewes, however, saw no difficulty in visibility. The church he preached was the Church of Christ, he contended; it had continuity with apostolic times, and had been visible throughout its whole existence. He assured Sir Toby that in England hardly any learned man "had declared that there was no necessity of a continual visibility in the Church."[26] That Andrewes actually held for perpetual visibility may be gathered from his general teaching on the Church and particularly from his contention that the

---

23 *Works,* IX, *Concio in discessu Palatini,* 91-92.
24 *Works,* IX, *Concio in discessu Palatini,* 92-93.
25 It does not include all the points of divergence from Roman Catholicism and Puritanism, of course, but it is reasonably complete.
26 Mathew, *Conversion of Sir Tobie Matthew,* 99.

Anglican and the Roman Catholic churches were indeed one and the same Church of Christ.[27]

The same note or characteristic follows logically from his teaching on the structure of church government which is found in his *Summary View of Government*. This rough, schematic essay attempts the vindication of episcopal government for the Church. Andrewes begins by analyzing the forms of government obtaining under the Old Testament from Moses onward. He finds therein counterparts for all the chief officers of the English Church of his own day: Christ is the counterpart of Aaron, who was head of the Mosaic Church; Eleazar, the chief overseer, corresponds to the archbishop; the princes of the priests to the bishops, priests to presbyters, and so forth.[28] In the New Testament, he explains, the whole ministry was at first invested in Christ alone. He then took unto Himself the Twelve, whose successors were the bishops; the Seventy, whose successors in turn were the priests; and finally the faithful people or the disciples. On Christ's departure from the earth the apostles became the shepherds of His flock. Each of them, singly[29] and jointly, had over all others in the Church authority or jurisdiction. They could impose hands in ordaining and confirming, command, countermand, censure. Then the apostles, to guarantee the continuance of the churches and the exercise of general care over them, ordained bishops to succeed them in power and place.

---

[27] Hunt, *Religious Thought in England*, III, 369. See also Mathew, *Conversion of Sir Tobie Matthew*, 99-100: Andrewes told Sir Toby "that he held the English Protestant Catholic Church, and the Roman Catholic Church, to be one and the same Church of Christ, forasmuch as he might conceive the fundamental points of faith, and the substantial worship and service of God; that we were both . . . the same house of God; and that the only question between us both was, in very deed, and might justly be, whether that part of the house wherein they dwelt, or else that other part which we inhabit, were the better swept, and more cleanly kept, and more substantially repaired."

[28] *Works*, VI, *Summarie View of Government*, 350.

[29] This constitutes a rejection of the primacy of Peter.

Seeing then God hath no less care for the propagation and continuance of His church than for the first settling or planting of it . . . it must needs follow that this power was not personal in the apostles, as tied to them only, but a power given to the church; and in them for their times resident, but not ending with them, as temporary, but common to the ages after and continuing, to whom it was more needful than to them, to repress schism and to remedy other abuses.

So that the very same power at this day remaineth in the church, and shall to the world's end.[30]

Hence, Andrewes concludes, "what a steward is in a house, a pastor in a flock, a captain in a camp, a master in a ship, a surveyor in an office: that is a bishop in the ministry."[31] And it is ever his desire and prayer, he writes to Du Moulin, that all those churches which are united in professing the same faith may be joined in the one ecclesiastical polity which derives from the earliest days of the Church—that is, in an episcopal government; for whosoever opposes that traditional form opposes the whole of antiquity as well as the consent of the universal Church.[32]

The Church has authority; as our mother "she hath the power of a mother over us, and a mother hath power to give laws to her children"; and though she have the tender heart of an indulgent mother, though she try as best she may to burden us with no more than we can endure, and searches the Scriptures to relieve us,[33] yet because people are sheep or goats she must have her rod of excommunication. "And if that will not serve, Moses hath another which he can turn into a serpent and sting them; yea, if need so require, sting them to death by the power secular."[34] How necessary is her guidance! exclaims Andrewes

---

30 *Works*, VI, *Summarie View of Government*, 356.
31 *Works*, VI, *Summarie View of Government*, 361.
32 *Works*, IX, *Responsiones ad Petri Molinaei epistolas*, 215.
33 *Works*, I, Ash Wednesday Sermon V, 391, 394-95.
34 *Works*, II, Lenten Sermon II, 28.

in another place; should every man be "left to himself for prayer, fasting, Sacrament, nay for religion too now and all? For God's sake, let it not be so, let us not be left altogether to ourselves, no not in prayer!"[35] We need her guidance indeed; when she calls us to something, it is "rather God by the Church, her ancient order and custom calls us to it."[36] In one of the warmest of his sermons Andrewes makes use of the story of Mary Magdalen's anointing of Christ to urge the laity's support of the Church on the ground that it is none other than the mystical body of Christ.[37] St. Paul, he says, expressly called the Church Christ's body, and well he might have, for "the first speech Christ ever spake to him, Himself calleth the Church *Me*—the word He useth."[38] Since Christ

> gave His natural Body to be bought and sold, rent and torn, cruci-fied and slain for His Body mystical; His Body mystical is cer-tainly dearer to Him, and better He loveth it. And then, if He will accept that is done to the less, and make it *bonum opus* [Magdalen's anointing]; He will much more that which is done to the more beloved; and it shall never go for less, never did I am sure.[39]

Lancelot Andrewes, therefore, preached a visible, authori-tative church whose constitution was episcopal and nonpapal. But an episcopacy which was the mere creation of the state—bishops who were nothing but civil officers, such as Elizabeth probably preferred—satisfied him not at all. The episcopal office, he tells us, was apostolic, and so divine, in origin; it was constituted a clerical order, distinct from and superior to the order of the priesthood. In a striking sermon preached on the

[35] *Works*, I, Ash Wednesday Sermon V, 392. The same holds for the sacrament and fasting, he says immediately, 393.

[36] *Works*, I, Ash Wednesday Sermon VI, 399.

[37] *Works*, II, Lenten Sermon III, 37-60. Its text is from Mark 14:4-6, where we read of the protest of some of the apostles over the seeming waste of an article which might have been sold to get money for the poor.

[38] *Works*, II, Lenten Sermon III, 50; see 1 Corinthians 12:12.

[39] *Works*, II, Lenten Sermon III, 52.

Second Commandment at St. Giles, Andrewes severely attacks the Presbyterian formula for church government. We have pretty well rid ourselves of images, he decides in a reference to the substance of the commandment; but many are the "imaginations" which various and sundry of late would have us take for "the Apostles' doctrine, and fellowship" (Acts 2:42). Some affect church government, "the Apostles fellowship." Since no society can endure without government, God has appointed in the Church governors and assistants with the power to receive accusations, to pass judgment, to censure, and to excommunicate. In this divinely established government there are but two degrees, both created by Christ Himself: the one of the twelve apostles, the other of the seventy disciples. It is utterly false to say that the apostles established an equality among the clergy, for the first order is superior to the second.[40] Bishops have succeeded the apostles; *presbyteri*, priests or ministers, have succeeded the Seventy, and until recently such has always been thought the proper form of church government. But there are some today who attempt to force on the Church, not simply as a mere convenient form but as one absolutely necessary and alone of Christ's institution, a government of lay elders, pastors, doctors, and, in some instances, of deacons as well. For such a government Andrewes finds no evidence in the Scriptures, the fathers, or the ecclesiastical writers, and so it is false—nothing but an "imagination."[41]

In this vigorous rejection of presbyterian government Andrewes did not trouble himself with anything more than the assertion, in contradistinction, of the episcopal form. A fuller development of his teaching of the *de jure divino* origin of episcopacy and its superiority as an order over the priesthood appears in his debate with Pierre du Moulin, a French Cal-

---

[40] *Works*, V, Occasional Sermon II, 62-63.
[41] *Works*, V, Occasional Sermon II, 64-65.

vinist.[42] The discussion was carried on in a series of three letters and three replies in 1618-1619, and is marked by unusually good temper and by the charge, so common in debate, that each did not entirely understand the other. Du Moulin had published in 1618 a book entitled *De la vocation des pasteurs*.[43] In his first letter to Andrewes he writes that he has heard James I was offended by certain references to episcopacy, and he hopes now to explain himself to James's satisfaction.[44] He had contended that the names *bishop* and *presbyter* were taken promiscuously for one and the same in the New Testament; that there was but one and the same order of both; and that the superiority of bishops is not *de jure divino* but merely *de jure ecclesiastico*. He had, he protested, no intention of lessening the dignity of bishops; there is only a difference of degree between episcopacy and priesthood, not one of order; and, in any case, as a French protestant he could not hold episcopacy as *de jure divino* without danger of being forced to recant.[45]

In reply Andrewes admits James was disturbed, for many in England were agitating similar ideas and Du Moulin's points might well be used to defame and calumniate the episcopal order. Conceding that the names *bishop* and *presbyter* are used indiscriminately, he warns Du Moulin of the danger that, since this is so, people might take the things themselves for one and the same. It is clear from the fathers that the offices are distinct.

---

[42] *Works*, IX, *Responsiones ad Petri Molinaei epistolas*, 205 ff.; published in English: *Of Episcopacy. Three Epistles of Peter Moulin Doctor and Professor of Divinity, Answered by . . . Lancelot Andrews, Late Lord Bishop of Winchester. Translated for the Benefit of the Publike* (no place, 1647). Quotations are from this English translation.

[43] Pierre du Moulin, *De la vocation des pasteurs* (Sedan, 1618). See *Works*, IX, 175, note b.

[44] Du Moulin had been one of James's literary assistants and had received several favors from the king. See Willson, "James I and His Literary Assistants," 49-51.

[45] *Of Episcopacy*, Letter I [Du Moulin], 1-6.

As to the second point, one order involves a power which the other does not; thus, bishops alone possess the power of conferring the priesthood, he writes as he refuses to accept the distinction suggested by his opponent. A degree involves superiority without any particular additional power; an order, on the other hand, includes both. The apostles and the seventy-two disciples constituted two distinct orders; bishops have succeeded the apostles, presbyters the seventy-two.[46] Further, anything done by the apostles was done by apostolic right, which is, "as I interpret it, by *Divine*. For nothing was done by the *Apostles*, that the *Holy Ghost*, the *Divine Spirit* did not dictate to them." Although we say these things be by divine right, he continues, we do not say they belong to faith; they belong rather to the practice of the Church.[47]

These first two letters practically complete the debate, for little doctrinal progress appears in the remaining four. Du Moulin strives to clarify his position in succeeding letters; Andrewes reiterates the stand of his first, but adds one or two points of interest. He emphasizes his conviction that episcopacy is *de jure divino*: "*Bishops* were formerly instituted by *Christ* in the *Apostles*; and *Presbyters* in the *Seventy Two*." The episcopal order "hath the strength and sinews thereof, not only from the Apostles, but even from our *Saviour* himself."[48] Though he holds firmly to this position, he does not contend that episcopacy is absolutely necessary:

> Though *Our Government* be by *Divine Right*, it follows not, either that there is *no salvation*, or that a *Church cannot stand*, *without it*. He must needs be *stone-blind*, that *sees not Churches standing without it:* He must needs be *made of iron*, and *hard hearted*, that *denys them salvation*. We are not made of that metal, we are none of those Ironsides; We put a wide difference betwixt

---

[46] Andrewes speaks sometimes of seventy, sometimes of seventy-two, disciples.
[47] *Of Episcopacy*, Letter I [Andrewes], 7-16; quotation from 16.
[48] *Of Episcopacy*, Letter III [Andrewes], 45, 53.

them. Somewhat may be wanting, that is of *Divine Right* (at least in the *external Government*) and yet *Salvation* may be had. So that you shall not need *to damn them to the pit of Hell, or pronounce the sentence of condemnation upon your flock.* This is not to *damn* anything, to *preferr* a better thing before it: This is not to *damn your Church*, to *recall it* to another form, that *all Antiquity* was better pleased with, i.e. to *Our:* but this, when *God* shall grant the opportunity, and your estate may bear it. If we do but agree upon *this* point, in all the *rest* we shall not fall out. But yet we wish not a concord, that is but pieced and patched up, but an intire, absolute agreement, without any piecing and patching: which, we doubt not but, *you* likewise wish with *us.*[49]

This passage is a curious combination of constancy and compromise, a clear manifestation of Andrewes' realization of the importance of antiquity and of his tolerant spirit—at least where Protestantism was concerned. *"Your Churches,"* he was to say again, "wanted somewhat that is of *Divine Right:* wanted, but not by your fault, but by the iniquity of the times." You did not have at the reforming of your church kings so propitious as ours. Thus he absolves the continental Protestants of sinning against the divine right.[50]

As the English Church developed through the early years of the seventeenth century, one major issue between the two great parties finally forced itself up through the petty squabbles over vestments and ceremonies and stood starkly revealed as the contest between presbyterianism and episcopacy. The early Puritans had been willing to tolerate episcopacy so long as it was held to be a mere civil delegation from the crown, yet they continued to strive for presbyterian government in the Church.[51]

---

49 *Of Episcopacy*, Letter II [Andrewes], 24.
50 *Of Episcopacy*, Letter III [Andrewes], 56.
51 Frere, *The English Church in the Reigns of Elizabeth and James I.*, 275-76; Davies, *The Early Stuarts*, 70: "Many puritans, like Bastwick, were indifferent about prelacy, so long as it was merely 'an order established by the king and state'; but their keenest antagonism was aroused when the theory of episcopacy *jure divino* was emphasized."

Andrewes fought for his order, not from mere self-interest as a member of a threatened episcopacy, but from the full conviction that in this matter he was theologically right.

Despite the professed aim of reformers generally to establish a worthy clergy in place of the old, the clerical state in England, both episcopal and sacerdotal, was by no means of a high order during Andrewes' day.[52] There were exceptions, of course, but few combined so many excellent qualities as Andrewes himself. He proposed to himself a fine ideal of priestly and episcopal service, and came very close to attaining it in practice. Careful and frequent preaching engaged a large share of his time; several hours a day he allotted to prayer; study, by which he said on one occasion the clergy are anointed,[53] remained ever a habit with him; of his interest in education we have already spoken;[54] his handling of temporalities was conscientious and prudent. Pembroke, in debt when he assumed the mastership in 1589, he left in 1605 with a surplus of more than eleven hundred pounds.[55] He had refused the bishoprics of Ely and Salisbury when they were vacant because he was unwilling to alienate any of their lands.[56] Yet he was in no way miserly; he spent great sums on the repair of the various houses connected with his preferments: four hundred and twenty pounds on the Chichester properties, more than twenty-four hundred on Ely's, and two thousand on those of Winchester. Aspiring

---

[52] Roland G. Usher, *The Reconstruction of the English Church* (New York, 1910), I, 205-43, an excellent study of the condition of the clergy at the beginning of James's reign.

[53] *Works*, III, Pentecost Sermon X, 287.

[54] *Supra*, 6.

[55] *Works*, XI, Isaacson, *Exact Narration*, xvii-xviii. A gap in the treasurer's accounts at Pembroke from 1596 to 1606 makes it difficult to determine how Andrewes built up the finances of the college, but figures actually extant confirm an increase of money in the "treasure-house" from £125 in 1589 to £726 in 1606 (Attwater, *Pembroke College*, 55).

[56] *Works*, V, Buckeridge, *Funeral Sermon*, 292.

scholars and the accomplished alike benefited at his hand;
among those he appointed to benefices were Samuel Harsnet,
later archbishop of York; Matthew Wren, one of Andrewes' successors at Ely; Meric Casaubon, son of Andrewes' great friend
Isaac.[57] A thoroughly delightful story of one of his typical bene-
factive gestures is to be found among the Rawlinson manuscripts
in the Bodleian Library. Unfortunately, it bears neither date
nor any indication of authorship.

> Mr. Fuller, the famous author of the *Miscellanea Sacra*, was a
> poor vicar, of an obscure parish near Salisbury called Alington;
> and notwithstanding his book was put out, and very well received,
> lived obscurely, and no notice at all taken of him. Till Erpenius
> coming into England, and being very freely and nobly entertained
> by Bishop Andrews he inquired of the bishop for this Fuller. The
> bishop answered he never heard of him. Erpenius replied, that he
> was a very excellent scholar, the best in his way of learning that
> was in England, or perhaps in all the world. This set Bishop
> Andrews on work to find him out, and after having given order to
> his chaplains and several others to inquire him out, at length he
> heard that he lived in such an place near Salisbury. The King
> going shortly after in progress lay at Salisbury. The bishop pres-
> ently sent for this Fuller; who being a poor and humble man was
> much affrighted, fearing lest the bishop had somewhat against him;
> but after much tergiversation, being confirmed by the messenger,
> he came to Salisbury. The bishop was at dinner; hearing of his
> arrival, [he] sent for him to come to dinner, made very much of
> him; and when sweetmeats came to the table, took a box out of the
> dish and sent it to Mr. Fuller. Mr. Fuller would not by any means
> accept of it, being a refreshment he needed not nor was accustomed
> unto. Yet with great importunity the bishop put it upon him, and

---

[57] *Works*, XI, Isaacson, *Exact Narration*, xv-xvii, and xv, note n. In the British
Museum, Sloane MSS., 118, f. 14, is a Latin letter from Meric Casaubon
requesting Andrewes' aid in the matter of a pension bestowed on Meric's
mother by the king over which a difficulty had arisen. Meric offers to
Andrewes all the books of his father's library which had come to him and
lists their titles. Meric Casaubon to the bishop of Winchester, September 13,
1618.

made him open it, where he found a presentation ready sealed to a very good benefice the bishop had conferred upon him.[58]

Nor did Andrewes overlook the poor, for whom he made several provisions in his will.[59]

He was not without his faults, of course, worst of which was sycophancy in his relations with James.[60] Still he stood out among his contemporaries remarkable, and indeed remarked— a man very close to the clerical ideal he preached. In a hard-hitting Latin sermon delivered to Convocation in 1593 he struck at the abuses in the Church of his day and urged his clerical brethren to meet the challenge of their high calling.[61] He reproves the selfish spirit which allows the clergy to behold with passive indifference the perils and troubles of the Church. Unworthy men are admitted to orders, he charges, men who follow the injunction of the text "Take heed to yourselves" (Acts 20:28) in so perverse a manner as to spoil their benefices to care for their heirs, their sons and daughters, instead of preserving them intact for their successors. We are accused, he says, of being " 'more concerned with shearing than shepherding the sheep.' "[62] Three things he lays down as necessary for the health of the Church: the care of doctrine, a higher standard of personal morality among the clergy, a true pastoral spirit. To the bishops, particularly, has been committed the office of teaching; they must see to the purity of doctrine, and unless it gets prompt attention, there will soon be no authoritative doc-

---

[58] Bodleian Library, Rawlinson MSS., B, 158, ff. 144-45 (spelling and punctuation modernized).

[59] *Works*, V, Buckeridge, *Funeral Sermon*, 294-95, where the provisions are summarized. "Neither did he stay to do good and distribute till his death, that is, then gave his goods to the poor when he could keep them no longer," says Buckeridge (294).

[60] See *supra*, 10.

[61] *Works*, IX, *Concio ad clerum*, 29-51. Ottley, *Lancelot Andrewes*, 32-35, has a good brief summary.

[62] Ottley, *Lancelot Andrewes*, 32-33.

trine left. Ignorant, foolish, fanatical preaching has turned the
church into a barbershop. What wonder that there be little
reverence among the people, that they behave in church as
though in a playhouse, since the clergy have not set them good
example! The clergy, he charges, are eager in pursuing their
own interests and remiss in caring for their flocks:

> If you attend not to the flock, the flock will attend to you. An
> unnatural state of things, portentous indeed, that this should come
> to pass: but you have already experienced it to some extent; while
> you are neglectful of the people, be sure that the people has its
> eye on you.[63]

Three things, Isaacson tells us, Andrewes particularly ab-
horred: he so hated usury that he loaned money to his friends
without expecting any return but the principal; he so detested
simony that he refused to admit men he suspected of simoniacal
practices to livings they sought, and as a consequence was frequently harassed by suits of law; and, as we have seen, he so
despised sacrilege that he refused preferment which involved
alienation of church revenues.[64]

The preceding pages have summarized Andrewes' observations on the Church of England; of necessity some of his
references to its two great enemies, Roman Catholicism and
Presbyterianism, have appeared. He had further and definite
ideas respecting each of them. In his first speech to the English
Parliament James I had said, " 'I acknowledge the Roman
church to be our mother church although defiled with some
infirmities and corruptions.' "[65] Such also seems to have been
Andrewes' sentiment. "The English Protestant Catholic Church"
and the Roman Catholic Church he held to be one and the same;

---

[63] Ottley, *Lancelot Andrewes*, 34-35. Ottley suggests that Andrewes refers here to
the Marprelate tracts.
[64] *Works*, XI, Isaacson, *Exact Narration*, xxvi-xxvii. For Andrewes exposition of
the duties of ministers see *Works*, VI, *Catechism*, 192-98.
[65] Davies, *The Early Stuarts*, 202, quotation from the *Commons Journals*.

the question was, he told Sir Toby Matthew, which part of this same house of God, yours or ours, is "better swept, and more cleanly kept, and more substantially repaired."[66] You Catholics are indeed members of the Catholic Church, "etsi *non sana membra*," he wrote in the *Tortura Torti*, while in the *Responsio ad Bellarminum* he makes a statement which sounds very like the "branch theory" of Christianity:

> *Roma* enim, pars Universi: *Romana*, particularis in universali: venit ergo contra et *fidem*, qui *Romanam Catholicae* aequalem facit: et vero *rationem*, qui *totum parte sua majus* non fatetur.[67]

His bitterest attacks centered on the papacy, of course; in his bitterness he occasionally misses the truth, as, for example, when he scornfully charges that the pope "perceives all that is to be perceived at once; can have nothing added to his knowledge from the first instant he is set down *in cathedrâ*; can have no new *comperi*, his *comperis* come in all together; gets Caiaphas' knowledge by sitting in Cephas' chair."[68] One need not be reminded that this is hardly an accurate statement of the claims of papal infallibility. Bitter, too, is a passage in one of the Pentecost sermons which accuses Gregory VII of hatching "a new misshapen Holy Ghost" and sending him into the world. The early Christians were meek and dovelike, but with this new Holy Ghost men "take arms, depose, deprive, blow up," and the dove, instead of an olive branch, has "a matchlight in her beak or a bloody knife." Would it not have been better for the Holy Ghost to have come down "in the shape of a Roman eagle, or of some other fierce fowl *de vulturino genere?*"[69] There

---

[66] Mathew, *Conversion of Sir Tobie Matthew*, 99-100; see *supra*, 82, note 27.

[67] *Works*, VII, *Tortura Torti*, 496; *Works*, VIII, *Responsio ad Bellarminum*, 218.

[68] *Works*, III, Pentecost Sermon XII, 328. Andrewes is commenting on the text "Aperiens autem Petrus os suum, dixit, in veritate comperi, etc." (Acts 10:34) ; the implication is that Peter could get new knowledge, but the pope cannot if his claim to infallibility be true.

[69] *Works*, III, Pentecost Sermon VIII, 255.

is no call to assemble further passages of this kind, of which there are several in the sermons.[70] The great attacks against the old Church and particularly the papacy occur in the *Tortura Torti* and the *Responsio ad Bellarminum*, which are not formally included in this survey: it is enough to notice that the attacks boiled over occasionally into the sermons.

Lancelot Andrewes had as little love for Puritans as he did for Roman Catholics. In his day Puritanism meant two things principally: a rigid Calvinism in doctrine, which looked to the Scriptures as the sole rule of faith and preached a gloomy predestination; and a presbyterian form of church government. His wariness of Calvinistic predestination and his sharp rejection of presbyterianism in church government is evident in his *Judgment of the Lambeth Articles*, and the *Concio in discessu Palatini*.[71] He seemed to think, however, that the important, in fact the crucial, difference between what he represented and what the Puritans stood for involved the business of discipline and not the essentials of religion:

> *Puritanorum* ea religio non est, quorum nulla est religio sua atque propria: disciplina est. Quod ipsum tamen de *Puritanis* generatim dictum volo, deque iis inter eos, qui praeterquam quod *Disciplinae* suae paulo magis addicti sunt, caetera sobrie satis sapiunt; Qui, quantumvis *formam* illam suam perdite depereant, in reliqua tamen doctrina satis Orthodoxi sunt.
>
> Mihi ab exteriori regiminis forma *Puritani* sunt, non autem a religione, quae eadem et est, et esse potest, ubi facies regiminis externa non eadem.[72]

---

[70] For example, in *Works*, V, Occasional Sermon I, 42, Andrewes charges that the pope has "dispensed with the oath and duty of subjects to their Prince against the fifth commandment; with the murder, both violent with dags, and secret with poison, of the sacred persons of Princes, against the sixth; with the uncleanness of the stews, and with incestuous marriages, against the seventh; so now of late, with the abomination of simony against the eighth."

[71] *Supra*, 5, 80

[72] *Works*, VIII, *Responsio ad Bellarminum*, 161, 162.

Andrewes profoundly loved order; in the Puritans he could
see nothing but disturbers of the peace and destroyers of the
proper hierarchy of society. They want equality to the utter
destruction of authority, he complains:

> No *super*, no superiority they; all even, all equal; fellows and
> fellows. "The right hands of fellowship," if you will; but not so
> much as imposition of hands, *super*. For if *super*, then *sub* follows;
> if "upon," then we 'under;' if above, then we beneath. But no *sub*
> with some; submit neither head nor spirit to any.[73]

They are meddlers spurred on by a hot humor they falsely
call the fire of the Holy Ghost; they take to themselves the style
of "godly brethren" and are forever "mending churches, states,
superiors—mending all, save themselves."[74] They are more than
sacrilegious, for "if but to spoil a church be sacrilege, as it is
granted, yet that leaves somewhat, at least the walls and the
roof, so it be not lead." The Pharisees loved the gold of the
Temple better than the Temple itself, and so do their posterity
to this day.[75] His striking sermon on the Second Commandment contains a number of sharp criticisms of Puritan pretensions respecting ceremonies, the manner of preaching, informal
prayers, and church government.[76]

Andrewes had not a great deal to do with Puritans in an
administrative way, though Macleane tells us that as bishop of
Winchester he won back from a "colloque" of Calvinist ministers the obedience of the Isle of Jersey, which was in the
jurisdiction of his diocese;[77] and among his Visitation Articles
for the year 1619 one aims at both Romanists and Puritans:
"Whether hath there been any secret conventicles or meetings
in your Parish by any Priest, Minister, or others, tending to the

---

[73] *Works*, III, Pentecost Sermon XI, 309.
[74] *Works*, III, Pentecost Sermon II, 133.
[75] *Works*, II, Easter Sermon X, 351, 352.
[76] *Works*, V, Occasional Sermon II, 60, 61, 68; see *supra*, 84-85.
[77] Macleane, *Andrewes and the Reaction*, 158-59.

depraving of the form of prayer, doctrine, or government of the Church?"[78]

Among the turbulent spirits of the day there were others, particularly Anabaptists and those whom Andrewes called "enthusiasts" or "voluntaries"—the radicals, we might say— who drew down upon themselves unmerciful castigation from the gentle bishop.[79] The "brain-sick Anabaptist"[80] he charged with being professedly against kingship and its authority, with denying all secular jurisdiction: "No law-makers they, but the Evangelists; no courts, but Presbyteries; no punishments, but Church-censures. These rise against the very estate of Kings; and that should they find and feel, if they were once grown enough to make a party."[81]

Andrewes himself did not escape the wrath of his enemies. Bellarmine, of course, drove merrily at him in the great controversy over the Oath of Allegiance; the Puritans, who suspected him of Romanizing tendencies, seem to have delayed the awarding of his doctorate in divinity at Cambridge;[82] and after his death a "profane and sawcy scribbler"

> not only defamed his doctrine as atheological, irrational, and worse than that of Arminius . . . but by an unchristian insinuation would make his Reader to believe, that Bishop Andrews was the worse for being Bishop Andrews, that Dr. Andrews was more a saint than the Lord Bishop of Winchester, and by consequence, that his last days were very unhappily his worst too.[83]

In spite of the bitterness of his opposition to Calvinism in England, Andrewes sincerely desired union among all the

---

[78] *Works*, XI, *Visitation Articles*, Article 27, 118.

[79] *Works*, III, Pentecost Sermon IX, 273; *Works*, III, Pentecost Sermon XI, 313-14.

[80] *Works*, I, Nativity Sermon XI, 186.

[81] *Works*, IV, Gowry Sermon I, 11; *Works*, V, Occasional Sermon VI, 130; and see *Works*, III, Pentecost Sermon XIII, 351.

[82] H. B. Swete, *Two Cambridge Divines of the Seventeenth Century* (London, 1913), 7-8.

[83] Andrewes, Ἀποσπασμάτια Sacra, Preface, xviii-xix.

reformed churches. He seldom refers to the great reformers
in the sermons, but he did cherish dreams of ecumenicity as
did Cranmer and Parker before him.[84] In the *Responsio ad
Bellarminum*, for example, he expresses his desire for a synod
among all who are not ashamed of Christ's name, or for a conference of internuncios, through which all might come "unum
per omnia sentire." Andrewes had a nostalgic longing for the
days of Christian unity. The people of the reformed churches,
he tells Bellarmine, have suffered no shipwreck of the faith,
they reject no creed of the old Church, they admit all.[85] The
reader will recall the hopes expressed for union in his debate
with Du Moulin on episcopacy.[86] This discussion took place in
1618 and 1619, and it is interesting to note that a tone of querulousness and discouragement, unusual in Andrewes, creeps
into the sermons of this period, possibly because he was disturbed by the growing Puritan clamor and the continued frac-
tionizing of Protestantism.

In his "bidding prayer" preceding the *Concio in discessu
Palatini* he prays publicly for unity in the Church "Catholica,
non Romana, sed Oecumenica, nempe, quam longe lateque patet
terrarum Orbis, longe lateque disseminata."[87] And in his Pentecost sermon of 1606 he exclaimed: "High shall be his reward
in Heaven, and happy his remembrance on earth, that shall be
the means to restore this 'accord' to the Church."[88] That man,
thought John Harington, might well be Lancelot Andrewes:

> I persuade myself, that whensoever it shall please God to give
> the King means, with consent of his confederate princes, to make
> that great peace which His blessed word, *Beati pacifici*, seemeth to
> promise,—I mean the ending of this great schism in the Church of

---

[84] Hunt, *Religious Thought in England*, I, 14, 42, for Cranmer and Parker.
[85] *Works*, VIII, *Responsio ad Bellarminum*, 448, 452.
[86] See *supra*, 86.
[87] *Works*, IX, *Concio in discessu Palatini*, 80.
[88] *Works*, III, Pentecost Sermon I, 113.

God, procured as much by ambition as superstition,—this reverend prelate will be found one of the ablest, not of England only, but of Europe, to set the course for composing the controversies; which I speak not to add reputation to his sufficiency by my judgment; but rather to win credit to my judgment by his sufficiency.[89]

---

[89] *Works,* XI, Harington, *Memoir,* xxxvii-xxxviii. Arnott, "Anglicanism in the Seventeenth Century," in More and Cross, *Anglicanism,* lxxii, asserts that Andrewes attempted negotiations with the Eastern Orthodox Church.

CHAPTER V

Andrewes
on Redemption

Lancelot Andrewes did not win fame among his contemporaries by preaching novel doctrine, nor simply because he
happened on a style which tickled the fancy of the moment and
set a fashion others tried to imitate, nor again because he knew
how to flatter two vain monarchs for whom adulation was the
spice of life; but rather because he preached with tremendous
conviction truths which in the last two thousand years have
come nearest to satisfying the longings in the hearts of men and
closest to providing a way out of the perpetual confusions into
which they persist in throwing themselves./Year after year he
took the old, orthodox truths of the honored creeds of Christendom, touched them with the genius of a fertile imagination,
soaked them in the rich flavor of his own sincerity, and preached
them with a brilliance and a striking directness which left his
hearers impressed, if not always improved./Whether or not the
Jacobean court was less vulgar, less immoral, more Christian,
more delicate in its sensibilities for his preaching than it would
have been without him is a question impossible to answer today.
It was, perhaps, not worse than any other European court of
the seventeenth century, yet one can hardly read the sermons
without contrasting their elevated moral tone with its traditional
reputation of coarseness and lack of refinement.

Andrewes faced the courtiers, the favorites, the king, and preached Christ, God incarnate, Christ poor, Christ suffering, Christ gentle, Christ reproving, Christ rewarding, Christ threatening, Christ risen; he preached as well the rottenness of sin, the pains of hell, the joys of heaven; the duty of repentance, the rigors of fasting; the monotonous necessity of personal effort in the performance of good works, the solemn obligation of prayer and the propriety of a cultivated liturgy. If he had given himself over to speculative theology, we might suppose that James had been intrigued, or if he had spent his hours in castigating Roman Catholicism and Puritanism, we might suppose he had found willing ears; the enemy from without and the enemy from within did not escape his attention, of course, but rarely did Andrewes make them tools of entertainment. He preached no "popular" topics, simply Christian doctrine and Christian moral practice—and strange as it seems, the court heard him.[1]

The focal point in all Andrewes' teaching was Christ: "To become like to Him we worship is the pitch of all religion";[2] "Find Christ and find all";[3] "There is no part of the whole course of our Saviour Christ's life or death but it is well worthy our looking on, and from each part in it there goeth virtue to do us good";[4] "All He did, all He suffered, all He bequeathed, all He was, He was for us";[5] "No man can be happy if he be not . . . taken prisoner by Christ. It is the only way to enjoy true liberty."[6] In such expressions as these he merely concentrates the theme which is quintessential to his thought. Bishop

---

[1] The one exception among his sermons perhaps would be those emphasizing divine right; surely these were welcome to James.

[2] See *supra*, 75.

[3] *Works*, I, Nativity Sermon XVI, 267.

[4] *Works*, II, Passion Sermon I, 120.

[5] *Works*, III, Easter Sermon XVIII, 92-93.

[6] *Works*, III, Pentecost Sermon VII, 230.

Andrewes was not a mystic; but union with Christ, union with God, which is so characteristically the end of mystical prayer, he made exactly the object of all spiritual effort. Nowhere does the Christocentricity of his teaching more completely or more beautifully reveal itself than in the sermons for Christmas, Passiontide, and Easter. Since he accepted the great fundamental creeds of Christendom, one has only to recall them to know the broad frame of his theology. What interests us, however, are the things that are specific to his teaching. What were the ideas on which he concentrated, which he emphasized as most suitable to the needs of his troubled Church? These three groups of sermons contain the answers. Random selections from any one or any combination of these, however they might be arranged, will all project the same picture—the incarnate Christ.

The Nativity sermons concentrate, of course, on the fact of the Incarnation of the Second Person of the Blessed Trinity and on the story of Christ's birth together with all its attendant circumstances: the shepherds, the angelic choirs, the coming of the Magi. Figuratively speaking, Andrewes keeps his eye on the two natures of Christ, never letting either completely out of sight. He plunges deep into the mystery to talk of the eternal generation of the Son of God, of His glory with God the Father in heaven, of His coeternity, coequality, and consubstantiality; of the union of the two natures in the one Person, of the necessity for such a union, of the purpose for which the Second Person became incarnate, and of man's consequent obligations. As can be imagined, these provide him with almost unlimited topics for development. If he had a tremendous appreciation for the infinity of God, His holiness, His mercy, and for the cardinal mystery of the Trinity, as indeed he did, it is his fine sense of the humanity of Christ and his gift for combining the two, the human and the divine, which most strikingly characterize his treatment of the Nativity. For example, in a series of powerful paragraphs from the first Nativity sermon we catch

echoes of the "Dies irae" which were to sound again in Francis
Thompson's *Hound of Heaven*. The angels sinned against God
and fell, he tells us, yet God made no pursuit. "And man fell,
and fled too, and 'hid himself in the thick trees' from the presence of God." God "made after him presently with *Ubi es?*
sought to reclaim him, 'What have you done? Why have you
done so? Protested enmity to him that had drawn him thus
away, made His *assumpsit* of 'the woman's seed.' " But God did
yet more: He "sent after him still by the hand of His Prophets,
to solicit his return," and when that was not enough, He went
after man in person; "this was exceeding much, that we fled,
and He followed us flying." And God "gave not over His pursuit, though it were long and laborious, and He full weary;[7]
though it cast Him into a 'sweat', a 'sweat of blood,' " until at
last, He seized upon man, took upon Himself man's very nature;
and now He can never put it off: "One we are, He and we, and
so we must be; one, as this day, so for ever."[8]

The following paragraph is typical of the sermon from
which it is taken and shows Andrewes at the pinnacle of the
mystery. The text on which he was preaching is from the famous
opening verses of St. John's Gospel, "And the Word was made
flesh, etc." (John 1:14). He considers God as the author of
the Scriptures:

> But He begins with the Word. His care being first to tell us of
> the pureness of His generation before of His generation itself; but
> after, by little and little unfoldeth Himself and tells, He is so the
> Word as the Son also. Indeed, it was best beginning with the Word.
> That term the heathen wise men, the philosophers, would never
> stumble at, but brook it well enough; as indeed they did not with
> approbation only, but with high admiration, read and magnify
> the beginning of this Gospel. Witness Tertul. in Apol., Euseb. in

---

[7] The reader will recall the verse "Quaerens me, sedisti lassus," from the hymn
"Dies irae," in the Mass of the Dead.

[8] *Works,* I, Nativity Sermon I, 6-9.

Praepar., August. de Civit. 10., and Theodoret. It was conform to
their reason, *Quod Deus ab aeterno intelligit,* and that Νοῦς and
Λόγος, 'the conceiving of the mind,' and 'the mind' must needs
be coeternal—the mind never without it; as the Prophet saith,
Egressus Ejus a diebus aeternitatis.[9]

From such heights Andrewes can descend to a simple hom-
ily on the shepherds and the sign given them for the finding
of the newborn Savior—Child, swaddling clothes, a manger:

> To Bethlehem they [the shepherds] will. Set the sign by, let
> them alone, say nothing to them. When they came thither, they
> would never go to an inn, or ostrie, but to the very best house in
> the town. Or if to an inn, to the fairest chamber in it; or to a
> chamber at least; never to the stable, there to look in the manger
> for *Christus Dominus.* To the stable we go to look for a horse, to
> the crib for *bos cognovit et asinus*—for one of them; never thither
> to seek for the Saviour of the world.
>
> Nay, if in their search passing by, by hap they had lighted
> upon such a birth—a Child so lying; it may be they would have
> pitied the poor Babe and the mother, but have gone on their way
> and sought farther. Never, I dare say, taken Him for Christ the
> Lord. And if one should have bid them, 'Stay, for this is the Child
> the Angel spake of,' they would have shaken him off and said with
> as great scorn as they, 1 Sam. 10. *Nunquid poterit iste salvari nos.*
> "What shall this be our Saviour trow?"[10]

Andrewes' freedom of movement in the Scriptures, his keen
insight into their correlations, are well illustrated in his explanation of the use of the word *ecce* in the prophecies concerning
the Nativity. The Holy Ghost, who never sets an *ecce* but " 'upon
matters of great moment,' " has strung a whole series of *ecces*
among the Scriptures prophetical of the Nativity:

---

[9] *Works,* I, Nativity Sermon VI, 88. Note that this paragraph contains typical
Andrean references to the fathers; that is, very indefinite ones. The editors
have verified the vast majority of such references and complete them in the
margin beside the text.

[10] *Works,* I, Nativity Sermon XII, 199.

This *ecce* here, to the last, *Ecce concipies* of the blessed Virgin; that, to Esay's *Ecce concipiet Virgo;* that to David's *Ecce de fructu ventris tui;* that, to Abraham's *Ecce in semine tuo;* and so up, till ye come to *semen mulieris.* There they first begin, and take light one from another, till they come to the *Ecce natus est hodie,* the *ecce* of all *ecces,* the last and highest of them all. And as a beacon serveth to call up and stir up men to have regard, so is this here [the text of the day, *Ecce enim evangelizo vobis,* etc. (Luke 2:10)] to excite them, and in them us all, with good attention to hear and to heed these so great good tidings.[11]

These passages barely suggest the variety of Andrewes' handling of the Nativity, but they should suggest the bishop's warm, penetrating presentation of this mystery of the redemption which involves so many basic Christian teachings. Since Andrewes followed the fathers and the scholastics in playing on the paradoxes of the Incarnation and the Nativity, the words he quotes from his favorite father, Augustine, may well be taken as an apt expression of his own understanding and appreciation of these two events:

Deus; quid gloriosius? Caro; quid vilius? Deus in carne; quid mirabilius?[12]

Of the three splendid sermons on the Passion of Christ it is difficult to prefer one above the others. Each exemplifies the meditative quality so common in Andrewes' work, each very signally illustrates the Christocentricity of his teaching, the real personal relationship he felt men should have with Christ, and, finally, each analyzes the mystery of the redemption. The second of these sermons drew its text from Lamentations 1:12:

Have ye no regard, O all ye that pass by the way? Consider, and behold, if ever there were sorrow like My sorrow, which was

---

11 *Works,* I, Nativity Sermon V, 72.
12 *Works,* I, Nativity Sermon III, 37-38; see also Mitchell, *English Pulpit Oratory,* 141.

done unto Me, wherewith the Lord did afflict Me in the day of the fierceness of His wrath.[13]

Andrewes' first business, as usual, is to break down the text and to establish its applicability to Christ. The keynote he introduces immediately—this is the voice of one in the depths of affliction, in the terrible extremity of having no one to "respect him or care for him." Here we have a complaint and a request, "Have ye no regard?" "Consider and behold." It is our task, then, to consider and to weigh the quality and the cause of Christ's suffering, that we may come to an understanding and an appreciation of its significance, for Christ here invites us to ponder the pains of His Passion; begs us to turn from the routine of business, however important that may be, to look upon Him suffering. And we are not simply to gaze upon, but to "consider" and "regard" what we behold.

There never was suffering and sorrow like this—consider both the torments themselves and the Person who bears them. They were not merely pains of the body, "so woeful as Pilate verily believed His very sight so pitiful, as it would have moved the hardest heart of them all to have relented and said, This is enough, we desire no more." No; terrible as were these, Christ's grief of soul was worse:

> Give me any grief, save the grief of the mind, saith the Wise Man; for, saith Solomon, "The spirit of a man will sustain all his other infirmities, but a wounded spirit, who can bear?"[14]

The sorrows of His soul are so great as to be unknown to us, as the Greek fathers have put it in their liturgy: " 'By Thine unknown sorrows and sufferings, felt by Thee, but not distinctly known by us, Have mercy upon us, and save us!' " Now, all these pains of body and of soul are *poena sensus*; there was yet

---

[13] *Works*, II, Passion Sermon II, 138-57.
[14] *Works*, II, Passion Sermon II, 144.

a more terrible pain which Christ had to suffer, the *poena damni*. His pain of loss and His dereliction during the Passion are absolutely unparalleled:

> They among whom He had gone about all His life long, healing them, teaching them, feeding them, doing them all the good He could, it is they that cry, "Not Him, no, but Barabbas rather;" "away with Him," "His blood be upon us and our children." It is they that in the midst of His sorrows shake their head at Him, and cry, "Ah, thou wretch;" they that in His most disconsolate estate cry Eli, Eli, in most barbarous manner, deride Him and say, "Stay, and you shall see Elias come presently and take Him down."[15]

Of those nearest Him on earth "some bought and sold Him, others denied and forswore Him, but all fell away, and forsook Him." Even His Father in heaven abandoned Him. Why did Christ cry out in His Passion, "My God, My God, why hast Thou forsaken Me?" when we read that the martyrs went cheerfully, even singing, through their torments? "Martyres non eripuit, sed nunquid deseruit," Augustine tells us in reply: God did not deliver their bodies, "but He forsook not their souls, but distilled into them the dew of His heavenly comfort, an abundant supply for all they could endure. Not so here." Christ had "no comfort, no supply at all."[16]

So much for the *dolor*, says Andrewes; what of *dolor Meus*, the Person who suffered? He was a man, He was a just man, said Pilate's wife in warning; He is innocent, said Pilate himself in judgment, and wrote that He was a king; all of these, this Person was infinitely more, as the centurion saw: He was the Son of God. It is because of the Person who suffered, then, that this Passion is absolutely unique:

---

[15] *Works*, II, Passion Sermon II, 145-46.

[16] Andrewes hastens to caution against a false understanding of God's forsaking of Christ. He quotes St. Leo: "'The union was not dissolved: true, but the beams, the influence was restrained.'" Andrewes does not strain the truth for dramatic effect (*Works*, II, Passion Sermon II, 147).

It is truly affirmed, that any one, even the least drop of blood, even the least pain, yea of the body only, of this so great a Person, any *Dolor* with this *Meus*, had been enough to make a *non sicut* of it. That is enough, but that is not all; for add now the three other degrees; add to this Person those wounds, that sweat and that cry, and pūt all together, and I make no manner question the like was not, shall not, cannot ever be. It is far above all that ever was or can be, *abyssus est.* Men may drowsily hear it and coldly affect it, but principalities and powers stand abashed at it.[17]

Now, the cause of all this unique suffering we must find in God's wrath, for it was God who so afflicted Christ. Only one thing arouses God's wrath, and that is grievous sin; but in Christ there never was any sin whatsoever; how, then, could God the Father have so punished His Son whose praise He had thundered from the very heavens? "There is no way to preserve God's justice, and Christ's innocency both, but to say as the Angel said of Him to the Prophet Daniel, 'The Messias shall be slain . . . but not for Himself.' "

The short is, it was we that for our sins, our many great and grievous sins,—*Si fuerit sicut*, the like whereof never were,— should have sweated this sweat and have cried this cry; should have been smitten with these sorrows by the fierce wrath of God, had not He stepped between the blow and us, and latched it in His own body and soul, even the dint of the fierceness of the wrath of God.[18]

No reason can be given for this action of Christ in taking on Himself our punishment, "but because He regarded us:—Mark that reason." He loved us who were nothing, who were even His enemies; let us not forget, says Andrewes, that the thing which sets the high price on this sacrifice is the fact that He who offers it to God is God. So far the causes of this affliction of Christ; but *cui bono*, for whose benefit all this love and suffering and

---

[17] *Works*, II, Passion Sermon II, 148-49.
[18] *Works*, II, Passion Sermon II, 150-51.

sacrifice? We are the ones to receive the benefit of all of these, he continues, for whereas the sins of men drove them away into exile and forfeited for them and all mankind any estate in the Land of Promise, yet by Christ's death, by the sacrifice of our high priest, by His very blood, we have gained a title to a heavenly inheritance.

Shall we not be moved, then, by this just plaint of Christ? All creatures except men seem to be aware of it, and in their own way, to show regard for it: "The sun in Heaven shrinking in his light, the earth trembling under it, the very stones cleaving in sunder, as if they had sense and sympathy of it, and sinful men only not moved with it." Andrewes then proceeds to make an important doctrinal point: If we have not regard for this sacrifice of Christ, "it may appertain to us, but we not pertain to it; it pertains to all but all pertain not to it." He then goes on to say:

> None pertain to it but they that take benefit by it; and none take benefit by it no more than by the brazen serpent, but they that fix their eye on it. Behold, consider, and regard it; the profit, the benefit is lost without regard.[19]

Here then, is Andrewes' teaching on the universality of the redemption; Christ suffered for all, but all do not participate in the benefit of that suffering—that is, in the redemption— without personal effort. This is no Calvinistic teaching of the theory of predestination, but rather a clear affirmation of the power of man's will to accept or reject salvation, an idea to which Bishop Andrewes returns in the conclusion of this sermon on the Passion of Christ:

> It is kindly to consider *opus diei in die suo,* 'the work of the day in the day it was wrought;' and this day it was wrought. This day therefore, whatsoever business be, to lay them aside a little; whatsoever our haste, yet to stay a little, and to spend a few

---

[19] *Works,* II, Passion Sermon II, 155.

thoughts in calling to mind and taking to regard what this day the Son of God did and suffered for us; and all for this end, that what He was then we might not be, and what He is now we might be for ever.

Which Almighty God grant we may do, more or less, even every one of us, according to the several measures of His grace in us![20]

Let these brief considerations of the Christmas sermons and this great sermon on the Passion suffice for an exposition of Andrewes' christology and his soteriology.[21] The allied doctrine of adoption he handles in his Nativity sermon of 1609. We were prisoners, and God freed us; but this was not all: "After our redemption we stood but as prisoners enlarged; that was all: but still we were as strangers; no part nor portion in God or His Kingdom, nor no reason we should hope for any." God took one step more, "the highest and farthest step of all." He translated us from the estate of condemned prisoners to the estate of children adopted, and with His Son, even by His Son, we

---

[20] *Works*, II, Passion Sermon II, 157. For a similar idea see *supra*, 71, where Andrewes says: " 'Want of faith makes that He, That is born to all, is not born to all though' " (*Works*, I, Nativity Sermon II, 28).

[21] The legalistic character of Andrewes' teaching on redemption may be noticed in the following: "Now, men's persons come to need redeeming by captivity; and in that case, there must be a ransom. Men's estates come to need it, upon a sale outright; and in that there needs a new purchase.

"We were gone both ways. Both are in the seventh to the Romans. At the twenty-third verse, 'there is a law in our members leading us captive;' when either we are taken, and carried away by strong hand, with a temptation, or overwrought by the sleights of the enemy. At the fourteenth verse there is a sale, 'carnal and sold under sin;' when, for some consideration as we think, but many times scarce valuable, we make away our estates by our own voluntary act.

"Christ redeems us from both. His 'ransom' ye shall find, ἀντίλυτρον. And His 'purchase,' *redemptionem* περιποιήσεως; that is 'of purchase,' plain. His purse went not for either, but His Person. His death, as the high priest's, freed us from captivity; His blood, as the blood of the covenant, was the price that cleared our estates from all former bargains and sales" (*Works*, III, Pentecost Sermon VI, 208-09).

have been made "joint-heirs" to the kingdom to which He was born—"is not this full on His part?"[22]

The truth of Christianity, the validity of its claims, and the completion of the redemption rest absolutely on the Resurrection of Christ. Bishop Andrewes, who preached this key mystery several times, warns his hearers in the first of the series of the obligations consequent on a knowledge of Christian truths:

> Christian knowledge is not a knowledge without all manner of account . . . we are accountants for it . . . we are to keep an audit of what we hear, and take account of ourselves of what we have learned.[23]

We must express the matter of a feast in the form of our lives: "By knowing Christ's death, we die to sin . . . by knowing His resurrection, we live to God . . . our estate in soul is bettered . . . the fruit of the words we hear, and the feasts we keep, do abound daily toward our account against the great audit."[24] The text of this first Easter sermon is taken from St. Paul's Epistle to the Romans:

> Knowing that Christ, being raised from the dead, dieth no more; death hath no more dominion over Him.
> For, in that He died, He died once to sin; but in that He liveth, He liveth to God.
> Likewise think (or account) ye also, that ye are dead to sin, but are alive to God in Jesus Christ our Lord (Romans 6:9-11).[25]

Andrewes' first concern, as is so often the case when he begins a series on one of the great mysteries, is to establish the fact. How do we know the fact of Christ's Resurrection? Paul knew because he saw the risen Christ; but the Romans, to whom he wrote, and we ourselves, know it only by "relation." We

---

[22] *Works*, I, Nativity Sermon IV, 59-60.
[23] *Works*, II, Easter Sermon I, 187-205; quotation from 188.
[24] *Works*, II, Easter Sermon I, 189.
[25] *Works*, II, Easter Sermon I, 187.

know "by relation in the nature of a verdict, of them that had seen Him, even Cephas and the twelve; which is a full jury, able to find any matter of fact, and to give up a verdict in it." And if the Twelve will not suit, we have the testimony of the five hundred who all together saw Him at one time.

The number of witnesses, however, is not so important as their quality. The testimony of people credulous and "light of belief" may legitimately be challenged, especially if they made no effort to set their knowledge on a firm basis. Andrewes argues that a thing "is ever best known that is most doubted of." Never, he continues, was any matter carried with greater scruple and slowness of belief, with more doubts and difficulties, than this matter of Christ's Resurrection. Mary Magdalen saw it, reported it, and was not believed; the two disciples met Christ risen on the road to Emmaus, reported it, and were not believed; so too the several women who had hastened to the tomb, and their words were dubbed " 'an idle, feigned, fond tale.' " Then all the apostles but Thomas saw Him, and seeing, doubted. Their doubt resolved, they tried to convince Thomas, and you know how peremptory he was: he made his conditions, and Christ met them. All this doubting at the beginning serves precisely to remove all our doubts and to assure us that Christ is truly risen, says Andrewes, quoting Augustine. All these witnesses took measures to establish their certainty, "and certainly they did know it, as appeareth. For never was any thing known in this world, so confidently, constantly, certainly testified as was this, that Christ is risen."

What did these witnesses get by testifying to this fact? Nothing, rather they lost by it:

> They lost by it their living, their life, all they had to lose. They might have saved all, and but said nothing. So certain they were, so certainly they did account of their knowing, they could not be got from it, but to their very last breath, to the very last drop of their blood, bare witness to the truth of this article; and chose

rather to lay down their lives and to take their death, than to deny, nay than not to affirm His rising from death. And thus did they know, and knowing testify, and by their testimony came the Romans to their knowing, and so do we.[26]

But our knowing is surer even than that of the Romans, for the "world that then was and long after in such opposition, is since come in." Thousands have laid down their lives since those early days in testimony of the fact, faith in the fact of Christ's Resurrection has conquered the whole world, so we have several additional arguments to prove it to us.

In some of the later sermons Andrewes returns to this problem of establishing the fact of the Resurrection. In the third of this series he proves that Christ could not have been spirited from His tomb:

> Though such a thing will be given out, that the Disciples stole Him away while the watch was asleep. But your reason will give you; 1. small probability there is, they could be asleep, all the ground shaking and tottering under them by means of the earthquake. 2. And secondly, if they did sleep for all that, yet then could they not tell sleeping, how, or by whom, He was taken away. 3. And thirdly, that His Disciples should do it; they you know of all other were utterly unlike to do any such thing; so fearful as miserably they forsook Him yet alive, and have ever since shut themselves up since He was dead. 4. And fourthly, if they durst have done such a thing, they would have taken Him away, linen, clothes, and all, as fearful men will make all the haste they can possibly, and not stood stripping Him and wrapping up the clothes, and laying them every parcel, one by one in order, as men use to do that have time enough and take deliberation, as being in no haste, or fear at all.[27]

The same Christ who died rose from the dead; did it not please Him to "retain the print, both of the nails and spear"?[28]

---

[26] *Works*, II, Easter Sermon I, 191.
[27] *Works*, II, Easter Sermon III, 233-34.
[28] *Works*, II, Easter Sermon V, 263.

As for the agency of the Resurrection, he writes in his last (and undelivered) Easter sermon:

> The resurrection is one entire act of two joint Agents, that both had their hands in it. Ascribed one while to Christ Himself, that He rose, that He came back; to shew that He had "power to lay down His life, and power to take it again." Another while to God, that He raised Him, that He brought Him back; to shew that God was fully satisfied and well-pleased with it, reach Him His hand, as it were, to bring Him thence again.[29]

In a sermon on the text from the Epistle to the Colossians (3:1-2), "If ye then be risen with Christ, seek those things which are above, where Christ sitteth at the right hand of God, etc.," Andrewes affirms our own resurrection: "As Christ died, so is He risen for all; and shall not all rise with Him? What do we then do with *si vos?* Yes, all rise with Him out of their graves, but not all rise to the right hand after-mentioned."[30]

Several other sermons of this series clamor for at least a brief mention: the twelfth, for example, which develops the typical sense of the Scripture story of Jonas and the whale— Jonas is the type and Christ risen the antitype;[31] or three later sermons dealing with Mary Magdalen and the risen Christ, which afford excellent instances of Andrewes' very human treatment of the utterly human scenes in which she figured on Easter morn.[32] The sermon with which the bishop finished his teaching on the subject of the Resurrection is a strikingly rich development of the text from the book of the prophet Isaias (63:1-3), "Who is this that cometh from Edom, with red garments from Bosrah? etc."—a text, it might well be remarked, which is customarily associated with the Passion. Andrewes here pictures

---

[29] *Works,* III, Easter Sermon XVIII, 89.
[30] *Works,* II, Easter Sermon VIII, 311.
[31] *Works,* II, Easter Sermon XII, 383-403.
[32] *Works,* III, Easter Sermons XIV, 3-22; XV, 23-38; XVI, 39-59.

Christ triumphant as having crushed His enemies and as being stained with the blood of vengeance.[33]

Andrewes' teaching on the Incarnation, the Nativity, the Passion, and the Resurrection practically completes the sermon material concerning major events in the foundation of Christianity which are at the same time subjects of doctrinal pronouncements and objects of Christian belief. There is yet one further event of capital importance in both respects which he also made the topic of an extended series of festal sermons. Christians generally regard the descent of the Holy Ghost upon the apostles on the first Pentecost Sunday as the final step in the establishment of the Church of Christ. Such too was Andrewes' position.[34] Intrigued by the wondrous nature of this mystery, Andrewes made it the occasion of some of his most learned exegesis. In these efforts, even more than in the Nativity sermons, he concentrates on the nature of the godhead; in the sermon for Whitsunday of 1612 he reviews the general Christian doctrine on the Holy Ghost and on the Blessed Trinity. There is a Holy Ghost, he says: He is God, God in unity of name, yet distinct in number and distinct as a Person by Himself. He is a Person by Himself, yet He is not of Himself; He "proceeds" from both Persons, that stand before Him, the Father and the Son, and the procession is "breath-wise."[35] In others of this fine series of doctrinal sermons delivered on the Feast of Pentecost, Andrewes develops numerous themes associated with the subject of the Holy Ghost: His threefold coming; His office, works, gifts; His place in the working out of the Redemption, and so forth.

---

33 *Works*, III, Easter Sermon XVII, 60-79.

34 See *Works*, III, Pentecost Sermon I, 110, where Andrewes holds it meet that the "first dedication of Christ's Catholic Church on earth" should occur on this day which was a great feast even under the Old Law.

35 *Works*, III, Pentecost Sermon V, 189; the procession Andrewes later calls by its technical name, "spiration" (*Works*, III, Pentecost Sermon XI, 307).

Andrewes' teaching was essentially Christocentric; even here, in these sermons on the Holy Ghost, he cannot get away from Christ, and two or three pages of his sermon for 1614 on the text "Thou art gone up on high. Thou hast led captivity captive, etc." (Psalm 68:18) richly portray Christ's redemptive work. Playing on the idea of captivity, he says we belong to Christ by the two titles of His creation and redemption of us. Adam sinned and was taken captive, and all men with him. Came Christ to suffer like a lamb, to rise like a lion, to break the gates of death, to take us captive unto Himself. So we, who had been captive to sin and error and Satan, are now captive to Christ:

> For all the world as an English ship takes a Turkish galley, wherein are held many Christian captives at the oar. Both are taken, Turks and Christians; both become prisoners to the English ship. The poor souls in the galley, when they see the English ship hath the upper hand are glad, I dare say, so to be taken; they know it will turn to their good, and in the end to their letting go. So was it with us, we were the children of this captivity. They to whom we were captives, were taken captives themselves, and we with them. So both came into Christ's hands; they and we His prisoners both.[36]

Christ has restored us to the " 'liberty of the sons of God,' " our enemies (sin, error, Satan), He has carried to confusion.

---

[36] *Works,* III, Pentecost Sermon VII, 230. This simile of the English capture of the galley is one of Andrewes' rare contemporary references. He was quite nautical in this sermon, for he shortly after makes an application of the story of the Spanish Armada: "In the year 88, the Invincible navy had swallowed us up quick, and made full account to have led us all into captivity. We saw them led like a sort of poor captives round about this isle, sunk and cast away the most part of them, and the rest sent home again with shame. Eight years, since they that had vowed the ruin of us all, and if that had been, the thraldom of this whole land; they were led captives in the literal sense, (we saw them) and brought to a wretched end before our eyes. So He that here did, still can, and still doth 'lead captivity captive' for the good of His" (*Works,* III, Pentecost Sermon VII, 230-31).

References to the Blessed Virgin Mary in the sermons are very few, though several times, particularly in the Nativity sermons, Andrewes had glorious opportunities to speak of her directly. Presumably his caution, his fear of being misinterpreted or of shocking his hearers, account for his reticence. In one of the *Two Answers to Cardinal Perron* he protested that Mary was not to be adored nor to be invoked, since each, he claimed, involved *cultus latriae* which is proper to God alone.[37] But that he reverenced her, particularly as the Mother of God, is clearly seen from his orthodox belief in the Incarnation, and from this brief passage in the *Preces Privatae:*

> Sanctissimae, intemeratae, super caeteros benedictae,
> Deiparae, et semper Virginis Mariae, cum omnibus Sanctis, memoria habita,
> Nos ipsos, et vicissim alios, et omnem vitam nostram,
> Christo Deo commendemus.[38]

Behind the whole economy of the redemption as its very necessary supposition lies the fact of sin. As one reads Andrewes' sermons he cannot but be impressed by his firm conviction that sin, the willful violation of God's law, is the worst thing in the world. I have never, he says in one of his Whitsunday sermons, seen any man "brought so low with any worldly calamity" as those whose eyes God opened to the sight of their own sins; and I speak, he says, of men "not of the common sort, but men of spirit and valour, that durst have looked death in the face." Their hearts were broken, "yea even ground to powder with it; contrite indeed."[39] It is very necessary for an understanding of the whole complex of Andrewes' thought to realize immediately that he taught man's personal power of

---

[37] *Works*, XI, *Two Answers to Cardinall Perron*, 46-47.
[38] *Works*, I, Nativity Sermon IV, 53-54, where Andrewes discusses the motherhood of Mary; *Works*, X, *Preces Privatae*, 141.
[39] *Works*, III, Pentecost Sermon X, 294.

will to reject or to indulge in such violations of God's commands. Man is not driven by necessary compulsion to sin, nor,
on the other hand, is he so confirmed in grace that, once justified, he can never lose sanctifying grace by willfully committing
sin. The importance of this position with relation to Andrewes'
teaching on predestination, justification, the priestly power of
remitting sin, and to the general character of his theology
simply cannot be overestimated.

Andrewes defined sin as a "turning from God," a turning
of our backs upon God, a forsaking of the way of His commandments.[40] Sin is an error, a rebellion, a fall which has
terrible consequences, "for it fouls as a fall, for it bruises as
a fall, for it bringeth down as a fall; down from the state of
Paradise, down to the dust of death, down to the bar of judgment, down to the pit of hell."[41] It is a brutish thing and so
against the "nobleness of reason," a shameful thing and so
against public honesty.[42] Sin was even the cause of Christ's
death.[43] In all sin there are two elements:

> 1. *Reatus*, and 2. *Macula*, as all Divines agree, 'the guilt,' and
> 'the soil,' or spot. The guilt, to which punishment is due; the spot,
> whereby we grow loathsome in God's eyes, and even in men's too.
> For even before them, shame and reproach follow sin. Take these
> two away, and sin is gone. And there is no people under Heaven,
> but have sense of these two; and nor religion is, or ever was, but
> laboured to remove them both.[44]

Andrewes taught, of course, the distinction between original
sin: "the mother-sin . . . the sin of Adam and Eve, and their

---

[40] *Works*, I, Ash Wednesday Sermon IV, 361. See also *Works*, II, Easter Sermon
   II, 296: "What is it [sin] but a transgression or passing over the lines and
   limits of our duty, set us in the law of God?"
[41] *Works*, I, Ash Wednesday Sermon III, 342.
[42] *Works*, I, Ash Wednesday Sermon IV, 372.
[43] *Works*, I, Ash Wednesday Sermon V, 385.
[44] *Works*, III, Pentecost Sermon XIII, 347.

motives to it, [which] are the lively image of all the after-births
of sin, and the baits of sin for ever" and "the actual sins of our
persons."[45] In one of the Nativity sermons he sets original sin
succinctly in its context. We were in union with God, through
Adam's sin the union was broken and we came to ruin, Christ
has repaired the break and we are gathered to God again:
"There was a former capitulation—the articles were broken:
then came this recapitulation here anew. An account was cast,
but it was mis-cast, and so it is here cast new over again."[46]

There are three capital sources of sin, Andrewes tells us in
the Ash Wednesday sermon of 1624: the spirit, the flesh, and
the world; sins deriving from each of these heads are corrected
by their contraries. Thus, the spirit, which loves to range at
liberty and scatter itself in all sorts of thoughts or fix itself on
some pleasing object, must be cured by confining it, by making
it undertake, for example, some "task of devotion," by setting
it to prayer, reading, meditating, "which is a dry object and
nothing pleasing to it; fix it so, and you punish it. For nothing
is more irksome."[47] Set the flesh, which "loves to fare well . . .
to sleep and take her ease," which "loves *vestiri mollibus*, mirth
and good company"—set it to fasting, to watching, to lying
"hard," clothe it in sackcloth, "make it retire and sit pensive:
abridge it of these all or any, and you punish it more or less I
warrant you." As for the world and the worlding, "they love
to part with as little as they can. Charge them with any thing
that shall be to them chargeable, it punisheth them shrewdly,
and is to them a punishment." Make them therefore do works
of charity and compassion, make them give alms.[48] The reader
recognizes the orthodox and traditional character of all this;

---

[45] *Works*, II, Passion Sermon III, 165; *Works*, I, Nativity Sermon VII, 113.
[46] *Works*, I, Nativity Sermon XVI, 270. In the paragraph following he speaks of
"Our separation, our ruin; our reparation . . . our 'gathering again.'"
[47] *Works*, I, Ash Wednesday Sermon VIII, 441-42.
[48] *Works*, I, Ash Wednesday Sermon VIII, 442.

what is impressive about it is that Andrewes preached it so clearly and vigorously to the gay Jacobean court, which one can easily imagine a little sensitive to such directness.

As a motive for avoiding sin, besides those implied in what he has said of its nature, the bishop suggests a healthy fear of God:

> Not to fear the next way is to fear. The kind work of fear is to make us "cease from sin." Ceasing from sin brings with it a good life; a good life, that ever carries with it a good conscience; and a good conscience casts out fear. So that, upon the matter, the way not to fear is to fear; and that God That brings light out of darkness, and glory out of humility, He it is That also brings confidence out of fear.[49]

Andrewes preached before Elizabeth at Richmond in 1599 just prior to the departure of the earl of Essex on his expedition to quell the insurrection of Tyrone. In one of the very few sermons wherein he makes reference to contemporary circumstances he proposed as a motive for giving up sin the blessings which in return God might grant to the expedition: "among our military points we would reckon the abatement of sin for one. . . . If we could be but persuaded to reform our former custom of sin, it would certainly do the journey good." Sin should be forborne at all times, of course, but in time of war, of national crisis, "we should have least to do with it."[50]

It is the part of true repentance, he said in another place, to give up the occasions of sin, the object, the bad company, or whatever it might be, that would lead us to turn back to our former folly.[51] We must pray to "God to take from us the

---

[49] *Works*, III, Pentecost Sermon XII, 336. The world "begins to grow from fear too fast," but fear is with God "a thing acceptable," he says in the same sermon (337).

[50] *Works*, I, Ash Wednesday Sermon II, 322, 329, 330.

[51] *Works*, I, Ash Wednesday Sermon IV, 364.

opportunity of sinning; so frail we are, it is no sooner offered
but we are ready to embrace it—God help us."[52] But for our
comfort let us remember "that even these sins which we commit
after baptism, after our calling, and when we come to the
knowledge of truth, are remissible."[53] In a Pentecost sermon
which occasioned some concern in the court Andrewes taught
that God had given the power to remit sin even to sinful men;
"Be the men what they will that have received it, no sin of man
shall make the power of God of none effect." He who is a sinner
himself may still remit sin and save others, though he himself
may not be saved.[54] On our part, however, there must be sorrow. While we cannot command physical tears, we must try, at
least when we review our sins and their circumstances, to have
sorrow for them; our indignation must arise not only for reasons affecting us, but from a consideration of God whom we
have by sin offended.[55] If all men are sinners, how is it then
that we are ordered to keep the commandments, how compose
keeping the commandments and the having of sin? Augustine
answers for us when he writes: *"omnia mandata facta deputan-
tur, quando quod non sit ignoscitur;* 'all are accounted as kept,
when what is not is pardoned out of His mercy.' "[56]

This introduces us to a notion as firmly held by Lancelot
Andrewes as was his conviction of the nature of sin: God's
mercy, which he throws back even to the act of creation:

It was mercy, and nothing but mercy, set the creation in hand.
For, it is well known, *in non ente* there could be no moving cause

---

52 *Works,* IV, Gowry Sermon VII, 159.
53 *Works,* V, Sermon on Prayer XIV, 430.
54 *Works,* III, Pentecost Sermon IX, 270-71, 277; see *supra,* 78, note 13. Besides
    this power of the keys for the remission of sin Andrewes also teaches that in
    the Church there are several means to purge us from our sins (*Works,* V,
    Occasional Sermon IV, 94-95) ; see *infra,* 145.
55 *Works,* I, Ash Wednesday Sermon IV, 370, 369, 373.
56 *Works,* III, Pentecost Sermon III, 153.

at all. Nothing we were, we and all His works: in nothing there can be nothing to induce why it should be brought out of the state of being nothing. So that His mercy it was that removed that universal defect of non-entity at the first.[57]

No need then for despair, for the God of mercy pleads with the sinner to turn to Him: "My outward calling by My word, inward movings by My Spirit, My often exhortations in your ears, My no less often inspirations in your hearts, *tactus Mei et tractus*, 'My touches and My twitches,' My benefits not to be dissembled"—all these God tells the sinner, all these are but to call him back to God.[58] God lays away His rigor and "will not go exactly to work, but be ready to relieve and repute that worthy that is not all out so."[59] God's mercy reaches even into hell that those there might not suffer as much as in justice they should.[60] Did not Christ risen appear first to two sinners, Mary Magdalen and Peter?[61] Anyone who will trouble himself to page through the *Preces Privatae* or the *Manual of Directions for the Sick* will find numerous passages of exquisite beauty and feeling dealing with the mercy of God. Andrewes surely had a fine sense of proportion and balance which kept his theology from being narrow, dour, and eccentric. While he did not hesitate to castigate sin, he was no less eager to point to the wide-open gates of divine mercy.

Bishop Andrewes was not above indulging in the preacher's plaint that his own day was far gone in sin. One of his sharpest references to his contemporaries occurs in the sixth Gowry sermon, in which he compared the plot against King Ahasuerus

---

[57] *Works*, IV, Gunpowder Sermon VII, 326-27.
[58] *Works*, I, Ash Wednesday Sermon III, 345-46.
[59] *Works*, I, Ash Wednesday Sermon VIII, 451. Note that Andrewes speaks here of "reputing worthy"; this is consistent with his teaching on justification and one of the points wherein he differs from Roman Catholic doctrine.
[60] *Works*, IV, Gunpowder Sermon VII, 326.
[61] *Works*, II, Easter Sermon III, 223-24.

by the two eunuchs, Bigthan and Teresh, as it is told in the
Book of Esther (2:21-23), to the attempt of the Gowries. Men
have become contemptuous of the very notion of sin; they have
ceased to regard it as something evil in itself; they fear only
penal consequences:

> What care men for sin, if there be no action at the common
> law for it? None but Westminster-hall sins do men care for. God
> saw it would come to this, men learn no more duty than penal
> statutes did teach them; He took order therefore to bring it within
> them too.[62]

Foreseeing this, God has, in this story of Bigthan and
Teresh, brought their sinful action within the penal laws, so
that their attempt, a grievous sin in itself and hence harmful to
the soul, is also a heinous and a capital crime which "will bear
not an action only, but an indictment of life and death."[63] The
application to the attack of the Gowry brothers is obvious. But
Andrewes, despite the vigor with which he denounced sin, rarely
became very specific; it may be that thus, while still being
quite clearly understood, he escaped arousing effective resentment among the courtiers, before whom, and to whom certainly,
he was speaking. With the exception of passages in the *Concio
ad clerum*, wherein he was addressing his brethren of the cloth,
the following paragraph represents him at about his most specific. He is playing on the word "consumpti" in his text from
Lamentations (3:22):

> We were in *consumpti*, if it were but our consuming sins; 1. if
> but of what then was and, may I not say, still is consumed and
> wasted. What huge sums in superfluity, riot, of belly and back, and
> worse matters! 2. Our time: if but the consuming of it in ease and
> idleness, and too well-known fruits of them both. 3. Of the service
> of God, that is quite consumed by most of us now, fallen to but a

---

[62] *Works*, IV, Gowry Sermon VI, 131.
[63] *Ibid.*

sermon, if that; and how little like a sermon we hear it, and less I fear after regard it! 4. Of God's name that runs waste, and our blessed Saviour, That is even piecemeal consumed in our mouths, by all manner oaths and execrations, and that without any need at all. These, with other sins, that fret like a moth and creep like a canker, to the consuming of our souls, we should find; that as it was our enemies' [the Gunpowder plotters'] purpose we should have been consumed, so it was our desert to have been consumed, and that it was His mercy only we were not consumed.[64]

Such was Andrewes' general teaching on the redemption and the major truths intimately connected with it. His teaching on the means by which the effects of the redemption are applied to individual men is the business of the next chapter.

---

[64] *Works*, IV, Gunpowder Sermon IV, 270-71. The text from Lamentations reads: "It is the Lord's mercies that we are not consumed, because His compassions fail not."

CHAPTER VI

Andrewes
on the Supernatural

The age in which Bishop Andrewes lived professed an almost universal belief in the supernatural. The confusions which tore at Christian unity had not yet issued into the rationalism which was to deny the supernatural and to exalt the power of human nature, but they had come to the point where, as Jeremy Taylor wrote before the middle of the century, every opinion was made an article of faith, every article of faith a ground of quarrel and envy which, in their turn, led to faction; and every faction, pretending in its zeal for God, went its busy way convincing men that, except they hated their brothers and persecuted every religion but their own, they lacked the very virtue of religion.[1] In their efforts to reduce the flaming bitterness of religious controversy and division which sprang from the confusion, men of the middle and late seventeenth century, moderates like Lord Falkland, John Hales, William Chillingworth, Jeremy Taylor, and after them the group known as the Cambridge Platonists, Henry More, Ralph Cudworth, Benjamin Whichcote, and others, set in motion a drift into rationalism

---

[1] John Tulloch, *Rational Theology and Christian Philosophy in England in the Seventeenth Century* (Edinburgh, 1872), I, 380. This sentiment occurred in Taylor's *Discourse on the Liberty of Prophesying* (1647).

which was entirely hostile to the old orthodoxy of the supernatural. What happened, of course, was that men, having begun by
disagreeing on what the supernatural was and what it implied,
at last agreed in very large numbers to deny that it existed, and,
therefore, that there were any implications.

We need not enter into the realm of contrary-to-fact conditions to imagine what Andrewes' reaction to all this would have
been, for he very clearly affirmed his faith in the supernatural,
and as clearly, if not as expansively, set reason, which he nevertheless respected, in its proper place. Probably while he was
catechist at Pembroke Hall he delivered the series of sermons
on prayer which has been published with his other *Works*.
Relying on the editors' judgment as to their authenticity, and
especially on the consonance of their doctrinal content with that
of the festal sermons, we may draw from them without fear of
misrepresenting Andrewes' teaching on the supernatural. The
series numbers nineteen sermons; the first six have the general
title, *Preparation to Prayer;* the remainder discourse upon the
Lord's Prayer.[2] The first group contains an affirmation of the
supernatural, distinguishes it from the natural order, and pro-
pounds man's inability to perform supernatural acts without
supernatural grace. From Andrewes' teaching on the supernatural, his doctrine of justification and his sacramental teaching
develop quite logically.

For the very first of these sermons on prayer Andrewes
chose an apt text from the Second Epistle of St. Paul to the
Corinthians (3:5): "Not that we are sufficient of ourselves to
think any thing as of ourselves; but our sufficiency is of God."[3]
We are not of ourselves able, he says, to do the things which
will lead us ultimately to heaven; but, given that inability, we

---

[2] *Works*, V, *Nineteen Sermons upon Prayer in General, and the Lord's Prayer in
    Particular*, 299-476.
[3] *Works*, V, Sermon on Prayer I, 301.

are not to despair, for God grants us the sufficiency necessary. In fact, it is a gift of God's goodness that we are able to do any good whatsoever. The realization of this truth should lead us to pray God that we may receive from Him what is wanting in ourselves. Our inability to do good is an insufficiency of nature—it pertains to all men, even to the apostles themselves.

In the undertaking of any good there are seven steps: the accomplishing of it, the actual doing of the thing, the beginning to do it, the speaking of what is good, the willing and desiring of it, the understanding, and the thinking of it. Without stopping to unravel Andrewes' psychology of human acts as illustrated here, let us note that he has arranged them according to the order of intention, accomplishment being the first thing intended, the last executed. Now, for all or any one of these acts, he tells us, we lack the power of ourselves, as the Scriptures prove to us, and we suffer this insufficiency even in the order of nature: "the actions of our life are not of ourselves but from God," he says in a reference to divine conservation and concurrence. However, the apostle is not speaking here of insufficiency in things natural; he is talking of an insufficiency in the "ministration of the Spirit." Thus, "no endeavour of men can endue us with the grace of repentance, with faith, hope, and Christian charity, except the inward working of God's Spirit." Further, St. Paul is not speaking of men "not yet regenerate by God's Spirit," but of himself and of his fellow apostles, who most assuredly were regenerate; if such as they lack this ability, how much more do we?

Now, the reason for our lack, for this insufficiency, for this inability to perform those acts which gain us our hoped-for reward, is precisely this: human nature simply cannot perform such acts in the estate of decay to which it was reduced by the fall of Adam, nor could it, even if it were restored to the highest degree of perfection possible to man before the fall. Thus, even Adam before the fall could not have performed them.

It is not in the power of nature to elevate and lift itself up to conceive hope of being partakers of the blessedness of the life to come, to be made "partakers of the Divine Nature," and of the heavenly substance: if men hope for any such thing, it is the Spirit of God That raiseth them up to it.

As the water can rise no higher than nature will give it leave, and as the fire giveth heat only within a certain compass, so the perfection which Adam had was in certain compass, the light of nature that he had did not reach so high as to stir him up to the hope of the blessedness to come; that was without the compass of nature, and comes by the supernatural working of grace.[4]

Whatever good we do by "the direction of natural reason, it is without all respect of God, except He enlighten us before." But in our regeneration the corruption of our will is healed and "a certain divine spark of fire and zeal of God's Spirit is infused into us, by which we are holpen to do those duties of piety, which otherwise naturally we have no power to do."

Our text was a general negative sentence, Andrewes recalls; how, then, do we account for other Scriptures which record good purposes that came into the hearts of God's servants? We need this qualification, he replies: some things "that come of us" are of ourselves; other some come from us indeed, "yet are not of us"; the first proceed naturally, the second are engrafted in us. Thus, "if any divine and spiritual thoughts come into our hearts, the Lord God is the 'potter' that frames them in us." The sin which dwells in us, for instance, is from us and of us, but "the grace of God's Spirit, which dwells not in us but doth tarry guest-wise, is that which is from us but not of us." Sins are of and from ourselves, but good actions are not:

It is dangerous to ascribe too little to the grace of God for then we rob Him of His glory, but if we ascribe too little to ourselves there is no danger; for whatsoever we take from ourselves, it cannot hinder us from being true Christians; but if we ascribe that

---

[4] *Works*, V, Sermon on Prayer I, 306.

to the strength of our own nature which is the proper work of grace, then do we blemish God's glory.[5]

God gives grace, we receive grace; and after God "by His Spirit hath thus enabled us, we are said to be able and meet to do those things which we are commanded." We need grace, therefore; we have it not of ourselves because it is a "divine thing"; where are we to get it but from Him who is "the well of grace" from which all men may draw? The means to obtain grace from God is prayer.

Such is one of Andrewes' developments of the supernatural. Succeeding sermons in this series return to many key ideas: "As well the ability which man had by nature, as our enabling in the state of grace, is from God." "To supply the defect that is in nature grace is added, that grace might make that perfect which is imperfect";[6] and again the emphasis on prayer:

> Now we cannot come to God but by prayer, as Augustine saith: *Non passibus sed precibus itur ad Deum, et nuncius noster oratio est quae ibi mandatum nostrum peragit quo caro nostra pervenire nequit;* 'It is not with paces but with prayers we go to God, and our messenger is prayer which there doth our errand where our flesh cannot come.'[7]

And prayer itself "is properly the effect of grace."[8]

The doctrine on the supernatural in these sermons is truly representative of Andrewes' thought on this important matter, as a comparison with one or two excerpts from the longer festal sermons will show. While speaking in one of the Easter sermons of the effects of Christ's Resurrection, Andrewes distinguishes the natural life which will be restored to all in our own resurrection from the higher life of eternal happiness which Adam

---

[5] *Works*, V, Sermon on Prayer I, 308.
[6] *Works*, V, Sermon on Prayer II, 311, 315.
[7] *Works*, V, Sermon on Prayer III, 321.
[8] *Works*, V, Sermon on Prayer VI, 351.

never actually possessed but to which before his fall he had a title. "All our thought," he says, "is to be for the latter, how to have our part in that supernatural life, for that is indeed to be restored to life."[9] And in the fifth Pentecost sermon he distinguishes again between the two orders:

> For as an absolute necessity there is that we receive the Spirit, else can we not live the life of nature, so no less absolute that we receive the Holy Spirit, else can we not live the life of grace, and so consequently never come to the life of glory. *Recepistis spiritum,* gives the life natural. *Recepistis Spiritum Sanctum,* gives the life spiritual.[10]

With the major propositions of Andrewes' doctrine of the supernatural in mind, the reader is prepared to appreciate the sermon on justification in Christ's name delivered at Whitehall on November 23, 1600. It is so closely articulated that it is more than usually difficult to brief the line of his thought, but three or four passages contain the climactic points of his argument. More nearly controversial than most other sermons, this reveals Andrewes disputing particularly the Roman Catholic teaching; hence its champions, Bellarmine and Stapleton, whose writings he knew well, are subjected to rather severe strictures, though his tone is decently elevated throughout.

The text, on which Andrewes works most diligently, is from Jeremias: "This is the name whereby they shall call Him, the Lord our righteousness [*Jehova justitia nostra*]" (Jeremias 23:6); the critical point is the interpretation of the word "righteousness."[11] To be justice, to be righteousness, is the name of Christ alone, Andrewes asserts. God gave Him this name, and the names He gives all have a meaning and a virtue in them; this name, for instance, has the power to justify, to forgive us our

---

[9] *Works,* II, Easter Sermon II, 218.
[10] *Works,* III, Pentecost Sermon V, 190.
[11] *Works,* V, Occasional Sermon V, 104-26.

sins, to give us salvation. Andrewes makes a division into two main points: the name, of which we are to consider the parts and the reasons thereof, and the sense of the name; and secondly, the calling Him by it, which includes our duty to do it and the benefit accruing to us for so doing. In his remarks on *justitia*—justice or righteousness—the preacher adumbrates the main argument. Righteousness is as a branch from which spring salvation and peace as its fruits. If this be had, so too are the fruits; sin, which is unrighteousness, yields the very contraries to salvation and peace—perdition of soul and unquietness of conscience.

Why, Andrewes speculates, was not Christ's name *Jehova misericordia nostra?* Is not mercy ours?

> True it is, mercy is ours, ours wholly there is no doubt; but justice is against us, and except justice may be made ours too, all is not as it should be. But if justice, if that in God which only is against, might be made for us, then were we safe.[12]

If Christ be "righteousness, and not only righteousness but ours too, all is at an end, we have our desires." Once He is with us and not against us, once He is our own, all is safe. St. Bernard tells us that we should *"uti Nostro in utilitatem nostram, et de Servatore salutem operari*—use Him, and His righteousness, use that which is ours to our best behoof, and work our salvation out of this our Saviour." This name, *justitia*, is abstract; and that is of set purpose. God made Christ not a sinner, but sin, not accursed, but a curse; similarly, according to this abstract name, we are not to be made "righteous persons," which in itself is a full enough favor, but "righteousness," the very righteousness of God Himself.

So much for the terms of the name, *Jehova justitia nostra;* all will grant it to Christ, but not everyone will give it its full sense. To say that it means Christ is the exemplary cause or the

---

12 *Works*, V, Occasional Sermon V, 111.

efficient cause of righteousness is true, but not enough. We find in both the Old and the New Testament that there is a double righteousness: a "righteousness accounted," and a "righteousness done." In the New Testament, in the fourth chapter of Romans, no fewer than eleven times we find the phrase "reputatum est illi ad justitiam"—a reputed righteousness; and in the First Epistle of St. John we read, "My beloved, let no man deceive you, he that doeth righteousness is righteous" (1 John 3:7)—a righteousness done, which "is nothing else but our just dealing, upright carriage, honest conversation." This latter the philosophers conceived and acknowledged; the other, "righteousness accounted," "is proper to Christians only." One is a personal quality; the other, reputed righteousness, "an act of the judge, declaring or pronouncing righteous. The one is ours by influence or infusion, the other by account or imputation." In our text the prophet refers to imputed justice, and the Holy Ghost would have it so understood:

> For the tenor of the Scripture touching our justification all along runneth in judicial terms, to admonish us still what to set before us. The usual joining of justice and judgment continually all along the Scriptures, shew it is a judicial justice we are to set before us. The terms of 1. A judge: "It is the Lord That judgeth me." 2. A prison: Kept and shut up under Moses. 3. A bar: "We must all appear before the bar." 4. A proclamation: "Who will lay any thing to the" prisoner's "charge." 5. An accuser: "The accuser of our brethren." 6. A witness: Our "conscience bearing witness." 7. An indictment upon these: "Cursed be he that continueth not in all the words of this law to do them." And again, he that breaketh one "is guilty of all." A conviction that all may be ὑπόδιχοι, "guilty" or culpable "before God." Yea the very delivering of our sins under the name of "debts," of the law under the name of a "hand-writing," the very terms of "an advocate," of "a surety" "made under the law;" of a pardon, or "being justified from those things which by the law we could not;" all these, wherein for the most part this is still expressed, what speak they but that the sense of this Name cannot be rightly understood, nor what manner of

righteousness is in question, except we still have before our eyes this same *coram Rege justo judicium faciente*.[13]

Hereupon Andrewes introduces from Scripture, the fathers, and the schoolmen arguments to prove that the righteousness in question is indeed imputed or accounted. He continues:

> And indeed, to do them no wrong, it is true that at this judgment-seat, so far as it concerneth the satisfaction for sin and our escaping from eternal death, the Church of Rome taketh this Name aright; and that term which a great while seemed harsh unto them, now they find no such absurdity in it; that Christ's righteousness and merits are imputed to us. So saith Bellarmine. . . . So saith Stapleton. . . . Thus they understand this Name in that part of righteousness which is satisfactory for punishment; and there they say with us, as we with Esay, *In Jehova justitia nostra.*

But when it comes to the question of positive justice,

> or that part thereof which is meritorious for reward, there fall they into a fancy they may give it over, and suppose that *justitia a Domino*, 'a righteousness from God' they grant, yet inherent in themselves, without the righteousness that is in Christ, will serve them; whereof they have a good conceit that it will endure God's justice, and standeth not by acceptation. So by this means shrink they up their Name, and though they leave the full sound, yet take they half the sense from it.[14]

This limitation we, on the other hand, do not accept, and we blame them for setting it. Why do they allow imputation in one place and not in the other? Challenge them for their reason for saying that in the question of satisfaction for sin we need Christ's righteousness to be accounted as ours, and they answer correctly with Bellarmine, "Non acceptat Deus in veram satisfactionem pro peccato nisi justitiam infinitam, quoniam peccatum offensa est infinita." Now,

---

[13] *Works*, V, Occasional Sermon V, 115-16. This passage is another instance of the legalism in Andrewes' theology.

[14] *Works*, V, Occasional Sermon V, 119.

If that be the reason, that 'it must have an infinite satisfaction, because the offence is infinite,' we reason *a pari*, there must also be an infinite merit, because the reward is no less infinite. Else by what proportion do they proceed, or at what beam do they weigh these twain, that cannot counterpoise an infinite sin but with an infinite satisfaction, and think they can weigh down a reward every way as infinite with a merit, to say the least, surely not infinite? Why should there be a necessary use of the sacrifice of Christ's death for the one, and not a use full as necessary of the oblation of His life for the other? Or how cometh it to pass, that no less than the one will serve to free us from eternal death, and a great deal less will serve to entitle us to eternal life?[15]

Andrewes presses the same idea further, condemning anything less than the imputed righteousness of Christ as defective, defiled, and no righteousness at all. Why, even the Church of Rome has "begun to cry . . . down" this notion of inherent righteousness, even Stapleton and Bellarmine have softened their positions! Our stand, then, is correct; "No abatement is to be devised, the Name is not to be mangled or divided, but entirely belongeth to Christ full and whole, and we to call Him by it, *Jehova justitia nostra*." In conclusion, we have the duty of calling Christ by this name and in its full sense, and, "calling Him by that Name which God hath prescribed, and which therefore is to Him most acceptable, we shall not do it for nought, for He will answer us, answer us, and answer for us; for us, as an advocate in our cause."

Lancelot Andrewes taught, therefore, a justification of imputation. The individual soul is established in the friendship and favor of God through having imputed to it the righteousness of Christ, who, by becoming incarnate and by suffering for His brethren, satisfied God for their offenses against Him. While denying to man an inherent justification, as did Luther, An-

---

[15] *Works*, V, Occasional Sermon V, 120. Quotations in the next paragraph are from 122-25.

drewes far outreached the German in assessing the value of good works in the scheme of salvation; yet he falls short of the full Catholic teaching of justification by faith and good works. In conformity with Article XI he taught that justification proceeded from faith and faith alone.[16] Whereas, however, Article XII merely declared that works come necessarily from a true and lively faith and so are signs of the life of that faith, Andrewes taught a necessity of good works which differed from Roman doctrine principally in denying them the quality of theological merit, an enormously important consideration in an appraisal of his thought, for his emphasis on personal responsibility (which has to include free will) and the necessity of personal effort stand out as prime characteristics of his whole theology. His apostolic labors were devoted to getting men to act, in short, to perform good works—and good works meant the observance of the Ten Commandments and the practice of Christian virtue. Our acceptance by God, he said in the Pentecost sermon of 1619, is not our work, but His gracious good will; nevertheless it is incumbent upon us to strive to render ourselves acceptable by avoiding sin, practicing faith, and doing good.[17] In fact, on the day of doom the "first and principal point of inquiry" will be whether or not we have fed the hungry, clothed the naked, and performed the other works of mercy.[18] In 1607 he delivered a sermon at Greenwich on the text from James, "And be ye doers of the word, and not hearers only, deceiving yourselves" (James 1:22). Throughout one finds a strong emphasis on doing the word of God and not hearing it only, for, as he threatens in conclusion, "hearing and not doing,

---

[16] *Works*, V, Sermon on the Temptation of Christ VII, 555-56: "The Papists ask where we find 'only' in justification by faith? Indeed we do not find it, but we do find that 'by faith' and nothing else we are 'justified,' and so we may well collect it by faith only."

[17] *Works*, III, Pentecost Sermon XII, 323-43.

[18] *Works*, I, Nativity Sermon X, 172-73.

we shall in the end be forced both to hear and to do a word, the
heaviest to be heard and the worst to be done of all others."[19]

In the eighteenth of the Easter sermons Andrewes quotes
St. Paul to the effect that we were created to do good works, and
redeemed "to be a people zealously given to good works."[20] In
the same sermon he establishes a relation between them and
faith; by works our faith is made perfect, for without them faith
is "stark dead." Every man on his death shall receive according
to his works: they that have done good works shall enter into
everlasting life. But, he reminds us, returning to the idea of
our insufficiency, we must first be made fit to do good works;
God had to enable us, and so He does:

> And by a fall things come out of joint, and indeed so they
> did; Adam's fall we call it, and we call it right. Sin which before
> broke the peace, which made the going from or departure which
> needed the bringing back; the same sin, here now again, put all
> out of joint. And things out of joint are never quiet, never at peace
> and rest, till they be set right again. But when all is in frame, all
> is in peace; and so it [the text of the day (Hebrews 13:20-21),
> "The God of peace . . . make you perfect in all good works to do
> His will. . . ."] refers well to "the God of peace" Who is to do it.[21]

God gives us the outward means by giving us the Church
and her ministry, and the inward by

> an inward operation of His own inspiring, His grace, which is
> nothing but the breath of the Holy Ghost. Thereby enlightening
> our minds, inclining our wills, working on our affections, making
> us *homines bonae voluntatis*. . . . What He works by us, He works
> in us, and what He works in us He works by us.[22]

And we do His will in every good work. In the *Two Answers to
Cardinal Perron* he made a firm declaration of his belief in the

---

[19] *Works*, V, Occasional Sermon IX, 202.
[20] *Works*, III, Easter Sermon XVIII, 93-94.
[21] *Works*, III, Easter Sermon XVIII, 96.
[22] *Works*, III, Easter Sermon XVIII, 98.

necessity of good works: "We hold *good works necessary to Salvation:* and that *faith without them saveth not.*"[23]

Bishop Andrewes had much to say on the subject of grace, which he considered of the greatest importance. Grace is necessary for the attainment of salvation, he says: "By grace we shall accomplish what truth requireth at our hands; that so, receiving grace, and walking in truth, we may come to the third and reward of both, glory."[24] Grace is an "enabling virtue," or power, divine in quality, which the Holy Ghost by ways unknown to flesh and blood inspires as a breath, distills as a dew, and derives as a secret influence in our souls.[25] The "Spirit of grace hath a working on our understanding by the light of faith, and secondly, in our will, by inspiring us with holy desires."[26] More than once Andrewes distinguishes between *gratia gratis data*, grace given to one for the profit of others, and *gratia gratum faciens*, the saving grace given to the recipient for his own salvation.[27] And finally, grace tarries "guest-wise" in the soul—it can be lost and regained.[28] As for merit, which is so closely related to the question of grace in Roman Catholic theology, merit availing to any supernatural reward, Andrewes denied it completely to human acts. Meriting, the performance of service worthy of reward, is exclusively the prerogative of Christ. To claim merit, as we have seen in the sermon on justification, is to derogate from the glory due Him alone.

In summary, then, Andrewes taught, not without some inconsistency, that faith alone is necessary for justification; that justification means to have Christ's righteousness imputed to us

---

23 *Works*, XI, *Two Answers to Cardinall Perron*, 29.
24 *Works*, I, Nativity Sermon VI, 97.
25 *Works*, II, Easter Sermon I, 204.
26 *Works*, V, Sermon on Prayer VI, 351; see also the similar quotation, *supra*, 135.
27 *Works*, III, Pentecost Sermon I, 121; *Works*, III, Pentecost Sermon II, 134; *Works*, III, Pentecost Sermon X, 276.
28 See *supra*, 127.

and to be restored to God's favor; that this is not enough for salvation, for faith must be live, operative, and must issue into good works by which we gain heaven; that good works are necessary, but have no power to justify nor to merit; that in order to perform such good works as God will notice and reward, our insufficient nature needs God's help in the form of grace.

Dom Gregory Dix has observed that the scriptural sacraments are intractable to Protestantism. Modern Protestants, he writes, have solved the difficulty by setting them aside and by denying that Christ "instituted or intended to institute the sacraments at all." But the men of the Reformation hesitated to dismiss the evidence of Scripture, "though they were unable to fit the external sacramental actions at all comfortably into their theological and devotional scheme of christianity."[29] Bishop Andrewes actually managed to fit "external sacramental actions" far more comfortably into his devotional scheme than into his theological, for in preaching and in practice he strongly supported most of those rites which the old Church called sacraments, but to which the Church of England denied the name stricte dictum; on the other hand, however, his Eucharistic doctrine is so ambiguous that modern scholars have been unable to affirm with confidence precisely what he held.[30] What has been

---

[29] Dix, *Shape of the Liturgy*, 633.

[30] C. W. Dugmore, who has made a careful study of Eucharistic doctrine among early Anglican writers, confesses: "It is not easy to determine how far Andrewes and his school actually went in their belief in the real presence" (C. W. Dugmore, *Eucharistic Doctrine in England from Hooker to Waterland* [London, 1942], 29). John Hunt regards Andrewes' "pious conceits" on the Eucharist as the very "germs of 'pernicious nonsense'" (Hunt, *Religious Thought in England*, III, 376). Macleane dares at least to say: "Whatever others may have been, Andrewes was clearly no mere 'virtualist'" (Macleane, *Andrewes and the Reaction*, 236). E. C. Messenger writes that only two Anglican writers of the seventeenth century "teach an Objective Presence, Andrewes and Forbes [bishop of Edinburgh], and even these employ language which makes their meaning somewhat doubtful" (Ernest C. Messenger, *The Reformation, the Mass, and the Priesthood* [London, 1937], II, 385).

intimated before with respect to Andrewes' teaching on the Eucharist—namely, that he tended to draw from the Eucharist all the devotional implications of the full Catholic position without admitting all its doctrinal bases—may equally be affirmed of his general teaching on the sacraments. In the first of his *Two Answers to Cardinal Perron* he concludes his discussion of the applicability of the name "sacrament" to the five rites so honored by the old Church, but not by the Church of England, in this fashion:

> The whole matter is a mere λογομαχία. If the thing were agreed upon, we should not strive for the name.[31]

In conformity, then, with Article XXVI Andrewes taught two sacraments *veri nominis:* baptism and the Lord's Supper. In the Pentecost sermon of 1619, after speaking of the reception of baptism, he continues, "and past the first there remaineth none but the second."[32] And in the following Pentecost sermon he quotes St. Augustine:

> *Haec sunt Ecclesiae gemina sacramenta*, saith Augustine. 'These are (not two of the Sacraments; so there might be more, but) the twin-Sacraments of the Church.' So but two of that kind, two famous memorials left us; in baptism, of the water; in the cup of the New Testament, of the blood He then came in.[33]

He was greatly embarrassed when he tried to explain to Bellarmine how Henry VIII, who defended seven sacraments, and James I, who professed two, could both legitimately bear the title of Defender of the Faith![34] Keeping still to the path of Anglican orthodoxy, he asserts, as does Article XXVI, that the sacraments are efficacious; they are signs "that shew and work both—work what they shew, present us with what they repre-

---

[31] *Works*, XI, *Two Answers to Cardinall Perron*, 26.
[32] *Works*, III, Pentecost Sermon XII, 343.
[33] *Works*, III, Pentecost Sermon XIII, 348.
[34] *Works*, VIII, *Responsio ad Bellarminum*, 71-73.

sent, what they set before us, set or graft in us."[35] But this efficacy does not depend upon the minister, for "he that ministereth the Sacrament hath no interest in the party by it, but God alone."[36]

Andrewes made baptism the topic of two of his Pentecost sermons. In the first, that of 1612, he uses it as a springboard to introduce a theological discussion of the Holy Ghost, who is mentioned in the Trinitarian formula of the rite, and graduates thereafter into a disquisition on receiving the Holy Ghost; we receive Him first in baptism, and are then made regenerate by Him.[37] Three years later he preached more at length on baptism itself, taking the Gospel story of Christ's baptism as his text (Luke 3:21-22).[38] The doctrinal assertions are quite traditional. He recalls the need of our being washed of our sins, even as babes, for we are all conceived of unclean seed. Christ needed no baptism; the very waters received a baptism from Him, and now they have power to cleanse us. Strictly speaking, he asks, can water do this, wash away sin?

> To clear it shortly; the truth is, it could not. It is no water-work, without somewhat put to it, to help it scour. But nothing on earth; not, if you put to it, "nitre," "much soap," "fullers'-earth," "the herb borith," say the Prophets, all will not do, it will not off so.[39]

The waters of the Jordan could not cleanse except in virtue of another baptism to follow—a baptism of blood, for without a mixture of blood, there is no doing away with sin. In Christ two streams of "water and blood" are met; and this is the "true Jordan, the bath or laver, wherein we are purged 'from all our sins.'" Christ gave us a lesson in His baptism that we "should

---

35 *Works*, II, Easter Sermon XII, 402.
36 *Works*, IV, Gowry Sermon III, 52.
37 *Works*, III, Pentecost Sermon V, 191.
38 *Works*, III, Pentecost Sermon VIII, 241.
39 *Works*, III, Pentecost Sermon VIII, 247.

and ought to be baptized"; and our baptism must be not only
of water, but of blood and the Spirit too. Of baptism in blood
Christ in His Passion has made us quit; whereas our obligation to undergo the others remains, as our Lord told Nicodemus
(John 3:5).

Christ prayed that the virtue of the Holy Ghost might be
joined to the water; and as the Holy Ghost descended upon
Christ in the form of a dove, so in baptism we are to receive of
Him dovelike virtues—peace, sincerity, patience, innocency,
"the 'silver feathers' " of this Dove, and preserve them in our
lives. By baptism, too, we become sons of God through adoption—being made by adoption what Christ Himself is. Would
that all this were enough! Andrewes exclaims in his peroration;
but we endanger all, "put it in hazard," when we fall into sin.
"His favour we may not finally lose, and to baptism we may
not come again." What then? We must come to His table, eat
and drink with Him, participate in the Holy Eucharist, "the
only means to renew" God's complacency in us, "and to restore
us thither, where our baptism left us."[40]

Andrewes, it will be remembered, functioned as a father-
confessor both at Pembroke and at St. Paul's, where he held
the prebendary stall of penitentiary. The practice of auricular
confession he commended, and in the *Preces Privatae* he thanks
God "Qui aperuisti mihi portam spei, confitenti et roganti, ex
mysteriorum et clavium potestate."[41] The various parts of penance the schoolmen demand he illustrates from the story of
David's repentance for having cut off part of Saul's garment
when he came upon the king sleeping in the cave (1 Samuel
24:5-8): "1. *contritio cordis* . . . his heart smote him for it;

---

40 *Works*, III, Pentecost Sermon VIII, 247-60.
41 *Works*, X, *Preces Privatae*, 279. Macleane cites several men who either com-
    mended or practiced oral confession themselves, among them Cranmer,
    Latimer, Ridley, Jewel, Hooker, Hobbes, Evelyn (Macleane, *Andrewes and
    the Reaction*, 64).

2. *confessio oris* . . . 'The Lord keep me' from doing more, this was too much; 3. *satisfactio operis* . . . in making amends, by not suffering his men to rise [against Saul when he was so completely in their power], but converting them from so sinful a purpose."[42] Though Andrewes respected the seal of confession, he held that it did not bind in all circumstances. Of Mordecai, who revealed his chance knowledge of a projected attempt on his king (Esther 2:21-23), the bishop said in bitter reference to the Gunpowder Plot:

> The mystery of the seal of iniquity, the seal of confession, it seems he knew not. It was not graven then, that seal; nor many hundred years after. That shuts up treason, as a treasure, under a sacred seal, at no hand to be broken; no, though all the Kings' lives in Christendom lay on it. This act of Mordecai's mars the fashion of that seal quite.[43]

Andrewes' sermon on the power of the keys, preached on the Sunday after Easter in Whitehall, 1600, discoursed upon the text: "Whosoever sins ye remit, they are remitted unto them; and whosoever ye retain, they are retained" (John 20:23). It created a stir in the court because of its very traditional tone.[44] Perhaps the commotion shook him a bit, or at least induced him to be more conservative in this matter, for six years later we find him asserting a little less confidently that the apostles, having received the grace of their calling,

---

[42] *Works*, IV, Gowry Sermon VII, 164. For a detailed enumeration of points for an examination of conscience and the stirring of sentiments of sorrow for sin see *Works*, X, *Preces Privatae*, 323 ff.

[43] *Works*, IV, Gowry Sermon VI, 141. The sixteenth of his Visitation Articles for 1625 contains this question: "And if any man confess his secret and hidden sins, being sick or whole, to the Minister, for the unburthening of his conscience, and receiving such spiritual consolation; doth, or hath the said Minister at any time revealed and made known to any person whatsoever, any crime or offence so committed to his trust and secresy, contrary to the 113 Canon?" (*Works*, XI, 131).

[44] See *supra*, 78, note 13; *Works*, V, Occasional Sermon IV, 82-103.

were "enabled to do somewhat about the remission of sins, that is not of like avail done by others, though perhaps more learned and virtuous than they, in that they have not the like *mitto vos*, nor the same *Accipite* that these have."[45] In a less qualified way this sentiment was the theme of the controverted sermon, as may be gathered from the following unusually fine summary with which Andrewes prefaces his remarks on the keys. Christ, he says, in this scene described by John, gave a commission to His apostles:

> To the granting whereof He proceedeth not without some solemnity or circumstance, well worthy to be remembered.
>
> For first, verse the twenty-first, He saith, "As my Father sent Me, so send I you;" which is their authorizing, or giving them their credence.
>
> Secondly, verse the twenty-second, He doth breathe upon them, and withal inspireth them with the Holy Ghost; which is their enabling or furnishing thereto.
>
> And having so authorized and enabled them, now in this verse here He giveth them their commission, and thereby doth perfectly inaugurate them in this part of their office.
>
> A commission is nothing else but the imparting of a power which before they had not. First therefore He imparteth to them a power, a power over sins; over sins, either for the remitting or the retaining of them, as the persons shall be qualified.
>
> And after, to this power He addeth a promise (as the lawyers term it) of ratihabition, that He will ratify and make it good, that His power shall accompany this power, and the lawful use of it in His Church for ever.[46]

This very carefully composed passage covers the essence of Andrewes' teaching on a power he considered resident in the ministers of the Church. Taken in conjunction with his own exercise of the office of confessor, it is another convincing proof of his nostalgia for the full devotional life of the old Church.

---

[45] *Works*, III, Pentecost Sermon IX, 277.
[46] *Works*, V, Occasional Sermon IV, 82-83.

The question of the commission of the power of the keys leads naturally to holy orders. The rite associated with the conferring of orders was not a sacrament, Andrewes contended, because it does not bestow *gratia gratum faciens,* as a sacrament does, but rather *gratia gratis data;* and again, the rite has been changed: whereas Christ ordained His apostles by breathing upon them, orders are now conferred through an imposition of the hands. The form, therefore, has changed; but it is of the very nature of a sacrament that it be both as to matter and to form of Christ's own institution.[47] Interestingly enough, the text for Andrewes' sermon on orders was taken from the same passage in John which supplied him with the text for the sermon on the power of the keys: "And when He had said that, He breathed on them, and said unto them, Receive the Holy Ghost" (John 20:22).[48] As baptism serves to make us Christians, he tells his hearers, so this "breath" which comes after it, serves to make men

> Christian-makers; such whose ministry Christ would use to make Christians; make them, and keep them; make them so by baptism, and keep them so by the power of the keys here given them in the next words, for the remission of sins.[49]

As a matter of fact, he continues, had not the Church of Rome retained these words, " 'Receive the Holy Ghost, whose sins ye remit, &c.,' " we might well doubt Rome had any validly ordained priests, for these are the words, and not the ones she adds ("Accipe potestatem sacrificandi pro vivis et mortuis"), which confer holy orders. Though the reception of orders involves an inward, it also requires an outward, calling, a manifestation of the fact of vocation through an external act such as Christ's ceremonial action in His ordination of the apostles.

---

[47] *Works,* III, Pentecost Sermon IX, 263.
[48] *Works,* III, Pentecost Sermon IX, 261-79.
[49] *Works,* III, Pentecost Sermon IX, 261-62.

For if nothing outward had been in His, we should have had nothing but enthusiasts—as we them have notwithstanding; but then we should have had no rule with them; all by divine revelation: into that they resolve. For sending, breathing, laying on of hands, have they none. But if they be of Christ, some must say, *mitto vos;* sent by some, not run of their own heads. Some say, *accipite;* receive it from some, not find it about themselves; have an outward calling, and an outward *accipite,* a testimony of it.[50]

This passage, it might be pointed out, is another affirmation of Bishop Andrewes' conception of a visible, authoritative Church. He would not leave the work of salvation to the fanciful impulses of interior experience. Similarly, he insists on the distinction between the person and the office. Orders bestow only the grace of office and not inward holiness: "He that is a sinner himself, may remit sins for all that, and save others he may, though himself be not saved; for it was not *propter se* he received this power, to absolve himself, but, as the next word is, *quorumcunque,* any others whosoever." Sever the office from the men,

leave the men to God to whom they stand or fall; let the ordinance of God stand fast. This breath, though not into them for themselves, yet goeth into and through every act of their office or ministry, and by them conveyeth His saving grace into us all.[51]

In the same sermon Andrewes takes the occasion to levy a charge of error upon those who foster the opinion that a person not in the state of grace has no right at all to any possession or place, an old Wycliffite position which was later sponsored by the Anabaptists.

In the light of such doctrine and of his teaching, in the correspondence with Du Moulin, that the episcopal order alone had the power of ordaining to the priesthood, it is easy to under-

---

[50] *Works,* III, Pentecost Sermon IX, 273.
[51] *Works,* III, Pentecost Sermon IX, 277, 278.

stand why Andrewes demanded that the three Scots bishops whom James had named to that office in his attempt to re-establish episcopacy in Scotland be first ordained deacons and priests before their elevation to episcopal rank; but it is not at all easy to understand how Andrewes yielded to Bancroft's argument that it was not necessary because, where there were no bishops, ordination by presbyters must be esteemed valid, otherwise there might be doubt whether there was any lawful vocation in most of the Reformed Churches. The consecration proceeded as a matter of fact, without any previous ordination; one cannot help but wonder whether Bishop Andrewes compromised himself in this instance.[52]

According to the bishop, the Church possessed five means for remitting sin, two of them sacraments: baptism, Holy Eucharist, the cleansing word of the Scriptures, the power of absolution, and

> a power in prayer, and that in the priest's prayer. "Call for the priest," saith the Apostle, "and let them pray for the sick person, and if he have committed sin it shall be forgiven him.[53]

This last, of course, is a reference to the rite which the old Church called the sacrament of extreme unction. Of its value as a rite Andrewes seems to have had no doubt, although one or two of his very few references to it are surprisingly irreverent—perhaps because in making them he was chiding his hearers for the "foul indignity" of never seeking God "but when He kills us." In the sermon where this charge occurs he speaks of our "having a little opiate divinity ministered to our souls, and so

---

[52] *Works*, XI, xi, note x, quotes an account of the incident from Spottiswoode's *History of the Church of Scotland.* We have seen something of Bishop Andrewes' ideals respecting the lives of the clergy in his *Concio ad clerum* (*supra*, 91-92) ; for a detailed exposition of the duties of the ministry as he conceived them see *Works*, VI, *Catechism*, 192-98.

[53] *Works*, V, Occasional Sermon IV, 94-95.

[being] sent away."[54] And in another of the same series he writes that at death

> must one come and as we call it, speak comfortably to us, that is, minister to us a little Divinity laudanum, rather stupefactive for the present than doing any sound good; and so take our leaves to go meet with *ira ventura*.[55]

To the formal rite of confirmation Andrewes makes only scattered references; for instance, while listing the offices of the Holy Ghost in the working out of our salvation, he cites our confirmation by Him "in the imposition of hands."[56] He speaks but rarely of matrimony. Celibate himself, he did not see the necessity of imposing celibacy upon the whole clerical order. Marriage he held to be indissoluble; in the *Discourse against Second Marriage* he maintained that not even adultery availed to the breaking of the bond.[57]

Andrewes' theology of the Holy Eucharist has received relatively great attention from competent scholars, yet it is so indecisive and involved as to leave them in uncertainty as to his exact doctrinal position. What is more important here is the pattern of ascetical practice the bishop constructed thereon. It was not easy for Andrewes to formulate within the limits of the Thirty-nine Articles a doctrine which would at the same time satisfy his devotional appetite. Dom Dix tells us that the reformers, realizing that the New Testament clearly reveals Christ's institution of the Eucharistic action,

> tried hard to retain a central importance and meaning for the eucharist in christian worship. But in every case they failed to carry their followers with them. Throughout the churches of the Reformation the eucharist rapidly assumed the position of an occa-

---

[54] *Works*, I, Ash Wednesday Sermon I, 306, 319.
[55] *Works*, I, Ash Wednesday Sermon VIII, 451.
[56] *Works*, III, Pentecost Sermon V, 191.
[57] *Works*, XI, *Discourse against Second Marriage*, 106.

sional addition to a worship which ordinarily consisted only of praises, prayers, exhortation and reading.[58]

Andrewes demanded a central and an essential place for the Eucharist in the liturgy: "No fulness there is of our Liturgy or public solemn Service, without the Sacrament. Some part, yea the chief part is wanting, if that be wanting."[59] After reading his Eucharistic prayers among the *Preces Privatae*, after noticing his constant pleading with his sermon audiences to partake of the Lord's Supper, one wonders how much it would hurt Andrewes, were he alive, to read this sincere confession of a modern Eucharistic scholar:

> Ever since the sixteenth century we Anglicans have been so divided over our eucharistic doctrine, and we are to-day so conscious of our divisions, that there is scarcely any statement that could be made about either the eucharist or our own rite which would not seem to some of one's fellow churchmen to call for immediate contradiction on conscientious grounds.[60]

Three major problems connected with the Eucharist deeply exercised the theologians of the sixteenth and seventeenth centuries, Andrewes no less than others: the real presence, transubstantiation, and the question of sacrifice. If we take for a norm of comparison the Tridentine teaching on all three doctrines, we shall find Andrewes differing therefrom in all except perhaps the real presence.[61] What he denies is far clearer than what he positively affirms.[62] Perhaps we would do well to attend to the conclusions of two or three able scholars for a summary of the

---

58 Dix, *Shape of the Liturgy*, 600.
59 *Works*, I, Nativity Sermon IV, 62; see *supra*, 27.
60 Dix, *Shape of the Liturgy*, 613-14. For Andrewes' Eucharistic prayers see *Works*, X, *Preces Privatae*, 239 ff.
61 See *supra*, 137, for lack of clarity in Andrewes' pronouncements with regard to the real presence.
62 Dugmore declares that the most definite point in Andrewes (and Laud) on Eucharistic matters is their rejection of transubstantiation (Dugmore, *Eucharistic Doctrine*, 40).

bishop's formal teaching. Unfortunately they enlighten us only a little. E. C. Messenger asserts that Andrewes teaches

> some form of Objective Presence, not *in*, but *associated with* the bread and wine, repudiates Transubstantiation, oral manducation, and denies the Catholic doctrine of the Sacrifice of the Mass.[63]

C. W. Dugmore decided that on the Eucharist as a memorial Andrewes taught a view midway between the position that it was simply a reminder to Christians of Christ's work and death, and the position that the Church's remembrance of Christ in the Eucharist was in addition a presentation of Him before God.[64] Bishop Frere thought that Andrewes refused to define the relation of the sacrifice of Calvary to the sacrifice of the Eucharist, but that he

> uses a term which comprehends both—viz. the term "Sacrifice of Christ's death." Moreover he uses it in such a way as to make it clear that he means to imply the Eucharistic sacrifice as well as the Sacrifice of Calvary: for when he speaks of its being available for present and absent, he must be speaking of the service, not of Calvary. Andrewes' definition is brief, but sound, deep and conclusive: it is a statement and at the same time an *eirenicon*.[65]

In the sermon preached at Andrewes' funeral John Buckeridge developed an extremely interesting conception of the Eucharist as a sacrifice, which Dugmore considers representative of Andrewes' teaching.[66] I am not prepared to contest that assertion, but confess that I do not find in Andrewes so fully elaborated a doctrine. Buckeridge's position seems to be completely compatible with Andrewes' pronouncements and partic-

---

[63] Messenger, *The Reformation, the Mass, and the Priesthood*, II, 381.

[64] Dugmore, *Eucharistic Doctrine*, 36-38. He refers the reader to a passage in *Works*, II, Easter Sermon VII, 300-01.

[65] Frere, *Andrewes as a Representative of Anglican Principles*, 17. See *Works*, XI, *Two Answers to Cardinall Perron*, 19-20, for the term "sacrifice of Christ's death."

[66] Dugmore, *Eucharistic Doctrine*, 38.

ularly with the spirit of his Eucharist teaching. There was only
one true sacrifice, Buckeridge says—the sacrifice of Christ on
the cross. Christ, the head of the mystical body which is His
Church, is not offered again in the Eucharist properly, but only
by commemoration. The fathers held the Eucharist a sacrifice
only because it is a representation or commemoration of the
true sacrifice of the crucified Christ. Christ is not sacrificed
daily in the Eucharist. But something indeed is offered to God:
the Church offers not Christ's natural body, but His mystical
body, which is the Church itself. We, therefore, as members of
Christ's mystical body the Church, offer ourselves in this sacrifice of the Eucharist.[67]

Far more impressive than Andrewes' formal doctrine is his
constant insistence on participation in the Eucharist as a means
toward the fulfillment of our religious duties and the nourishing
of our spiritual life. By the time of James I's accession to the
English throne the practice of partaking of the Eucharist had
fallen very much into abeyance.[68] A few years earlier Andrewes
had complained to his congregation at St. Giles that

> we do many times discontinue this action a whole year together.
> These long intermissions—so that if it be *panis annuus*, once a-year
> received, we think our duty discharged—are also, no doubt, a sec-
> ond imagination in our common practice. For sure we should con-
> tinue also in this part and the frequenting of it, if not so often as
> the Primitive Church did—which either thrice in the week, or at
> the furthest once, did communicate—yet as often as the Church
> doth celebrate; which, I think, should do better to celebrate more
> often.[69]

Whenever he had the chance, Bishop Andrewes urged his
hearers to communicate. When he preached the various festal

---

[67] *Works*, V, Buckeridge, *Funeral Sermon*, 259-66.
[68] Frere, *The English Church in the Reigns of Elizabeth and James I.*, 285.
[69] *Works*, V, Occasional Sermon II, 67.

sermons he usually linked the mystery of the day with the Eucharist. In sixteen of the seventeen Nativity sermons his peroration urges to participation in the Eucharist. It was his manner to point to the Eucharist as the best means of sharing in the benefits intended in the mystery, or of performing the duty imposed thereby, or of returning thanks to God for the gift bestowed upon mankind. Christ is born and given to us, the bishop says in the fifth of his Nativity sermons, and "To a gift the duty that belongeth properly, is to receive it." How shall we receive Him then?

> Who shall give Him us? That shall One That will say unto us within a while, *Accipite*, "Take, this is My Body," "by the offering whereof ye are sanctified." "Take, this is My Blood," by the shedding whereof ye are saved. Both in the holy mysteries ordained by God as pledges to assure us, and as conduit pipes to convey into us this and all other the benefits that come by this our Saviour.[70]

And he tells us in another place, "Our thanks are surely not full without the Holy Eucharist, which is by interpretation, thanksgiving itself."[71] The Eucharist is our means of union with Christ, for "never can we more truly, or properly say, *in Christo Jesu Domino nostro,* as when we come new from that holy action, for then He is in us, and we in Him, indeed."[72] Through the Holy Eucharist we receive also the Holy Ghost:

> For *Accipite corpus,* upon the matter, is *Accipite Spiritum,* inasmuch as they two never part, not possible to sever them one minute. Thus, when or to whom we say *Accipite corpus,* we may safely say with the same breath *Accipite Spiritum;* and as truly every way. For that body is never without this Spirit: he that receives the one, receives the other; he that the body, together with it the Spirit also.[73]

---

70 *Works,* I, Nativity Sermon V, 83.
71 *Works,* I, Nativity Sermon IV, 62.
72 *Works,* II, Easter Sermon I, 205.
73 *Works,* III, Pentecost Sermon IX, 278-79.

So too the reception of the Eucharist imparts grace to us; grace which is the very breath of the Holy Spirit, "the true and express character of His seal, to the renewing in us the image of God whereunto we are created."[74] And finally, Bishop Andrewes assigned to the Eucharist a power for the remission of sin: "The words are exceeding plain," he says; " 'This is My blood of the New Testament for the remission of sin.' "[75]

As Bishop Andrewes made Christ the center of his whole theology, he also set the Holy Eucharist at the very center of all those actions pertaining to life supernatural and the establishment of union between the individual soul and Christ. His Eucharistic teaching, then, can be said to be the high point in his conception of the Christian scheme of things. He was not only instant in preaching the Holy Eucharist, but careful to surround the service with the greatest reverence and honor, as may be seen from the attention he bestowed on preparing a decent liturgy, the detailed adornment of his own chapel, and the vigilance with which he supervised the rites within his own diocese.[76] Speaking of the scandal Andrewes gave by his practice of functioning as father-confessor while he was at St. Paul's, John Harington writes:

> The like scandal was taken of some, though not given by him, for his reverent speaking of the highest mystery of our faith and heavenly food, the Lord's Supper, which some are so stiff in their knees, or rather in their hearts, that they hold it idolatry to receive it kneeling. But whatsoever such barked at, he ever kept one tenor of life and doctrine, exemplar[y] and unreprovable.[77]

John Harington thoroughly appreciated Lancelot Andrewes!

---

[74] *Works*, III, Pentecost Sermon VI, 219.
[75] *Works*, V, Occasional Sermon IV, 94.
[76] *Works*, XI, Appendix F, "Bishop Andrewes's Chapel" (including floor plan and list of accoutrements), xcviii-xcix; *Works*, XI, *Visitation Articles*, especially those touching the ministry, service, and sacraments, 114-18, 129-33.
[77] *Works*, XI, Harington, *Memoir*, xxxvii.

CHAPTER VII

Andrewes as Moralist
and Ascetic

On the solid doctrinal foundation he constructed from
the rich traditions of the Christian heritage Bishop Andrewes
developed a logically consequent moral and ascetical super-
structure. He was not one to stand content with the learned
exposition of a doctrine. So profound was his knowledge of
human nature, so intense his convictions, so real the vitality of
his spiritual life, that he must always hasten to urge men to
the translation of their faith into action—and not only to urge
and exhort, but to detail the means for the fulfillment of their
great vocation as God's chief creatures on earth. Here again
the positive character of his thought reveals itself, a quality
which may well account for a large measure of his popularity.
He castigated vice as

> pernicious, as shutting us out of Heaven whither we would come,
> the greatest loss and *poena damni*, and pressing us down to hell
> which we fainest would fly, the greatest torment and *poena sensus*.[1]

He preached sin, hell, and damnation, the "*poena poena-
rum*, the penalty of all penalties most penal,"[2] and a healthy

---

[1] *Works*, I, Ash Wednesday Sermon IV, 372-73.
[2] *Works*, I, Ash Wednesday Sermon VII, 430.

152

fear of the Lord, but he knew human nature far too well to hold that sufficient, and was too thoroughly a Christian not to know that the God he worshiped had set for men a goal which should be wholly desirable in itself, that "visio Dei" which "all along the Scriptures, is made our chief good,"[3] and which we should not seek simply and solely as an escape from an almost inevitable and everlasting doom. Union with God forever was the goal. Sin, delectable in its own false and fleeting way to our weakened wills and clouded intellects, was the great challenge which had to be met and overcome. Violence must be done our feeble nature, that in striving it might grow strong and run with giant strides toward its appointed end. But the violence was to be reasonable, calculated, and inspired, for there was nothing of the enthusiast or the fanatic in Lancelot Andrewes. Rejecting servile fear on the one hand and mere emotionalism on the other, Andrewes laid down a careful plan of action which was to exercise the faithful in a vigorous conquest of their passions and a confident pursuit of eternal happiness. As Christ was the center of his doctrinal theology, so too was He the direct object of his ascetical striving—*"assimilari Ei quem colis,"* was for him the "pitch of all religion."[4]

To his teaching as a moralist and an ascetic Andrewes brought a keen insight into human nature, without which his practical teaching could hardly have been realistic. Christian living involves two things: Christian truth and the nature it seeks to direct. A little reflection on the bishop's career will show how excellent were his opportunities for knowing men. As student, fellow, and master of Pembroke he had that opportunity which only a teacher, perhaps, can appreciate. It would be difficult indeed to specify the knowledge he gained as father-confessor at Pembroke and as penitentiary at St. Paul's, but

---

[3] *Works*, II, Easter Sermon V, 261.
[4] See *supra*, 75.

foolhardy to suppose that this did not serve to enrich his intimate acquaintance with the secrets of men's hearts. His taste of parish life during the years of his vicarage at St. Giles later expanded into a broader pastoral experience as he administered successively three dioceses during some twenty years. With great men, academic, ecclesiastical, and civil, he was associated during more than half his long life, and he knew the business of government from his position as privy councilor and his frequent service on commission. With James I he was a favorite, and even an intimate, often in his company; and at least on the numerous occasions of his preaching at court, he came to know court life at first hand. That he was conscious also of the needs and the fortunes of the poor one may gather from the generous bequests bestowed on them in his will. Lancelot Andrewes was indeed a man of wide experience, but most important for his education in the ways of men were the hours he snatched from a busy routine for the seclusion and the wisdom of private prayer. Here was his opportunity for reflection, the *sine qua non* of profound knowledge. How well he reflected, how deeply he penetrated into the secrets of human nature, a few passages from his works will reveal.

Andrewes had a definite conception of the human nature for whose information, instruction, and moral guidance he so laboriously preached. Man, he tells us, is the special handiwork of a God who deliberated over his creation, who resolved to make him in His own image and likeness, who Himself framed his body and breathed into him a soul, and who finally set him in place as count palatine over the world.[5] That whole nature, not just the soul, is destined for heaven:

> For the soul is but half; though the better half, yet but half, and the redeeming it is but a half redemption; and if but half,

---

[5] *Works*, IV, Gunpowder Sermon VII, 330.

then imperfect. And Our Redeemer is God, and God's works are all perfect; if He redeem, He doth it not by halves.

Redemption is full, then, "when both soul and body shall enjoy the presence of God."[6] Though this be our noble origin and our noble destiny, we are sinners all and "our will is wholly inclined to that which is evil."[7] So indifferent are we to our true good that the threat of the loss of heaven will not lead us to true repentance or the abandonment of sin, whereas the threat of hell will. Andrewes was very much aware of that perversity of human psychology, which allows the highest motives an effectiveness in inverse proportion to their exaltation and sets greater store by those which are less sublime. As a motive in our lives "the present fear of future wrath for sins past," says Andrewes on one of his Ash Wednesday sermons, carries more weight with us than does the promise of the kingdom of heaven or the threat of its loss.[8]

Of real interest are the flashes of insight which the bishop manifests throughout the sermons, some of them trite, of course, but true: "So cross is our nature, none is so great an enemy to *recordare* as it," he says in a reference to ingratitude;[9] while other observations, at least in the manner in which he expressed them, reveal originality. Of the perverseness of human nature Andrewes says, commenting on the incident of Mary Magdalen's anointing of Christ:

---

[6] *Works*, II, Easter Sermon V, 262.

[7] *Works*, V, Sermon on Prayer XI, 401. It is clear from succeeding passages in this sermon on the petition of the Lord's Prayer, "Thy will be done," that Andrewes does not mean to imply that the will so inclines to evil as to be necessitated to it. He is emphasizing at this point the necessity of grace for the doing of God's will: "We pray not that we of ourselves may do the will of God, for no man can rise up to heaven unless he first receive a grace from heaven. . . . Our suit is not only for good thoughts, and heavenly desires, but also for ability of grace" (402, 403).

[8] *Works*, I, Ash Wednesday Sermon VII, 425, 427, 424-25.

[9] *Works*, II, Lenten Sermon V, 79.

Be a thing done to never so good purpose, yet some Judas will mutter and malign, and come forth with his *Ut quid?* some Judas will cast his dead fly into Mary Magdalene's box of ointment.[10]

And again, "What is so plain," he asks, "but by man's wit somewhat may be said to it?"[11] True to his own mild character, he suggests that the proper answer to hard language and verbal abuse is disregard,[12] and that the best victories are won by quiet persuasion,[13] for the gentler emotions are often effective: sorrow, for instance,

many times worketh us to that, by a melting compassion, which the more rough and violent passions cannot get at our hands.[14]

Men love praise, especially from people of importance: "Never did the dew of Heaven more sweetly refresh the grass, than doth a favourable saying pierce the inferior from the mouth of a prince";[15] and they are ever scrambling to climb above one another. To gain glory

we are content to deprive ourselves of all rest, which otherwise we love well enough. And a restless course we enter into, and hold out in it all our life long, and all to win it, though it be but a little before our death. For no rest will satisfy or give us full content, unless it be on the right hand.[16]

For the hypocrite Andrewes had nothing but scorn:

And mark it when you will; there is no animal so ambitious, no chameleon so pants after air, as doth the hypocrite after popular praise: for it he fasts, and so hungry and thirsty he is after it as you shall hear him even beg for it.[17]

---

10 *Works*, II, Lenten Sermon III, 57-58.
11 *Works*, XI, *Discourse against Second Marriage*, 108.
12 *Works*, VI, *Catechism*, 229.
13 *Works*, IV, Gowry Sermon VII, 171.
14 *Works*, I, Ash Wednesday Sermon III, 340.
15 *Works*, II, Lenten Sermon I, 14.
16 *Works*, II, Easter Sermon VIII, 319, and see 317.
17 *Works*, I, Ash Wednesday Sermon VI, 411.

In the same sermon he makes a brilliant attack upon religious hypocrisy, which he brands as play acting:

> The heathen man long since observed, that *Mundus scena,* that in his conceit, 'the world for all the world was like a stage or theatre,' scarce a true face in it, all in a manner personate; and the actions in the world not much unlike to their acting of their parts in the acts and scenes of a stage-play; but our Saviour Christ He goes farther, He tells us here [Matthew 6:16] of a stranger matter. That there want not that make His Church a very stage, and play with religion, and play religion and every part of it, so carrying themselves in things pertaining to God as if they had some play or pageant in hand. It is but too true this. If you will set up a stage, I will find you actors for it enow.[18]

Earlier in this sermon he had observed in defense of fasting that the sheep is not to leave his fleece, nor the Christian his fast, "because otherwhile the wolf is found in the one, or the hypocrite at the other."[19] Again he warns that we are apt to be oversensible of our own joy; a truer estimate of it would come from those who are not party to it.[20] And in another place he acutely observes:

> Do we evil, we will not know it, we excuse it, we lessen it. Do we well, we know it straight; nay we over-know, and over-praise it.[21]

Indeed, we scarcely give God credit for the good we do, and are quick to put all our faults from ourselves to others.[22] We have a great tendency to "reprieve ourselves and stay the execution" of punishment due us at our own hand.[23] The point is very well taken!

18 *Works,* I, Ash Wednesday Sermon VI, 406-07. Through the next three or four pages Andrewes develops this further.
19 *Works,* I, Ash Wednesday Sermon VI, 403.
20 *Works,* IV, Gunpowder Sermon II, 230.
21 *Works,* III, Pentecost Sermon XII, 342.
22 *Works,* IV, Gunpowder Sermon IV, 269.
23 *Works,* I, Ash Wednesday Sermon VIII, 449.

Upon another common foible Andrewes touched more than once. There is a humor "that we are all given unto by nature," which leads us to try conclusions in rare and unknown matters, "contemning things common, and to be fond after strange novelties."[24] We love to meddle with what neither pertains to us nor will do us good, but "that which is our duty and would do us good, that we care not for."[25] Perhaps the following blast in the Christmas sermon of 1622 reflects a certain discouragement in Andrewes over the state of religion in England. In any case, it is another instance of his dislike of private authority in religious matters, and is of a piece with the preceding complaints. He is referring to the request of the Wise Men for information regarding the birthplace of the King of the Jews:

> For they in the East were nothing so wise, or well seen, as we in the West are now grown. We need call no Scribes together, and get them tell us, "where." Every artisan hath a whole Synod of Scribes in his brain, and can tell where Christ is better than any learned man of them all. Yet these were wise men; best learn where they did.[26]

And we have a strong tendency, Andrewes tells us, to misuse the virtue of hope:

> The truth is, hope hears evil without a cause. The fault is not hope's, the fault is our own; we put it where we should not, and then lay the blame upon hope, where we should blame ourselves for wrong putting it. For if ye put it not right, this is a general rule: as is that we hope in, so is our hope. "Ye lean on a reed," saith Esay. "Ye take hold by a cobweb"—Job. "Ye catch at a shadow," saith the Wise Man.[27]

---

[24] *Works*, V, Sermon on the Temptation of Christ V, 528.

[25] *Works*, III, Pentecost Sermon XI, 319.

[26] *Works*, I, Nativity Sermon XV, 260. In this sermon Andrewes says in a similar vein: "Our proverb is you know, 'The nearer the Church, the farther from God,'" and, "All our religion is rather *vidimus*, a contemplation, than *venimus*, a motion, or stirring to do ought [sic]" (258).

[27] *Works*, II, Easter Sermon XI, 374.

The "cast virtue" of humility, completely neglected by the philosophers, was the very reason for the exaltation of Christ and the "ground of His mother's *magnificat*"; it is "a glory for humility, that even proud men take a pride to shroud themselves in her mantle, that pride wears humility's livery."[28] It is as unnecessary to record more of Andrewes' observations on human nature as to say that they could be multiplied far beyond what have been here indited to show that he had keenly observed and thoroughly understood men, whose welfare in society and particularly in the things of the spirit were his major concern.

Bishop Andrewes had a more finished and integrated moral teaching than what can be gleaned from the sermons, as his *Catechism* and his several written opinions on specific moral problems will reveal. Thus, at one time or other, he dealt with the Ten Commandments, usury, marriage after divorce, oaths, vows, and so forth more formally than he did when he was preaching.[29] Moral or ethical discussions, however, do occasionally crop up in the sermons, and throw no little light on the general character of his theology. In a rather fanciful sermon on the text "I will preach the law, whereof the Lord said to Me: Thou art My Son, this day have I begotten Thee" (Psalm 2:7). Andrewes inserted one paragraph which seems to set him with those who taught a traditional concept of the natural law:

> God hath His Law in the same division that man hath his; His statute and His common law. "The law of nature which is written in the hearts of all men," that is the common law of the world. Of that every man is to take notice at his peril. But this law here is no part of that law; *Filius Meus Tu* is not written in the heart, it must be preached to the ear. No light of nature could reveal it from within—preached from without it must be. And so and no otherwise come we to the knowledge of it. The very word gives it for such, which is properly 'a statute' as this is, enacted and decreed

---

28 *Works*, II, Easter Sermon IX, 325, 326.
29 See *supra*, 12, 15, 17.

in the High Court of God's Council above, and reserved "to be revealed in the latter times;" and of that we cannot "hear without a preacher," and the preaching thereof was committed to Christ.[30]

It is only to distinguish it from the higher law about which he is discoursing that he mentions the natural law in this passage, of course; but a comparison with his teaching on the law of God in the *Catechism* with this brief mention of the natural law confirms the impression of a traditional doctrine. This common law of the world written in men's hearts, this "light of nature, for rebelling against which all that are without Christ suffer condemnation,"[31] is made manifest to us from within ourselves; when we stray from the path of right

> there takes us sometimes . . . "a throbbing of the heart;" or, as the Apostle, certain "accusing thoughts" present themselves unto us which will not suffer us to go on quietly, our minds still misgiving us that we are wrong.
>
> Besides, when any danger of death is near; nay, if we do but sadly think on it, a certain chillness takes us, and we cannot with any comfort think on our journey's end, and hear as it were a voice of one crying behind us, *Haec est via,* That is not the way you have taken; "This" that you have lost "is your way, walk in it." Which voice if we hear not, it is long of the noise about us. If we would sometimes go aside into some retired place, or in the still of the night hearken after it, we might peradventure hear it.[32]

Although Andrewes has not used the term here, he is presumably speaking of the voice of conscience which issues the moral dictates of human reason and is the expression of the natural law within us.

For the sermon which preceded the departure of Essex to suppress rebellion in Ireland in 1599 and in which he discussed the morality of war, Andrewes chose a likely text from Deu-

---

[30] *Works*, I, Nativity Sermon XVII, 290-91.
[31] *Works*, III, Pentecost Sermon XIV, 372.
[32] *Works*, I, Ash Wednesday Sermon IV, 361.

teronomy: "When thou goest out with the host against thine enemies, keep thee then from all wickedness" (Deuteronomy 23:9). War and divinity, he argues, have a bearing on one another; there is a "double use"

> 1. of war in divinity; that our going forth might procure the giving over sin. 2. Of Divinity in war; that our giving over sin might procure good speed to our going forth, even an honourable and happy return.[33]

He reasons from the text that, if those who go to war must keep themselves from sin, it follows that war itself is not sinful but lawful, and may be undertaken without sin. This does not mean, of course, that war may be irresponsibly entered upon, for the text says "when," which indicates that there are certain times or circumstances in which war is lawful. War, then, "is not so secular a matter, but that it hath both his lawfulness and his holiness," for it is clear from many places in Holy Writ that war has its time and even its commission from God.[34] War, then, is sometimes justifiable. Furthermore, this kind of war on which we are about to engage, "not defensive war, but offensive too, hath his 'when.' " Does not our text say " 'when thou goest forth against them,' " and not "when they come forth against thee"?[35] Relying entirely on Scripture, Andrewes continues his justification of offensive war; he is not especially convincing, it must be admitted. From the same source he seeks to establish that a war against rebellious subjects is most just and lawful. And finally he turns to the war in hand:

> Here have been divers princely favours vouchsafed, and most unkindly rejected; means of clemency many times most graciously offered, and most ungraciously refused; yea, faith falsified and expectation deluded; contempt upon contempt heaped up, that the

---

33 *Works*, I, Ash Wednesday Sermon II, 323.
34 *Works*, I, Ash Wednesday Sermon II, 323-24.
35 *Works*, I, Ash Wednesday Sermon II, 324.

measure is full. These then are the enemies "against," and this the time "when." When not only we may but must, and that not with God's leave only, but with His liking and full commission, "go forth" in this cause. So that war is lawful; and this kind, "to go forth;" and against these enemies most just and most lawful. At this time against these enemies it is a war sanctified; they shall "consecrate their hands," they shall *praeliari praelia Domini*, that fight against them.[36]

Such a war is "an act of justice, and of justice corrective, whose office is to punish sin."[37] Therefore (and this is the "use" of war in divinity), the time of war especially is a time for us to give over sin.

While reflecting on this idea Andrewes had a happy thought: this business of avoiding sin, which has a very necessary use in war, is entirely "within the compass of our [clerical] profession." Perhaps, then, this

> may serve to answer the question, more usually than advisedly oft cast out, What good do these Churchmen? What use is there of them now at such times as this? Yes, there is an use of them, and that in war we see. The camp hath use of this place [church], and they that serve there of them that serve here.[38]

Andrewes always stood for order and authority, and opposed action on private authority alone. This did not lead him, however, to deny the right of self-defense. There is only one occasion, he said in a Gowry sermon, when one cannot await the magistrate's aid; the law of nature grants one the moral right of opposing force to force in the case of an attack on his life

---

[36] *Works*, I, Ash Wednesday Sermon II, 325.

[37] *Works*, I, Ash Wednesday Sermon II, 330.

[38] *Works*, I, Ash Wednesday Sermon II, 327-28. The foregoing development of the moral rectitude of war may be compared with the three conditions for a just war laid down by Andrewes in the *Catechism* (*Works*, VI, 223-24): war must be commanded by just authority, it must be in a just cause, and it must be undertaken with a right end and purpose. "And ever," he says in another place, "the end is above the means" (*Works*, II, Easter Sermon IX, 336).

by a private enemy. Yet this must be done *"cum moderamine inculpatae tutelae,"* or *"se defendendo."*[39] In another reference to lawful authority Andrewes made this interesting distinction regarding obedience:

> An obedience there is that cometh from the *dictamen* of natural reason; in some things we so obey, we will do it because our reason so moveth us. That is, *obediens natus.* But some other there be, wherein there is no other reason to lead us to do it but only this, that it is enjoined us by a lawful superior, and therefore we do it, and for no other cause. This is *obediens factus,* and that in true proper terms is the right obedience indeed.[40]

Very closely related to the question of sin, and therefore within the province of the moral theologian, is the problem of temptation, to which Andrewes gave a great deal of attention. This led him quite naturally to speak of the devil, whose nature, wiles, and purposes he was most anxious to uncover. His confidently realistic approach to Satan will more than likely amuse many of our contemporaries, though Andrewes would surely find a kindred spirit in the author of the *Screwtape Letters.* Satan, he tells us, "is of God's making as an Angel, of his own marring as a devil," and he is the "enemy of all peace."[41] The bishop made his seventh sermon on the Gunpowder Plot the occasion for a full exposé of the devil's aims and ambitions:

> The enemy of God he is, and so of all God's works; and of those His works most, that God most sets by, that is, mankind; and of that part of mankind most God hath done most for, and so may be thought most to favour, that is, Christian men; and then of them, if there be a *Non taliter* in His mercy, a *Non taliter* too in

---

[39] *Works,* IV, Gowry Sermon VIII, 187.

[40] *Works,* II, Easter Sermon IX, 326. The text for this sermon included the phrase [*Christus*] *factus obediens usque ad mortem, mortem autem crucis* (Philippians 2:8). Andrewes remarks: "We love obedience in a whole skin; *usque* anything rather than that" (327).

[41] *Works,* IV, Gunpowder Sermon VII, 329; *Works,* II, Easter Sermon IV, 243.

his malice straight. If a *super omnes* with God, a *super omnes* with him, *in sensu contrario.*

To any creature, only because it is a creature, is he cruel; he will into the hog-sty to shew it, rather than not to shew it at all.

But to man, to one man rather than to a whole herd of swine.

And among men, his malice is most at Christian men; they are nearer to the kingdom of God. To keep them from that himself hath irrecoverably lost, that is, Heaven, and to plunge them into eternal misery, whereunto himself is fallen, without all redemption.

And among Christian men to the best sort, to public persons rather than to private mean men.

But if he could get a whole parliament together—a King, his nobles, his commons, that is, a King, kingdom and all, and up with them all at once, all together, there were none to that; that, lo, he would over sea and land to compass. For that were indeed with him a *super omnia*, he never had done the like.[42]

Yes, the devil is back of every treachery; *"inter duos proditores diabolus est tertius."*[43]

Now it "is exceeding behoveful for us . . . to know the length of the devil's chain," that we may beware our danger from him. Know you, that neither full nor fasting are we out of his reach, for he attends our feasts, attends our fasts, our almsgivings, and our prayers, striving always to corrupt the manner, pervert the end, and to turn them into sin. He tries to get us not to do what is good; if we do it, to get us to do it poorly; or even to do what God commands, but for his vile ends—such, as Revelation calls them, are the "deep fetches, or policies of Satan" (Revelation 2:24).[44] Wherever we turn

he meets with us still. These are his designs; this doth he *diversis itineribus,* 'by contrary ways' seek to circumvent us. First, down he sits in his court, and offers us a license not to keep Lent, to keep what diet we will; and if we refuse it threatens us he will get us

---

[42] *Works*, IV, Gunpowder Sermon VII, 335.
[43] *Works*, IV, Gowry Sermon VIII, 189.
[44] *Works*, I, Ash Wednesday Sermon VI, 401.

presented for hypocrites. But if that move us not, but we stand out resolute for all his scarecrow, then out he comes in a new style, falls to commend us as good orderly men, but withal to advise us friendly to do all so as may be for our best behoof, which is to have it seen in any wise. And, that which is strange, scares us with that in the beginning which he brings us to in the end; even to do that in hypocrisy that before he wished us in no wise to do for fear of hypocrisy.[45]

In his sermon on the text from the Lord's Prayer, "And lead us not into temptation," Andrewes discusses both the devil and temptation.[46] We have prayed God to forgive our sins, he says; now we petition Him that we may not contract further sin. We are not forever secure once God has pardoned us, for the devil is most malicious against those who have been snatched from his thrall; therefore must we pray that we enter not into temptation. Temptation is a trial and a proof, and is of two sorts: good, and that proceeds from God; evil, and that proceeds from Satan. In His wisdom God judges it good to test our faith and patience by afflicting us, not because He does not know us sufficiently, but that men and angels might know the purity of our faith He tries us in the fire. Satan, on the other hand, tempts us, not for our own good, but to draw us away from God. Some temptations, of course, we suffer by reason of the corruption of our human nature: "From sins lighting upon our thoughts it is impossible, it cannot be; but from making there a nest or hatching ought, that we are willed to look to, and that by God's grace we may,"[47] for to us the devil "needs bring but a pair of bellows, for he shall find fire within us."[48] But temptations which come to us from without are from the devil, who makes use of both prosperity and adversity as he tries now to

---

[45] *Works*, I, Ash Wednesday Sermon VI, 404-05.
[46] *Works*, V, Sermon on Prayer XVI, 441-48.
[47] *Works*, I, Ash Wednesday Sermon II, 334.
[48] *Works*, V, Sermon on the Temptation of Christ II, 494.

allure us with pleasures, now to frighten us with violent danger, and all the while to confuse us into magnifying the one and the other. "If he cannot prevail as a tempter, he will endeavour that he may hurt us as a tormentor."[49]

For our comfort we must remember that, though we have not the strength to conquer the least temptation of ourselves alone, God's grace will enable us to overcome; and again, that the devil cannot tempt us without God's permission—he is chained by God and so cannot go further than God will give him leave. Nor can he tempt us beyond our strength:

> The Holy Ghost is not a stander by, as a stranger, when we are tempted . . . but He leads us by the hand, and stands by as a faithful assistant. He makes an issue out of all our temptations, and "will not suffer us to be tempted beyond our strength."[50]

Tempted indeed we will be. And God wills to use Satan to try us; hence we pray "*ne Deus nos inducat,*" and not "*ne tentet nos Satanas.*"[51] If we do not wish to be led into temptation

> we must not lead ourselves, nor tempt ourselves, nor grope for sin, for the devil's temptation cannot hurt us, it shall be a means to grace us, if we withstand it; but if we will be drawn away of our own lusts, then we cannot but be led.[52]

We must forego the occasions of sin, and guard our eye, which is "the broker between the heart and all wicked lusts that be in the world."[53] And we must pray, not vaguely and in general, but precisely that we may be delivered from the temptations to those sins to which we are most inclined.

The sermons on the temptation of Christ enlarge upon this quite orthodox pastoral theology. An idea or two culled from

---

49 *Works*, V, Sermon on Prayer XVII, 450.
50 *Works*, V, Sermon on the Temptation of Christ I, 485.
51 *Works*, V, Sermon on Prayer XVI, 446.
52 *Works*, V, Sermon on Prayer XVI, 447.
53 *Works*, V, Sermon on the Temptation of Christ VI, 540.

these will enable one to realize how much a master of the spiritual life Bishop Andrewes was. From this temptation of Christ,
he suggests, we should learn how to deal with the devil, for He
sanctified temptation in undergoing it Himself. We should not
be discouraged, then, should temptations assail us or come to
us at the holiest times or in the holiest places. Not even the
monks and hermits of the desert could escape them for all their
solitude.[54] In some instances we are to stand to the devil, keep
an eye on his temptation; in others, as "in a case of lust, or
filthy desire, then do ye fly from him."[55] Both presumption and
despair, the bishop quite correctly warns in the same sermon,
should be avoided in our attitude toward temptation; "blessed
is he that so loveth God, that he can be content to creep on hands
and feet to Him."[56]

One will not read many of the sermons before deciding that
their author knew and practiced a high Christian asceticism, for
they bear an extraordinary degree of sincerity, conviction, and
sane balance which is wholly different from superficial emotionalism and empty fancy. Fortunately we have the direct
testimony of a member of his household as to the virtues for
which he was noted. His life, if not in every way perfect (as
whose is?), can well be held a striking example of Christian
living. Henry Isaacson singled out in Andrewes several qualities, of which zeal and piety were the principal. Many hours
daily he spent in private prayer with God, falling even into
tears in the intensity of his devotion. In public prayer his reverent behavior inspired others to imitation. Even before he came
into great preferments, Isaacson continues, he practiced charity
and compassion, so that poor parishioners, prisoners, debtors,
and the aged benefited from his hidden acts of charity, often

<hr />

54 *Works*, V, Sermon on the Temptation of Christ II, 480, 486, 488.
55 *Works*, V, Sermon on the Temptation of Christ VII, 551.
56 *Works*, V, Sermon on the Temptation of Christ VII, 535.

performed "under other men's names."[57] In the administration
of offices of both a spiritual as well as a temporal nature, in the
handling of matters financial or the cure of souls, and in the
granting of preferment the bishop gained a just renown for
fidelity and integrity.[58] As almoner, for example, it is recorded
of him that,

> he would never suffer one penny of that which accrued to him
> by that place to be put or mingled with any of his own rents or
> revenues; and wherein he kept a more exact account than of his
> own private estate; and secondly, being so separated, he was as
> faithful in the disposing of it; not only in the general trust of his
> sovereign, in the daily charges incident to that place, expended by
> the sub-almoner, and other yearly ordinary charges; but when he
> perceived that he had a surplusage, those charges defrayed, he
> would not suffer it to lie by him; but some of it he disposed to the
> relief of poor housekeepers, some in releasing of poor prisoners,
> and comforting them which lay in misery and iron; and some in
> furnishing poor people with gowns, hose, shoes and the like: for all
> which, many, so bestowed by him, had he reserved to his own use,
> (his patent being *sine computo*,) no man could have questioned
> him: but he was a faithful steward in this, as in the rest.[59]

---

[57] *Works*, V, Buckeridge, *Funeral Sermon*, 295.

[58] "In hoc uno tamen infirmitas quaedam apparuit, quod nimis fuerit intentus
gratificandis amicis, non sine aliorum praeiudicio; attamen in homines indig-
nos nil contulit," wrote one Roger Ley in his manuscript "Gesta Britannica."
See British Museum, Stowe MSS., 76 [Roger Ley], Gesta Britannica prae-
sertim Anglorum adjectis aliquot observationibus maxime in ijs quae ad
Ecclesiam a temporibus retroactis ad A.D. MDCXLVIII spectant, f. 247. The
"Gesta Britannica" was completed on April 28, 1664, according to a note in
Ley's hand on f. 364v.

[59] *Works*, XI, Isaacson, *Exact Narration*, xix-xx. Andrewes' precise care of finances
entrusted to him may be seen in British Museum, Additional MSS., [12, 222],
Original accounts of the churchwardens of the parish of St. Giles, Cripplegate, from 11 May, 1570, to 18 May, 1580, and from 27 May, 1596, to
2 June, 1608, ff. 39v, 44v, 48v, 52v, 56v, 61, 66, 71v, 76, where there appear in
his hand signed notifications of the auditing of the annual accounts. Andrewes
seems also to have been present at the audit nearly every year of his mastership at Pembroke, as is attested by his signature in the *Audit Book*. See
Attwater, *Pembroke College*, 55.

To people or institutions to whom he was indebted for favors and benefits he always manifested a sincere practical gratitude. His hospitality and munificence were bestowed, the one on people of quality and respect, especially on scholars and strangers, and the other upon the poor scholars of both Cambridge and Oxford. For James's entertainment he once spent three thousand pounds during a three-day royal visit at Farnham Castle in the Diocese of Winchester. His table was bountifully supplied, yet he seldom knew himself when he came from his study what meat he was to have; but he "strictly observed in his provisions of diet, the time of Lent, Embers, and other fasting days, according to the laws of this kingdom, and the orders of the Church."[60] Affable, modest, indefatigable in his studies, writes Isaacson,

> it may truly be said of him, that he had those gifts and graces, both of art and nature, so fixed in him, as that this age cannot parallel him; for his profundity and abyss of learning was accompanied with wit, memory, judgment, languages, gravity, and humility; insomuch, that if he had been contemporary with the ancient fathers of the primitive Church, he would have been, and that worthily, reputed not inferior to the chiefest among them.[61]

There can be no reasonable doubt that Lancelot Andrewes was an extraordinary figure, nor that the driving force and wellspring of his holy life was the Christian asceticism he preached and lived. Asceticism too frequently evokes in the modern mind dour visions of watchings, fastings, mortifications, self-denial, penance, and little else. All indeed are among its weapons and recommendations, but they do not exhaust the list of practices in which it seeks to exercise men as they pursue the positive goal of their salvation. Andrewes knew this, of course; hence the positive character of his sermons generally. Yet he con-

60 *Works*, XI, Isaacson, *Exact Narration*, xxiii.
61 *Works*, XI, Isaacson, *Exact Narration*, xxvi.

stantly underlined and urged the more rigorous demands of
Christian asceticism.

With us, he once remarked, "men be good because they be
great; with God they be great because they be good."[62] Good
and great by God's standards we must all strive to be. We are
created to seek after God, but are more concerned to have "days
and elbow-room enough to seek other things, and to shrink up
His seeking into a narrow time at our end." We consider the
time spent in seeking God a loss to the fruits and joys of living,
"As if the fruit of life were not to find God, or as if any true
hearts' joy God being not found." Does not Augustine tell us
that in the tears of a penitent there is "more sound joy than
in risu theatrorum, 'in all the games the theater can afford' "?[63]
Let love be our motive, for

> *Solus amor erubescit nomen difficultatis,* 'love endureth not the
> name of difficulty,' but shameth to confess any thing too hard or
> too dangerous for it.[64]

The pursuit of good is no easy thing, for often will evil be
spoken of it, "*regium est . . . bene cum feceris, audire male
. . .* but *divinum . . . de bono opere lapidari.*"[65] But we must
persevere in difficulty lest we suffer for hesitating as did Lot's
wife—how sudden and extraordinary was her punishment![66] If
we do the best we can, God will be satisfied. Nowhere, perhaps,
has Andrewes better displayed the fine balance of his ascetical
teaching than in the following passage from his sermon on the
zeal of St. Paul:

> *Fecit quod potuit,* saith our Saviour in Mary Magdalene's case;
> and *dedit quod habuit,* in the case of the poor widow's mites; and

---

[62] *Works,* III, Easter Sermon XVIII, 92.
[63] *Works,* I, Ash Wednesday Sermon I, 316.
[64] *Works,* II, Lenten Sermon VI, 108.
[65] *Works,* II, Lenten Sermon III, 58.
[66] *Works,* II, Lenten Sermon IV, 61-77; this is the burden of the whole sermon.

that is as much as God doth, or man can require. But be it little, or be it much, he that giveth all leaveth nothing ungiven.[67]

Against the three fonts of sin Andrewes proposed three specific remedies:

> For spiritual sins, prayer and works of devotion; for fleshly, works pertaining to *castigo corpus meum;* for worldly, alms, and works of charity and compassion.[68]

Quite aware of our readiness to say to ourselves *"Propitius esto tibi,"*[69] of our "pangs and qualms of godliness,"[70] and of our nature's common resentment at being urged, as to something needful, to things beyond what we "have a liking to perform,"[71] Andrewes nevertheless insisted often upon work, action, and personal effort on the part of the individual as essential for the fostering of the spiritual life. In the sermon preached before King James at Whitehall on Easter Sunday of 1613 he says it is foolish "when we see daily things here beneath without travail will not be come by, once to think things above will drop into our laps without any seeking."[72]

Prayer, then, is our first task in the spiritual life. Had the *Preces Privatae* never been published, even had Andrewes never composed his sermons on prayer, one would easily gather from his familiarity with the Scriptures, his penetration into the depths of religious ideas, and his insights into human nature that Bishop Andrewes was a man of prayerful reflection and meditation. "He was," says Bishop Frere, "what his prayers

---

[67] *Works,* II, Lenten Sermon VI, 103.

[68] *Works,* I, Ash Wednesday Sermon VIII, 442. These three, he says in a previous sermon, "to offer to God our 1. soul by prayer, 2. our body by abstinence, 3. our goods by alms-deeds, hath been ever counted *tergemina hostia,* 'the triple or threefold Christian holocaust, or whole burnt-offering'" (*Works,* I, Ash Wednesday Sermon V, 381).

[69] *Works,* I, Ash Wednesday Sermon IV, 368.

[70] *Works,* II, Easter Sermon I, 202.

[71] *Works,* I, Ash Wednesday Sermon IV, 366.

[72] *Works,* II, Easter Sermon VIII, 314.

made him."[73] Canon Brightman has pointed out the relation between the *Preces Privatae* and the sermons:

> The devotions are in fact an abstract of the sermons, the ser-
> mons a development and expansion of the devotions. The things
> which he delivers to the Church are the things in which he habitu-
> ally 'exercises himself day and night;' they have been proved and
> tested in his own heart; and the essence of his public teaching is
> distilled into suggestion for his own devotion.[74]

One need only notice the heavily scriptural character of the
Preces Privatae, the simplicity of their devotional spirit, the
confessions of sins, professions of faith, petitions for divine
favor, the requests for blessings on all sorts of people—the
kingdom, magistrates, dioceses, colleges, farmers, artificers, and
so forth, all aptly calculated to stir sentiments of piety, contrition, or duty—to realize how true it is that "the theology of
the *Preces* is that of the *Sermons.*"[75]

Taken in conjunction with the *Preces Privatae* and with the
section on prayer in the *Catechism,*[76] the nineteen sermons on
prayer, delivered probably at Pembroke during Andrewes' days
as catechist, form a fairly complete treatise.[77] These are the
sermons, it will be remembered, which contain his teaching on
the supernatural, wherein he explained the interrelationship of
the supernatural, grace, and prayer. Grace is necessary for
supernatural life, and the means to obtain grace is prayer,[78] yet
prayer itself is properly the effect of grace.[79] So necessary is
prayer that its neglect is sinful, for only by prayer can we come

---

[73] Frere, *Andrewes as a Representative of Anglican Principles,* 26.

[74] Brightman, *The Preces Privatae,* li.

[75] Brightman, *The Preces Privatae,* liii.

[76] *Works,* VI, *Catechism,* 97-101.

[77] *Works,* V, Sermon on Prayer XV, 432; Andrewes uses the term to describe
these sermons.

[78] See *supra,* 128.

[79] *Works,* V, Sermon on Prayer VI, 351. In the *Catechism* (*Works,* VI, 106) he
says: "Prayer is the means of all other graces."

to God. We are to pray with confidence, diligence, and perseverance—reasonably, with cause; such prayers will God answer. What is hurtful to us He will not grant, so that even "*non accipiendo accepimus.*"[80] Of the many things Andrewes taught regarding prayer, few beyond these two—its necessity and the manner of it—need comment. One relates quite directly to asceticism as such. When we pray "Thy will be done," says he, we actually pray not so much that God's will be done, but rather that what God wills may be our will, for there is one will of God (His revealed will), which we can resist, another (His secret will), which is irresistible. It is not for us curiously to inquire and search out God's secret will touching reprobation or election, but simply to adore it. The effort of our lives should be to frame ourselves to God's will as it is revealed in the Ten Commandments, and to submit with patience to whatever His secret will has determined for us.[81] Thus does Andrewes preserve God's omnipotence in the final disposition of man and man's free will to serve or not to serve—not a moral freedom, of course, but a physical. We may confidently expect the Holy Spirit to direct our prayer, to give us words to speak, to fix our attention and to enkindle our hearts; and we must remember that the faithful, as being of one body, the Church, benefit each other by their prayers.[82] Both private and public prayer he recommended,[83] and he strongly approved vocal prayer.[84] His teaching on prayer for the dead is not wholly clear. In the *Discourse of Ceremonies*, for instance, he wrote that such prayer is but an idle imitation of the heathen,[85] though he once confessed: "For *offering* and *prayer for the dead*, there is little to

---

80 *Works*, V, Sermon on Prayer III, 321-28.
81 *Works*, V, Sermon on Prayer XI, 396-404.
82 *Works*, V, Sermon on Prayer IV, 337-39.
83 *Works*, V, Sermon on Prayer VI, 357.
84 *Works*, V, Sermon on Prayer V, 349.
85 *Works*, VI, *Discourse of Ceremonies*, 373.

be said against it; it cannot be denied, that it is ancient."[86] Petitions for the dead apparently appeared in the *Preces Privatae*,[87] and in at least one place in the sermons Andrewes calls for "A prayer for Mordecai, that for his so sitting in the gate he may sit in a better place."[88] Whatever his personal practice, in the sermons Bishop Andrewes did not make a great deal of prayer for the dead.

To the second of his remedies for sin, works pertaining to "castigo corpus meum," he devoted several of the Ash Wednesday sermons. They bear entirely upon the ascetical practices of fasting and repentance, and aim at arousing his audience to works of self-denial. Summoning the resources of his great learning and raising himself to an unusual emotional pitch, he methodically hammers at the necessity, the value, and the appropriateness of repentance and fasting. It was not by accident, indeed, that a great number of the bishop's observations on human nature occur in this particular series of sermons, for he made it clear to his congregations that he knew the difficulties, as well as the benefits, in terms of human psychology and spiritual necessity, which are inherent in these elements of Christian discipline.

Andrewes attacked the subject of fasting with a refreshing directness not always apparent in his preaching. We preachers, he says for example, have been accused of entertaining you with nothing but discourse about "the mystery of godliness," and never with exhortation to its exercise, while you are charged with falling into gloom at the mere mention of fasting. How we practice it, let each one answer for himself; as for me, I take

---

[86] *Works*, XI, *Two Answers to Cardinall Perron*, 24.
[87] Most of these, Brightman says, were omitted in Samuel Wright's manuscript copy (Brightman, *The Preces Privatae*, xvi-xvii). The Anglo-Catholic edition made use of an edition of 1675 which in turn was based on Wright's copy (*Works*, X, vii). Wright was once Andrewes' secretary.
[88] *Works*, IV, Gowry Sermon VI, 152.

you all now to witness that we preach it.[89] As a matter of fact, he later said, excess "in fare and feeding" is accounted England's national fault:

> So no fruit that our nation is more bound to bring forth than it [fasting]. For *esca ventri* and *venter escis*, "meat for the belly, and the belly for meat," it no where reigneth so much.[90]

Physicians are wont to enjoin fasting to aid digestion, philosophers advise it as a means "to keep the sense subtile," and states politic proclaim it "to preserve the breed of cattle, or increase of strength by sea," but we prescribe it to a religious end; "So no physical, philosophical, political, but a prophetical, yea an evangelical fast," is this we preach to you.[91] The religious motives for fasting are numerous: it is an act of the virtue of temperance, of corrective justice as the penal part of penitence; it humbles the soul, and prevents the lusts of the body from rising against it; by fasting we perform an act of the service of God, especially since it involves sacrifice; and the exercise of fasting, "by inuring ourselves to this part of true Christian discipline, serves to enable us to have *ventrem moratum*, 'the mastery of our belly' against need be."[92]

Expanding a little on some of these ideas, Andrewes proceeds to the ends which fasting prosecutes. Fasting punishes the flesh; by fasting we "amerce ourselves, as it were, for abusing our liberty before, and making it an occasion to the flesh," and so we prevent God's judgment of us by judging ourselves. God is inclined to mercy when He sees us angry with ourselves; He had rather we punish ourselves than He should have to do it. Since our bodies have joined in the sins we commit, they too should suffer, even as the soul does, in repentance. Again,

---

[89] *Works*, I, Ash Wednesday Sermon V, 376.
[90] *Works*, I, Ash Wednesday Sermon VIII, 443-44.
[91] *Works*, I, Ash Wednesday Sermon IV, 367.
[92] *Works*, I, Ash Wednesday Sermon V, 380-81.

chastisement for sin has a "medicinable force, a special good remedy to prevent sin, when it is not yet fallen on us or we into it."[93] But fasting has its use not only in evil things and as an aid in repelling them, for we often have some particularly desirable favor to ask of God and are willing to commend it to Him with more than ordinary prayer.

> We have otherwhile extraordinary occasions in our worldly affairs, and then we make no account of a meal's loss: have we none such *in spiritualibus* to God-ward? None but vulgar there? Never any but such as we can entertain with our common dull devotion? Need none other, but as if the business between God and our soul were the silliest and poorest business we had to go about.[94]

When our devotion is dull and "our prayers full of yawning, when the brain is thick with the vapour and the heart pressed down with the charge of the stomach," fasting is a special friend to prayer, for it "feathers" it, gives it vigor and fervor. It is far more important to speak of the need of fasting than to prescribe the manner: "We cannot get men to it, to fast; what need we then spend any speech how they should not do it, when they do it not?" he asks as he launches into his sermon on the avoidance of hypocrisy.[95] On another occasion he took time to advise his audience that fasting need not involve rigid abstention, so that our knees grow weak; "The Church, as an indulgent mother, mitigates all she may," and requires only that we forego *"cibos desiderii . . .* meats and drink provoking the appetite, full of nourishment, kindling the blood."[96] Once more, then, we find in Bishop Andrewes that balance, moderation, and sweet reasonableness which are so exactly characteristic of this significant figure in Anglican history.

---

[93] *Works*, I, Ash Wednesday Sermon V, 388.
[94] *Works*, I, Ash Wednesday Sermon V, 389-90.
[95] *Works*, I, Ash Wednesday Sermon VI, 399.
[96] *Works*, I, Ash Wednesday Sermon IV, 368.

As Andrewes insisted on the external manifestation of religion, so did he insist on interior virtue and spirit. He considered repentance, for example, as closely associated with the external practice of fasting. So important and so necessary is this virtue, he tells us, that in respect of it we face these two alternatives: "1. Repent, or 2. Perish . . . there under God's wrath for ever, not to repent and not to perish, is not possible."[97] In the fourth Ash Wednesday sermon Andrewes delved into the nature of repentance. His text foreshadows the development:

> Therefore also now, saith the Lord, Turn you unto Me with all your heart, and with fasting, and with weeping, and with mourning.
> And rend your heart, and not your clothes, and turn unto the Lord your God (Joel 2:12-13).[98]

In accordance with the text he defines repentance as a "*redire ad principia,* 'a kind of circling,' to return to Him by repentance from Whom by sin we have turned away."[99] Two turnings make up this circle—one is to be made with the whole heart, and this is our turning to God, and the other, "wherein we look backward to our sins wherein we have turned from God," should break our hearts into contrition. Thus we have a conversion from sin and contrition for sin:

> One resolving to amend that which is to come, the other reflecting and sorrowing for that which is past. One declining from evil to be done hereafter, the other sentencing itself for evil done heretofore. These two between them make up a complete repentance, or, to keep the word of the text, a perfect revolution.[100]

But the "very true essence of repentance" consists neither in conversion nor in sorrow, but rather in indignation—anger

---

[97] *Works,* I, Ash Wednesday Sermon VII, 429. This position is quite opposed to Calvinistic predestination, for it attributes the choice of salvation or damnation to each individual.

[98] *Works,* I, Ash Wednesday Sermon IV, 356-74.

[99] *Works,* I, Ash Wednesday Sermon IV, 358.

[100] *Works,* I, Ash Wednesday Sermon IV, 359.

at myself for the sin committed; this is the essential passion which will rend my heart.[101] We must pray for this true spirit of repentance, which is a gift of God,[102] and must see that it issues into acts, for if neither acts nor fruits follow from repentance, "*fingitur non agitur poenitentia,*—it is Augustine, 'we do but dally, all is but counterfeit.' "[103] While justice sometimes destroys, "so doth repentance never but saves always."[104] A little reflection on Bishop Andrewes' teaching on the nature of sin, the redemption, Christ's Passion, and man's supernatural destiny will make clear how consistent this traditional doctrine on repentance is with the general pattern of his thought. He often related repentance to prayer, fasting, and almsgiving, the last of the three main ascetical practices he recommended.[105]

Except when he preached at St. Mary's Hospital on Easter Wednesday of 1588, Andrewes devoted little attention to almsgiving other than urging it in passing and referring briefly to its ascetical value as an antidote for a worldly spirit.[106] In this remarkably full "Spital" sermon of some fifty pages Andrewes covers practically the whole of his social teaching in connection with a strictly ascetical topic. He rarely had anything to say directly upon social questions, though his awareness of them induced him to associate them with the problems of religion. His plan, if such it was, for fostering the nation's social well-being called for an indirect approach rather than a frontal attack. He would have men influence society through the moral improvement of their own lives, and through the steady practice of Christian virtue.

---

101 *Works*, I, Ash Wednesday Sermon IV, 372.
102 *Works*, I, Ash Wednesday Sermon IV, 357.
103 *Works*, I, Ash Wednesday Sermon VIII, 440.
104 *Works*, I, Ash Wednesday Sermon VIII, 445.
105 *Works*, I, Ash Wednesday Sermon V, 381; *Works*, I, Ash Wednesday Sermon VIII, 441-42; see *supra*, 171.
106 *Works*, I, Ash Wednesday Sermon VIII, 442.

Of moral duties, both "Christian" and "Civil," he writes:

> The *Christian* duty of bearing wrong, where it is well per-
> suaded, doth mainly strengthen the *Civil* of doing no wrong; and
> the Christian, of departing with our own charitably, doth strengthen
> the Civil of not taking other men's injuriously; and so of the rest.
> That he called it not amiss, that called Divinity the backbone of
> the Prince's law; and consequently Religion of the common-
> wealth.[107]

And again, with respect to prayer:

> When the Apostle willeth that, "first of all, prayers and suppli-
> cations should be made for Kings and all in authority" [1 Timothy
> 2:1-2], the reason is, as Augustine noteth, because both man's sal-
> vation, the honesty of life, knowledge of the truth, quietness of
> kingdoms, duties of Kings, and whatsoever tendeth to the public
> benefit, come by and from prayer; so that not only the Church and
> spiritual matters, but the commonwealth and temporal things, are
> stayed upon the pillar of prayer.[108]

As is almost invariably true of the texts he chooses for his
sermons, Andrewes' text in the "Spital" sermon supplies an
excellent outline of what he will discuss.

> Charge them that are rich in this world, that they be not high-
> minded, that they trust not in the uncertainty of riches, but in the
> living God, Which giveth us all things to enjoy plenteously;
> That they do good, be rich in good works, ready to distribute
> and to communicate;
> Laying up in store for themselves a good foundation against
> the time to come, that they may lay hold of eternal life (1 Timothy
> 6:17-19).[109]

This text was peculiarly suited to his audience, which included "lords, knights, aldermen, masters, wardens," and probably members of the clergy for whom special accommodations

---

107 *Works*, II, Lenten Sermon I, 8.
108 *Works*, V, Sermon on Prayer IV, 334.
109 *Works*, V, Occasional Sermon I, 3-53.

were provided.[110] After making the proper applications with some grace and as much vigor, Andrewes, then master of Pembroke, turns to the practice of almsgiving. The papists, he says, very openly accuse you of not doing good works:

> One of them saith that our religion hath comforted your force attractive so much, and made it so strong, that nothing can be wrung from you. Another, he saith that our religion hath brought a hardness into the bowels of our professors, that they pity little, and the cramp or chiragra into their hands, that they give less. Another, that our preaching hath bred you minds full of Solomon's horseleeches, that cry "Bring in, bring in," and nothing else. All of them say that your good works come so from you, as if indeed your religion were to be saved by faith only.[111]

And they accuse us, the clergy, of not preaching good works to you. "Here I call for them now, I take witness, I call you to record, I call heaven to record . . . I have made them a part of my charge, and the most earnest and vehement part of my charge, even the charge of doing good." To you, therefore, that be rich, I make this charge; if you do not good, "talk not of faith, for you have no faith in you." On the last day you will not be asked of the highness or lowness of your minds, of your trust and confidence, or any other virtues, but of "your feeding, clothing, visiting, harbouring, succouring . . . of your well-doing only. This I say to you, bear witness I say it." Andrewes remained true to this position throughout his life.

He was stung by the Catholics' taunt, and in defense of his coreligionists he challenged them to show him any "popish city Christian," be it Rome or Rheims, where more charity had been done to orphans, for instance, than had been during this Easter week in London.[112] He continued:

---

110 *Works*, V, Occasional Sermon I, 39; and 1, introductory note.
111 *Works*, V, Occasional Sermon I, 35-36.
112 *Works*, V, Occasional Sermon I, 36.

I will be able to prove that learning in the foundation of schools and increase of revenues within colleges, and the poor in foundation of almshouses, and increase of perpetuities to them, have received greater help in this realm within these forty years last past, since not the starting up of our Church as they fondly use to speak, but since the reforming ours from the error of theirs, than it hath I say in any realm Christian, not only within the self-same forty years, (which were enough to stop their mouths) but also than it hath in any forty years upward, during all the time of popery, which I speak partly of mine own knowledge, and partly by sufficient grave information to this behalf. This may be said, and said truly.[113]

Be ye then rich in good works, he urged; "Rich in coffer; so ye are: rich in conscience; be so too. Your consciences you shall carry with you, your coffers you shall not. Thus you are valued in the Queen's books; what are you in God's books?" As you are "sessed" in the one, so are you in the other; "each one according to his ability."[114] In one of his rare excursions into the field of social theory Andrewes next urges the wealthy to support necessary foundations and societies; to avoid eating up and converting to their own use companies and institutions which are for the good of the many "by out-buying and out-bidding" everyone else; to desist from capturing civil livings and from turning common into private, as though they, the rich, were seeking to dwell alone upon the earth. Some people think the world is toward an end—if any reason were to convince me that this is so, he says, none would be more effective than this, "that every man doeth what in him lieth to discommon communities, and to bring all to the first privation."

For the world being itself a main society, these men by dismembering under-societies seek and do what they can to dissolve the whole. So that God must needs come to make an end of the

---

113 *Works*, V, Occasional Sermon I, 37.
114 *Works*, V, Occasional Sermon I, 38-39.

world, or else if this hold on we should shortly make an end of it ourselves.[115]

I have heard, he says, that, though charitable donations have been made for the maintenance of the poor, the poor are still in want and that they who "have the receiving of the profits do yet increase mightily." If that is really true, it is a sin crying to heaven.

> It is good for you to know what things are said abroad. For my part, in God's presence I protest, I know none; and if there be none, present none. It is that I desire; the charge is now given, may be given in vain.[116]

Seldom is Lancelot Andrewes so direct.

He assigns as the proper objects of almsgiving, first, the Church,"You must have a wing stretched abroad to cover it"; and secondly, the poor:

> You must have a bosom wide open to receive them. Lazarus in a rich man's bosom is a goodly sight in Heaven, and no less goodly in earth. And there shall never be a rich man with Lazarus in his bosom in heaven, unless he have had a Lazarus in his bosom here on earth.[117]

When we are able to do great good for others, we "would have doing good too good-cheap." The charges are great, doubtless, but doing good to the needy will "quit the charges," in the benefits it confers. Not only do the poor then profit in soul and body, and the commonwealth in recovering useful citizens, but God's blessings will descend upon the whole country in return for our favors bestowed on the poor.[118] One further idea from

---

[115] *Works*, V, Occasional Sermon I, 41.

[116] *Ibid.*

[117] *Works*, V, Occasional Sermon I, 43.

[118] *Works*, V, Occasional Sermon I, 43-44. Andrewes in this passage is speaking specifically of London and its people, but the ideas seem to be of broader application.

this sermon sums up neatly the intimate relation between religion and society as Andrewes conceived it. In helping the poor
and the needy, he points out, you are actually helping yourselves. God does not command us to works of charity so much
for the sake of those we aid as for our own. He does not need
us that the poor be fed; did He not once feed Elias by means
of the ravens, and could He not do so still? God could so have
created the world that for all men there would ever be sufficiency, but He did not so will.

> He ordered there should ever be "poor" in the "land." Why?
> To prove them, and to prove you by them; that He Which feedeth
> you might feed them by you, that your superfluities might be their
> necessaries; that they of their patience in wanting, and you of your
> liberality in supporting, might both together of Him That made you
> both receive reward. . . . We have need of them as they have need
> of us, yet that we make theirs remaineth ours still.[119]

Had Andrewes no word for the prosperous other than re-
minders of their obligations in charity, warnings against en-
tanglement in their riches, and threats of ready doom? In the
Catechism, which is nearly contemporary with the "Spital" sermon in origin, he writes under the Fifth Commandment that
our duty is

> 1. To place them with the elders in the gate, to prefer them that
> are wealthy; and the reason, because *nervus reipublicae argentum*,
> 'money is the sinew of the commonwealth;' there may come much
> benefit to the commonwealth by them. . . .
> 2. The second duty of the meaner sort towards these noble or
> wealthy men is, to account them their fathers, and themselves their
> sons . . . and to give them honour and reverence accordingly.[120]

---

[119] *Works*, V, Occasional Sermon I, 46-47.
[120] *Works*, VI, *Catechism*, 206-07. Each of us, he writes later in the *Catechism*,
must be content with his own estate (264). Andrewes had a hierarchic conception of society which was based partly on class, though in himself he had
a fair instance of the possibilities of raising oneself in status, and he acknowledged that honor is due men of excellent gifts (203 ff.).

In Lent of 1595 Andrewes preached at Richmond on the Gospel story of Dives and Lazarus, and undertook to assure the wealthy that, since Abraham, a rich man, was in heaven, "There is hope . . . for rich men in a rich man's bosom."[121] Dives, he said, did not go to hell because he was rich, but because he received his goods of God without remembering that he had received them, why he had, or on what condition. Dives received them as his sole alone and lived his earthly life as though there were no other life which he could gain only by helping others, by supplying others, who had little from God, from the abundance he had received for precisely that purpose.[122]

Bishop Andrewes had a lively sense of time, if that be the correct term to express the tremendous urgency which seems to have haunted him. With great frequency he devoted parts of his sermons to the time element in his subject matter: the fullness of time in the story of Christ's Nativity, the circumstance of time in the question of the morality of war, the appropriateness of certain times for fasting, and so forth.[123] No less than seven times does he refer to the words of the governor Felix, "when I find a convenient time" (Acts 24:25). "I like not his saying," Andrewes comments. "He that said it never found it; had it then, never found it after." When it came to religion, Bishop Andrewes was every bit an apostle of the "now."[124]

---

[121] *Works*, II, Lenten Sermon V, 78-97; quotation from 88.

[122] *Works*, II, Lenten Sermon II, 89-92.

[123] *Works*, I, Nativity Sermon IV, 45-63; *Works*, I, Ash Wednesday Sermon II, 321-37; *Works*, I, Ash Wednesday Sermons, *passim*.

[124] *Works*, I, Ash Wednesday Sermon VII, 431. Reference to the other occasions when this appeared may be found in the index in *Works*, XI, 377.

Andrewes'
Political Theory

Jewry, Bishop Andrewes explained to his audience of Easter, 1616, "was the scene or stage whereon the errors or virtues of all governments were represented to all posterity."[1] What more natural, then, than that he look to the Scriptures when the burden was upon him of speaking about government, or kingship, or the right by which monarchs reigned and ruled their people? The early seventeenth century, a "scriptural" age not only in matters which we would willingly call theological, tended generally to cast the net of Scripture very freely and thus drew almost every topic of debate within the province of theology; and that "queen of the sciences" stood for much more than a negative norm with which the conclusions of reason must check, or else be rejected; theology was a positive source in which ideas, theories, and arguments destined for application in the secular order were most earnestly sought and easily found. Toward the end of the century the increasing difficulty of constructing a watertight and probative argument from Scripture and the ease with which one text was used to drive out another led Filmer, for one, to argue from nature rather than from Scripture when he sought to establish the theory of divine-right

---

[1] *Works*, II, Easter Sermon VI, 273-74.

monarchy.[2] But Lancelot Andrewes was quite content with Scripture and, while not disdaining natural reason, argued his political theory as a theologian. He looked, then, to the scenes of Scripture, and beheld the virtues of divine-right monarchy— thus God instituted government and so should we acknowledge, honor, and preserve it.

Andrewes would never have called himself a political theorist, yet he devoted a relatively large number of his authentic sermons—some sixteen—to expounding the origins, the nature, and the sacredness of kingship as it existed in Jacobean England, and some four to government as such. He talked not as one seeking a change, but as defender of a *status quo* which was *de jure*, and what was more important in his mind, *de jure divino*. We shall approach his teaching on government and divine-right monarchy more or less chronologically. Some sermons will demand more attention than others which are repetitious in doctrinal content, but the repetitions, as they occur, will indicate the emphasis the bishop deemed necessary in a matter dear to him, and, as events were to prove, so significant in seventeenth-century England. The first three sermons on political thought, preached in 1590, 1591, and 1601, deal principally with government in general; in 1622 he composed, but did not preach, another on the general subject of government. Thus the long series on divine-right monarchy is practically bracketed within general observations on government, though in each instance divine-right monarchy is basic to his thought.[3]

---

[2] John Neville Figgis, *The Divine Right of Kings,* second edition (Cambridge, 1922), 148. In view of Andrewes' prominence in the Jacobean court it is difficult to understand why Figgis, J. W. Allen, Margaret Judson, and Godfrey Davies have failed to accord his political teaching more than occasional comment or have neglected it entirely in their studies of seventeenth-century English political theory.

[3] *Works,* II, Lenten Sermon I, 2-15 (1590); *Works,* II, Lenten Sermon II, 16-36 (1591); *Works,* V, Occasional Sermon VI, 127-40 (1601); *Works,* III, Pentecost Sermon XV, 377-401 (prepared, but not delivered, 1622).

The two controversial works, the *Tortura Torti* and the *Responsio ad Bellarminum*, along with the earlier *Catechism*, contain other statements of his political thought.

In the *Catechism* discussion of the Fifth Commandment Andrewes proposed a "compact" theory of the origin of government. To work out their salvation as God desires, he declares, men must live godly and honest lives. Hence they must be taught the knowledge of God; for this they must be free of "outward invasions" and of "inward tumults." If the fathers and mothers of families could have provided the necessary security and peace, there had been no need of any other government; but came Nimrod and his hounds (Genesis 10:8) to trouble men, so "God first allowed, and after instituted, that there should be" governors to protect us from evil men and government to resist foes from without and restrain strife within that men might live in "godliness and honesty."[4] Further on Andrewes explains again how there came to be magistrates. Authority, he says, first and principally pertains to God and comes afterward to man "by God's approbation and appointment."[5] He continues:

> The power ecclesiastical would have been sufficient to have governed the world, but that Cain building a city . . . made the godly first take order for their defence; and so city against city was the occasion of civil government, because some men . . . would

---

[4] *Works*, VI, *Catechism*, 175. Andrewes' teaching here resembles Hobbes' famous passage: "The finall Cause, End, or Designe of men, (who naturally love Liberty, and Dominion over others,) in the introduction of that restraint upon themselves, (in which wee see them live in Commonwealths,) is the foresight of their own preservation, and of a more contented live thereby; that is to say, of getting themselves out from that miserable condition of Warre, which is necessarily consequent . . . to the naturall Passions of men, when there is no visible Power to keep them in awe, and tye them by feare of punishment to the performance of their Covenants, and observation of those Lawes of Nature set down in the fourteenth and fifteenth Chapters" (Thomas Hobbes, *Leviathan*, Ernest Rhys, editor, 87).

[5] *Works*, VI, *Catechism*, 198.

still be offering violence and injury if there were not a power to bridle them.

Now seeing they must have government, the main reason why they would be under one man, and give *potestatem vitae et necis*, 'power of life and death,' to one particular, was, *praestat timere unum quam multos*, ' 'tis better to fear one than many;' better one wolf than a great many, and so a man's life to be continually in hazard of every man.

After the flood God gave the sword into man's hand . . . to shed the blood of him that should shed another man's blood; and then Sem, called Melchizedek king of Salem, took upon him to defend God's people from Nimrod and his fellow-hunters.[6]

Bishop Andrewes seems, therefore, to have taught originally that governments arose among men as the result of threatening circumstances which induced them to confer power on a leader, and that such a *regimen* was allowed and approved by God. Some twenty-five years later, however, he declares flatly that God is the cause institutive of both the world and of its government. Any idea that a king is "ex importunitate populi" he just as flatly rejects.[7] Beyond this change, he taught a fairly consistent theory of divine-right monarchy. Kingship was established by God; kings rule therefore by divine right; their persons are sacred; they may not be resisted; to them by that same divine right subjects owe allegiance and obedience; over kings God exercises a special protection.

Resting his argument upon the Old Testament from which he drew his text, "The earth and all the inhabitants thereof are dissolved: but I will establish the pillars of it" (Psalm 75:3), Andrewes opened his series of political sermons before Elizabeth at Whitehall in 1590.[8] Two pillars, two strengths there are which support the nation, the worship of God (religion) and

---

[6] *Works*, VI, *Catechism*, 198-99.
[7] *Works*, IV, Gunpowder Sermon V, 283-84. Macleane calls attention to this change in Andrewes' teaching (Macleane, *Andrewes and the Reaction*, 37).
[8] *Works*, II, Lenten Sermon I, 2-15.

the execution of justice or right. To the prince is committed the trust of bearing up each and of seeing to their care; without him there would be no " 'sheep of the pasture,' " only " 'sheep for the slaughter;' " " 'no people, but a rout;' no building, nor pillars, but a heap of stones."[9] In his governing the prince has for his model David, "skilful upholder of these two main pillars, which bear up and give strength to every land."[10] Andrewes insists once more on the essential importance of religion for the well-being of society in this sermon, for he makes it basic to government: "where Religion thrives not," he asserts, "the other of Justice will not hold long."[11]

The lenten sermon of the following year, 1591, assigns a sacred character to government. Another verse from the Psalms suggested the development: "Thou didst lead Thy people like sheep, by the hand of Moses and Aaron" (Psalm 77:20).[12] The "leading" of the text is a gift God bestowed upon His people—the gift of guidance and government. We are to see God in every government, for those who rule are "but hands under Him and unto Him," and He is " 'King over kings themselves,' " and ruler of all peoples.[13] He appoints all rulers, whether good or bad, wise or foolish, religious or otherwise; the Person and power of God are chief in every rule. The very great demands the task of ruling imposes upon governors, and the natural wildness or unwillingness in inferiors to brook the rule of anyone over them, argue the miraculous and supernatural character of government. Government is therefore in a sense divine and sacred.[14] Now, the chief end and "principal intendment" of government, that to which all its other functions

---

9 *Works*, II, Lenten Sermon I, 6-11.
10 *Works*, II, Lenten Sermon I, 15.
11 *Works*, II, Lenten Sermon I, 12; and see *supra*, 179.
12 *Works*, II, Lenten Sermon II, 16-36.
13 *Works*, II, Lenten Sermon II, 17-19.
14 *Works*, II, Lenten Sermon II, 20-21.

are subordinate, is to lead men to "the land of the living."[15] In succeeding paragraphs of real beauty Andrewes muses upon God's providential leadership of His people of England as He guides her counselors, judges, army, and even "our navy in the sea by unknown paths to the place it would go."[16] Though there is but one God and one guide, He did not keep the "estate of guiding" wholly to Himself, but chose to associate with Himself in the commission of leading His servants both Moses and Aaron—"to make *hominem homini deum*, 'one man a guide and god to another.' "[17] They rule by His authority, for they wear His name, sit in His seat, and bear His rod. Over these two God set another "power and authority regal, in place of the head, as Himself termeth it; and to it, as supreme, united regiment of both." Andrewes excuses himself from further comment upon this supreme power on the grounds that he is dealing here "only with the hands of regiments Ecclesiastical and Civil. Which . . . overspread and preserve every state."[18] Both hands are necessary; one needs the other. Moses and Aaron make a complete government: Aaron strengthens "mainly Moses' *debita legalia*, 'duties of Parliament and common law,' by his *debita moralia*, 'duties of conscience and divinity' "; Moses preserves Aaron's honor and right.[19]

Two years later Andrewes preached on the text from Matthew (22:21) concerning the rendering unto Caesar his due.[20] His exposition follows traditional lines, but the thesis states an important principle of his political theory. There is no conflict between God and Caesar, for Caesar is of God's ordaining, "be Tiberius what he will," he asserts, as he distinguishes between

---

[15] *Works*, II, Lenten Sermon II, 22.
[16] *Works*, II, Lenten Sermon II, 24-25.
[17] *Works*, II, Lenten Sermon II, 30.
[18] *Works*, II, Lenten Sermon II, 32.
[19] *Works*, II, Lenten Sermon II, 34-35.
[20] *Works*, V, Occasional Sermon VI, 127-40.

the office and the particular individual who may be holding it at a given time.[21] To God and to Caesar certain things are due of duty; to fail to render these is unrighteous and unjust. Since God is Lord over all, those things only which He committed to Caesar when He associated him with Himself in the government of mankind do we owe to Caesar. We owe him honor, inward and outward; we are not to speak evil of him; we owe him our prayers and the service of our bodies. Caesar rules over us with his sword and his scepter to protect us from foreign enemies and from injustice within the land. To the one we owe customs and tribute or tax; to the other the fees due his courts of justice, fines, and the right of confiscation—current and ordinary expenses all. For the extraordinary expenses of military preparedness we owe subsidies; and in all of these duties we are obliged in conscience.[22]

When Christian IV, king of Denmark and brother of James I's queen, visited England during the summer of 1606, Andrewes had the opportunity of preaching before two monarchs on August 5, which was the anniversary of the Gowry Conspiracy.[23] The following summary paragraph pulls together most of his ideas:

> But I may not keep you too long in the thesis; ye have seen, I suppose, already both why it should be just with God to give salvation unto Kings. 1. Because there is a wicked one who would destroy them. 2. Kings are in God's place. 3. God's honour is concerned in saving them. 4. In their safety the safety of many nations consists. You have also seen how God brings this to pass, by His word, and by His work. 1. He reveals it by His lightning. 2. He touches them, and turns their counsels into smoke. 3. The contrivers

---

[21] *Works*, V, Occasional Sermon VI, 132-33.

[22] *Works*, V, Occasional Sermon VI, 134-39.

[23] *Works*, V, Occasional Sermon XII, 235-56. The sermon was preached in Latin (see *Works*, IX, 53-74); we follow the English version. Its text came from the Psalms, "It is He that giveth salvation unto Kings, Who delivereth David His servant from the perilous . . . sword" (Psalm 144:10).

themselves, He shoots them through with His arrows. And thus He works salvation for Kings in the middle of 'the earth.[24]

More particularly, he continues, does God protect believing kings because they are His servants, and as such He governs them. In the event we commemorate today and in the Gunpowder incident we have splendid examples of how God saved His servant James from the sword and destruction.[25] Once again Andrewes asserts the dependence of religion upon the prince: here in England we have seen four princes successively altering religion and the people changing with them; he seems to regard each change on the part of the people a legitimate one, precisely because it was dictated by the prince.[26]

On September 28 of the same year Andrewes delivered another sermon with political implications before James at Hampton Court. In the Book of Numbers we read that God bade Moses make two trumpets of one whole piece of silver to be used for calling together the congregation and for removing the camp.[27] It is generally agreed, says Andrewes, that this passage records the original warrant for calling assemblies of God's people. It involves a twofold power, one respecting war, the other peace. Moses, and Moses alone, has the prerogative and the power of calling and dissolving assemblies concerning public affairs. An assembly of all estates in the body politic is an extraordinary event, but very necessary on occasion for consultation and for action in times respectively of peace and war. Since all more willingly submit to "that whereof all do agree," the making of laws is the chief business of an assembly in time

---

[24] *Works*, V, Occasional Sermon XII, 248.
[25] *Works*, V, Occasional Sermon XII, 252-54.
[26] *Works*, V, Occasional Sermon XII, 245.
[27] *Works*, V, Occasional Sermon VII, 141-68. Its text: "Then God spoke to Moses, saying, Make thee two trumpets of silver, of one whole piece shalt thou make them. And thou shalt have them . . . to assemble . . . the congregation, and to remove the camp" (Numbers 10:1-2).

of peace.[28] Assemblies have their use not only in civil matters, but in ecclesiastical as well, for the Church has her laws to make and her wars to fight. Power is executed *organice*, by an instrument, by the trumpet as our text indicates, and its sound is the sound of God—its authority, therefore, divine, he implies. The trumpets are of one piece to show that both assemblies (civil and ecclesiastical) are *"unius juris,* both 'of one and the same right.' "[29] Now, God gave this power to call assemblies directly to one individual "without first settling it in any body collective at all."[30] Though you would expect that Aaron, the priest, had the power to call religious assemblies, Moses received even this; he alone has the right and it is to pass on to those who hold his place. Moses was the chief magistrate and not a king, of course; but he held this power as a power regal, and the power of calling assemblies is universally held to belong to dominion.[31] Not only is it consonant with the law of God that the power of calling public assemblies belong to Moses and his successors, but it is entirely agreeable to the law of nature, which makes the head supreme over the body, and to the law of nations, which, by the light of reason, sets such power in the "chiefest person."[32] Andrewes devotes several pages of this sermon to a historical review of the exercise of the power by both Jewish and Christian rulers, and confesses that by 1180 (the date of the Council of the Lateran) the pope had taken unto himself

---

[28] *Works,* V, Occasional Sermon VII, 143-45. "This sermon was preached 'for the reduction of the two Melvilles, and other Presbyterian Scots, to a right understanding of the Church of England' " (*Works,* XI, lxiii; quotation from Wood's *Athenae Oxonienses*).

[29] *Works,* V, Occasional Sermon VII, 146-47.

[30] *Works,* V, Occasional Sermon VII, 148. Andrewes says immediately: "It is from our purpose to enter the question, whether the power were in the whole body originally? seeing though it were, it is now by the positive ordinance of God otherwise disposed" (148).

[31] *Works,* V, Occasional Sermon VII, 148-50.

[32] *Works,* V, Occasional Sermon VII, 153.

one of the two trumpets and left in the hands of the prince only one trumpet.

> [which] hath hitherto been holden a plain usurping, and an usurping (not upon the congregation, but) upon princes and their right, and that they in their own wrong suffered it to be wrung from them.[33]

What makes this action of the pope a usurpation? "Not to Aaron, but to Moses it was said, *Et erunt tibi*," he replies. "With some ado it was recovered not long since."[34] Thus, early in the reign of James, Andrewes justifies the power of the king in matters ecclesiastical. He does not bother to specify those powers any further, but remains content with a general declaration of the king's superiority.

On the anniversary of James's coronation, March 24, 1607, Andrewes preached again on the importance of kingship and its relation to religion—themes which could not but have been pleasing to James. He found a pertinent text in the Book of Judges: "In those days, there was no King in Israel, but every man did that which was good in his own eyes" (Judges 17:6). Because there was no king in the days to which this passage refers, he tells us, "religion first, and after it all went to wrack."[35] Terrible confusion reigned in Israel, especially in religion, for men fell into idolatry. When a king is set in place, religion will be free of idolatry, men's lives and goods will be in safety, and their vessels in honor, for a king is the most effectual bar to *"Fecit quisque quod rectum in oculis."*[36] Israel did not lack all government in those dark days; but because

---

[33] *Works*, V, Occasional Sermon VII, 163-66.
[34] *Works*, V, Occasional Sermon VII, 166. The reader will recognize this as the familiar argument for the Reformation in England. On the following page Andrewes notes that in his day Presbyterians and Congregationalists (he does not name the latter) are striving to take away the king's power over ecclesiastical assemblies.
[35] *Works*, V, Occasional Sermon VIII, 171.
[36] *Works*, V, Occasional Sermon VIII, 175-76.

kingship is the best of God's means for ordering society, He thereupon instituted kingship among them. Had there been a better, He would have established it. Kingship is the most perfect form of government—a multitude ruled by unity, all by one.[37] A king sees to it that everyone does not do what is good in his own eyes and evil in God's; he punishes evildoers; he will care for religion, and no one need wonder how important that is in our day when so many set up their own religion. This, indeed, is the "first and chief article in his charge."[38] Religion was the first cause that made God think of setting up kings. Andrewes concludes his "matter of instruction" by favoring hereditary kingship:

> It agreeth with His will there be not only Kings but a race of kings; that so soon as the breath is gone from one, instantly it may be rested in another.

For thus will the evils of *interregna* be avoided.[39]

May we pray for evil to befall a person? asks Andrewes in the first of the Gowry Conspiracy sermons.[40] Not only may we do so, as Scripture clearly reveals, he replies, but sometimes we are even obliged to do so, for to pray for the king's safety, which we must do, is to pray also against those who would undermine him.[41] Underminers of the king may be divided into international enemies (other states) and inferiors (traitors). Kings must suffer both as did David, as Christ and God Himself do; but at the moment James has no international enemies. Of the second class of enemies, those who think, speak, and act against the king—all of which are forbidden—there are two kinds: those who rise against kingship and its authority and

---

[37] *Works*, V, Occasional Sermon VIII, 175-77.
[38] *Works*, V, Occasional Sermon VIII, 178-80.
[39] *Works*, V, Occasional Sermon VIII, 182.
[40] *Works*, IV, Gowry Sermon I, 3-23.
[41] *Works*, IV, Gowry Sermon I, 7-9.

those who rise against the person of the king. Of the first class are the Anabaptists, who deny all secular jurisdiction, and those who seek to bring parity into the Church. These latter want no dependence, no superiority, no subordination; and though they gloss it over, they want the commonwealth fitted to the Church. We shall soon hear them say Moses must not exalt himself above the congregation, for all God's people are holy no less than he! "Risers" against the person of the king, on the other hand, are the ambitious, and the seekers of revenge like the two brothers Gowry.[42]

These, then, we are to curse as enemies of God. Kings are by God, of or from God, for or instead of God; they sit in His place and represent His Person. So close is the knot between God and king that whosoever resists the king, resists God also. Further, "risers" against kings are enemies of mankind, for rulers are appointed for man's good. Without them the strong would devour the weak; hence the safety of the kingdom is fast linked with the health and safety of the king. Again, the king is "nutritius Ecclesiae," and enemies of the nurse are enemies of the child. Destroy the Church, which is the apple of God's eye, and the whole world is brought to dissolution. "Risers" against the kings give offense therefore against God, the state, and the Church—truly it is permissible for us to pray against such as these.[43]

On the same anniversary a year later, 1608, Bishop Andrewes discussed the inviolability of kings. "Who can lay his hand on the Lord's anointed, and be guiltless?" (1 Samuel 26:8-9). Saul had been persecuting David, he relates, had given David ample reason for wanting to retaliate; yet when David came upon the sleeping king, had him completely at his mercy, he stayed his hand and did not lift it against the Lord's

---

[42] *Works*, IV, Gowry Sermon I, 9-12.
[43] *Works*, IV, Gowry Sermon I, 13-17.

anointed.[44] And he went to the sanctuary for his middle term, explains the bishop; it was not *Dominus Rex,* but *christus Domini,* that carried weight with him. Any violation or touching of the Lord's anointed is a sacrilege.[45] This charge of David's, "Quis erit insons?" is a "triumphant negative," for none can rise up against it; it allows no exception. No one can violate the Lord's anointed and be guiltless. Nor does it apply only to cases of private vengeance. Some today tell us that misgovernment— tyranny they call it—usurpation of ecclesiastical power, bloody persecution, are not excluded by this charge as just grounds for attacking a king; but they are wrong. As a matter of fact, says Andrewes, I think God let all these faults appear in Saul, His first king, all the faults that would ever appear in any king after him, precisely to enforce a king's position, for thus we received our answer at the very beginning—"Ne perdas."[46] In applying this story to the Gowry, Andrewes found himself in the difficulty of having James parallel Saul, about whom he had said many fierce things (for example, that Saul was possessed by an evil spirit) in order to make his point of absolute inviolability. Out of this delicious embarrassment he very neatly escaped by bravely calling James greater than Saul, ruler of a larger kingdom, and "better without all comparison!"[47] James must have grinned!

In the third Gowry sermon, delivered at Holdenby in 1610, Andrewes resumed his thesis respecting the sacredness and inviolability of kings. His claims were exorbitant. The argument derives principally from a brief text in Chronicles: "Touch not mine anointed" (1 Chronicles 16:22).[48] This commandment, he contends, was in force long before Moses in the

[44] *Works*, IV, Gowry Sermon II, 24-42.
[45] *Works*, IV, Gowry Sermon II, 32.
[46] *Works*, IV, Gowry Sermon II, 35-38.
[47] *Works*, IV, Gowry Sermon II, 41, and see also 38.
[48] *Works*, IV, Gowry Sermon III, 43-75.

time of the patriarchs under the law of nature; and it is the greatest commandment,

> not only because it is of the greatest in Heaven, and concerning the greatest in earth, but for that it is the original main precept touching Princes and their safety, or as the phrase is, the fundamental law, upon the which all the rest are grounded, unto the which all the rest reduced, and from the which all the rest derived.[49]

The "anointed" of the text were the patriarchs, who had fatherhood and government, whom kings have succeeded, so that *jus regium* comes out of *jus patrium*. Our opponents quite incorrectly try to apply the term *christi Domini* to the pope, cardinals, and so forth, for of all persons who are anointed only kings, after the patriarchs, are called *christi Domini*.[50]

Three claims are made upon kings; one by the pope, one in the name of the "people," and one by God.[51] The pope bases his claim over rulers on the ceremony of anointing: as master of the ceremony he wants to be master also of the substance; but rulers were God's anointed long before the ceremony was instituted in the time of Moses. The anointing merely declares what is a fact antecedent to and independent of the ceremony—no *christi pontificis*, then, says Andrewes.[52] Cardinal Bellarmine speaks as though rulers were *christi populi*, as though they held power of the people. He

> waxeth very earnest for it;—I think, because he seeth the Pope's arm groweth short, and loath he is but there should be still some hands to touch them;—he will not so much as give God leave to appoint Saul or David of Himself, but he taketh upon him to suspend them both, until the people with their suffrage come in, and ratify God's doing.[53]

---

[49] *Works*, IV, Gowry Sermon III, 45.
[50] *Works*, IV, Gowry Sermon III, 47-50.
[51] *Works*, IV, Gowry Sermon III, 51-53.
[52] *Works*, IV, Gowry Sermon III, 51-52.
[53] *Works*, IV, Gowry Sermon III, 52.

But this falls to the ground, because God says "meos." By God, as Irenaeus tells us, kings are born men and by His appointment alone they are made princes. And very exalted is their anointing, for kings partake of " 'such a chrism as wherewith Christ is anointed.' "[54]

Andrewes next addresses himself to the problems of rebellion and the deposition of monarchs. Some fancy that God's anointed may "forfeit their tenure," cease to be *christi Domini,* and that then "who that will may touch them." But they are entirely wrong. They suppose anointing implies some grace, *gratia gratum faciens,* which makes rulers religious and good Catholics, or some *gratia gratis data,* which makes them able or apt to govern; that if he will not hear a Mass, a ruler is therefore no Catholic and no anointed; that if after anointing he grows defective, proves to be a tyrant, or favors heretics, his anointing may be wiped or scraped off; that then you may write a book *De justâ abdicatione,* or make a holy league, touch him, or blow him up as you will.[55] At this point in his sermon the bishop makes an assertion which is critical in his theory: that the royal anointing is not religion, nor virtue, nor any spiritual grace, otherwise there would be "now no kings, but those that be Christians."[56]

> *Unxit in Regem,* Royal unction gives no grace, but a just title only, *in Regem,* 'to be King;' that is all, and no more. It is the administration to govern, not the gift to govern well; the right of ruling, not the ruling right. It includes nothing but a due title, it excludes nothing but usurpation. Who is "anointed?" On whom the right rests. Who is *inunctus?* He that hath it not. . . . David, or

---

[54] *Works,* IV, Gowry Sermon III, 53, 56.

[55] *Works,* IV, Gowry Sermon III, 56-57. The book referred to seems to be Jean Boucher's *De justâ abdicatione Henrici Tertii, 1589.* The "league" may refer to the alleged Papal League of 1580. See Pollen, *English Catholics in the Reign of Queen Elizabeth,* 233-43.

[56] *Works,* IV, Gowry Sermon III, 57.

he that first beginneth a royal race, is as the head; on him is that right of ruling first shed; from him it runs down to the next, and so still, even to the lowest borders of his lawful issue. . . . It is for ever. God's claim never forfeits; His character never to be wiped out or scraped out, nor Kings lose their right, no more than Patriarchs did their fatherhood.[57]

Allegiance, he continues, is not due the king because "he is virtuous, religious, or wise, but because he is *christus Domini*."[58] Kings, therefore, are not to be touched to their hurt; neither knife, nor pistol, nor poison, nor a virulent tongue may be used against them. Nor may their crown and dignity be touched: "If their state hold not holy, no more will their persons. It hath ever been found, if their crown once go, their life tarrieth not long after."[59] "Nolite tangere" is a universal prohibition binding both people and countries, "neither subject, nor alien, nor enemy, nor King, nor people; nor one religion, nor other; nor one, nor many," may even will to touch God's anointed.[60]

Three years later Bishop Andrewes turned again to the problem of the source of royal authority.[61] He called the words of his text, "By Me Kings reign" (Proverbs 8:15), the royal charter of kings, for on these four words, he contended, all kings and kingdoms of the earth depend. "Per Me" kings were first settled in their reigns and have ever since been upheld. "Me" indicates a personal causality; neither stars, nor pope, nor high priest, nor body collective, nor kings themselves are the cause of kings' reigning; the sole cause is a divine Person, the Son of God, the Wisdom of God, who became man, and upon whom God conferred all kingdoms on earth. Royal authority, therefore, derives from God the Father through God

---

[57] *Works*, IV, Gowry Sermon III, 58.
[58] *Works*, IV, Gowry Sermon III, 58-59.
[59] *Works*, IV, Gowry Sermon III, 61.
[60] *Works*, IV, Gowry Sermon III, 64.
[61] *Works*, IV, Gunpowder Sermon V, 277-95.

the Son. Since there is no permissive sense attached to this "per," kings are not *ex importunitate populi;* "per Me" expresses the cause institutive of the world and of the government of the world. By Christ's will, expressed in His words and deeds, kings are given, sent, placed on their thrones, vested with their robes, girt with their swords, anointed, and crowned. All things, especially good things, come from God, and kings be good things.[62]

Kings are "by" God without reference to their religion—all kings, even tyrants; and God alone can unmake them. Usurpers may reign, of course, but they are not kings; on the other hand, some true kings, driven from their thrones, have not reigned; it is one thing indeed to be a king, and another to reign. "Per Me" each *(de jure)* king begins to reign, and the ruling power remains with his heirs. Kings are not irresponsible, for they are answerable to God in that they should rule rightly, "per Me"—that is, according to wisdom. Both people and kings must take note of this text, then. If princes weigh it well, they will rule better; if people reflect upon it, they will obey the sooner, for both the power of sovereignty and the duty of allegiance derive from God, and he who attacks a king, attacks God Himself.[63]

The Gowry sermon of 1614 adds nothing to the doctrinal position Andrewes has thus far expounded, but one proposition therein shows us how utterly he depended on Scripture for arguments to support his teaching. In his mind David was the great type of all kings; what the Scriptures say of him, therefore, may be applied to all kings:

> King David, he is in Scriptures, not *persona Regis* only, 'the person of a King,' but *persona Regum,* 'a person representing all Kings' to come after him; such specially as, with David, serve and

---

[62] *Works,* IV, Gunpowder Sermon V, 278-85.
[63] *Works,* IV, Gunpowder Sermon V, 285-93.

worship God in truth. We do safely therefore, what is said to him, apply to them all, since he is the type of them all.[64]

The Gunpowder sermon of the same year was linked with the previous one of the series when Andrewes declared in his exordium that he had shown in the one how "per Me" kings reign, and explained that he was presently carrying the idea further to show that "per Me" seditious persons come to ruin and destruction.[65] His text was very suitable: "My son, fear thou the Lord, and the king; and meddle not with them that are given to change. For their destruction shall rise suddenly, etc." (Proverbs 24:21-23). Andrewes explains Solomon's words:

> To have regal duties rightly settled, he goes up as high as God, begins with *Time Deum*, the fear of God. And thither we must if we shall go soundly to work. It is not the common law, or any act of parliament, that breeds *Time Regem* kindly. If our fear to the King be taught us by the law of man, it is not yet upon his true base, his right corner-stone. To divinity we must, to this book, the book of the fear of God; if it be right, ground it there. And if that might take place, there should need no law else to sustain or preserve Kings or states.
>
> Set this down then for a rule, that there is no surer friend, no surer stay to Kings and their rights, than *Time Deum*, that is, true religion. And set down this with it, that it is a sure sign of a good religion if it will join with *Time Regem*, the duty to the prince, well. For if it be a true *Time Deum*, it strengthens *Time Regem*, it weakens it not.
>
> And on the other, that it is an infallible note of a bad one, if either it shoulder the King from God, or shrink up the sinews of civil obedience.[66]

"Time Deum," and you are a good Christian; "Time regem," and you are a good subject. But the Catholics have turned "Time regem" into "Time, Rex," and they try to get us

---

[64] *Works*, IV, Gowry Sermon IV, 76-100; quotation from 77.
[65] *Works*, IV, Gunpowder Sermon VI, 296-317; 296.
[66] *Works*, IV, Gunpowder Sermon VI, 302-03.

to change our religion for one "wherein for your comfort you shall not understand a word, not you of the people, what you either sing or pray; and for variety, you shall change a whole communion for a half"; while others advise us: "You shall change for a fine new Church-government: a presbytery would do much better for you than a hierarchy; and, perhaps, not long after, a government of states than a monarchy."[67] Whether or not Andrewes really feared at so early a date (1614) that such would actually come to pass, he seems to have read the logic of events in England very shrewdly. In the Gowry sermon of 1615, for example, he boldly asserted that he who takes away the king's crown will not long after have also his life.[68] The thesis of this particular sermon is that to God alone belongs the power of instituting kings and the destruction thereof, but Andrewes carefully avoids specifying how or in what circumstances God might choose to do away with one.[69]

Apparently Andrewes felt that the common law had evolved to such importance in men's minds that he must appeal to it also in support of the king. Though he had very recently said that "It is not the common law, or any act of parliament, that breeds *Time Regem* kindly,"[70] in a Gowry sermon of 1616 he turned to the common law to underline the heinousness of attempts against a prince.[71] The appeal aborts, for throughout the common law is swallowed in divinity, and what might have proved a more interesting sermon falls back into a familiar pattern. From the Book of Esther (2:21-23) he relates the story of a frustrated plot against King Ahasuerus. Mordecai had overheard the plotters, Bigthan and Teresh, turned them in, and they promptly suffered condign punishment. We are in-

---

67 *Works*, IV, Gunpowder Sermon VI, 303-06.
68 *Works*, IV, Gowry Sermon V, 101-25; 113.
69 *Works*, IV, Gowry Sermon V, 115.
70 *Works*, IV, Gunpowder Sermon VI, 302; see *supra*, 202.
71 *Works*, IV, Gowry Sermon VI, 126-52.

formed, however, that the law by which the plotters suffered derived from the Persians (inscribed at the king's dictation), was enrolled in Esther at God's direction, and thus was made the law of God; that therefore it was the law of Jews and Gentiles, of man and God, an old law, a written law, and not a law "of Edward the Third then, *et a principio non fuit sic.*"[72] We may quite properly call in the Bible to justify the justice, or to strengthen the law, of the land; *facultas juris* and *facultas theologiae* should mutually support each other. Until a more ancient is found, this in Esther is the oldest "roll" we can adduce to show that plotting against a king is treason by both law and divinity. "Well we may talk of law, the law of the land; but when all is done, never do men rest with that quiet and full contentment as when they see it is warrantable by the word of God."[73] But, he says later,

> What care men for sin, if there be no action at the common law for it? None but Westminster-hall sins do men care for. God saw it would come to this, men learn no more duty than penal statutes did teach them; He took order therefore to bring it within them too.

Plotting against the king "will bear not an action only, but an indictment of life and death."[74] The remainder of the sermon is devoted to the inviolability of kings. It belongs to royal prerogative that mere plotting against a monarch involve the penalty of death; in no other case is it so. Furthermore, no seal of confession justifies withholding information regarding a projected plot, and in no case whatsoever is it lawful to lay hands upon the king.[75] Andrewes had merely nodded toward the common law.

---

[72] *Works*, IV, Gowry Sermon VI, 128; a reference to the Statute of Treasons, 1352.
[73] *Works*, IV, Gowry Sermon VI, 128.
[74] *Works*, IV, Gowry Sermon VI, 131.
[75] *Works*, IV, Gowry Sermon VI, 132-41.

The sermons of this latter part of the bishop's life betray with far greater frequency than his earlier efforts those faults of style for which he has been justly criticized. Whether he had run out of inspiration, had been caught in the web of his own "metaphysical" conceits, or had begun to suffer the disabilities of old age, his sermons from about this time (1616) generally make frightful reading. The Gunpowder sermon of this year, for instance, contains a fantastic development of the text: "The children are come to the birth, and there is not strength to bring forth" (Isaias 37:3).[76] The miscarriage is compared to the preparation of the Gunpowder Plot up to the very last moment before the discovery. God did not give strength for this birth, and so saved us, Andrewes comments![77] The prime purpose of this sermon, however, seems to have been to attack Bellarmine. The bishop charged him with teaching a doctrine which implied that neither allegiance, conscience, Christian duty, nor respect, but only the lack of strength to resist, restrained the saints and martyrs of the early Church: "Id fuit, quia deerant vires." But that is false, retorts Andrewes, else the Christian Roman army would have overthrown Julian the Apostate or Valens the Arian.[78] In a confused way he had touched a critical point, for the bull of excommunication issued against Elizabeth spoke of releasing Catholics from allegiance to her; it was later mitigated so that withdrawal of obedience was made dependent upon ability to effect the provisions of the bull.[79] Just why Andrewes failed to detail here this important point, where the parallel is so obvious, is a little difficult to understand. All that he says is simply:

---

[76] *Works*, IV, Gunpowder Sermon VIII, 341-60.
[77] *Works*, IV, Gunpowder Sermon VIII, 351.
[78] *Works*, IV, Gunpowder Sermon VIII, 354-55.
[79] For the mitigation of the bull of excommunication see Ludwig von Pastor, *The History of the Popes from the Close of the Middle Ages*, Ralph Francis Kerr, editor (London, 1930), XIX, 389-90.

You cannot but remember a clause not long since printed, and so as it were a child but lately born, a cardinal's child it is, I mean the tenet late taken up at Rome:—that all is now to go, all Christianity to stand or fall, by *Sunt,* or *Non sunt vires.*[80]

The Gunpowder sermon of 1618 argues that from Scripture "there is, in the regal power of all, yea even of heathen Princes, [authority] to confirm and to enjoin what may tend to the worship and service of God."[81] Kings, the bishop adds immediately, are responsible to God for the exercise of this power, though two "accordings" are requisite for every law: a law must be enjoined by the king, and it must be accepted by the people for observance;

Which observing is the life of every law; even the public approbation, or giving allowance of it, by the constant keeping it. The second "according" is added for the people's commendation; that what was prudently advised, and lawfully enjoined, was by them as dutifully observed.[82]

Andrewes preached before the king and lords at the opening of the fateful parliament of 1621 on a text which offered good possibilities for the occasion: "God standeth in the congregation of Princes. . . . In the midst will He judge the gods" (Psalm 82:1).[83] "Gods," he tells his audience, is a title of honor bestowed upon those in authority whom we must therefore respect. Among them are various grades; one is "supereminent above the rest, and the rest *ab eo missi* have their mission and commission from him. Many superiors, but one sovereign."[84] As

---

[80] *Works,* IV, Gunpowder Sermon VIII, 354.

[81] *Works,* IV, Gunpowder Sermon X, 385-405; quotation from 402. Andrewes mentions the establishing of feasts, laws against blasphemy (involving the death penalty), and the building of churches. In the *Tortura Torti* he denies that infidel princes have any primacy *(primatum)* in spiritual matters (*Works,* VII, *Tortura Torti,* 463).

[82] *Works,* IV, Gunpowder Sermon X, 403.

[83] *Works,* V, Occasional Sermon X, 203-22.

[84] *Works,* V, Occasional Sermon X, 205-06.

"gods" you in authority have a duty to be good and to prosecute the welfare of this assembly, which is the good of all. As God's lieutenant the king has received power to call you together in an assembly where God Himself stands in your midst. Since the cause of such a meeting is God's high pleasure, the public weal, its proper work is the making of laws—God's work, indeed. He has imparted to you His name and "His power and made you a congregation of lawgivers and of gods, both at once." You are the highest power on earth save one—"Next to the 'sceptre' in Judah's hand is the 'lawgiver between his feet.' "[85] God exercises two functions in and upon this congregation: He stands here to keep you "mortal gods" in your place and He judges your works, for you are herein responsible to Him. Parliament's duty is to believe Him present, to behave in a manner reflecting your belief in His presence, and in peace and concord, plain dealing, and not in cunning, without regard for any person, and with good cheer, to procure such results as will please Him.[86] Here, once more, Andrewes impresses upon us his key principle respecting the management of society: let religion guide us, king, parliament, and all, in the government of the nation.

The Whitsunday sermon prepared for 1622, but not delivered, was not a happy effort.[87] Uninspired, shot with play upon words, it rather unsuccessfully attempts to relate the trinity of gift (ability), calling, and work to the Blessed Trinity, from the three Persons of which each derives: ability from the Holy Spirit, appointments to office from the Son, who is wisdom and the source of order, and exercise of the office and of the abilities from the Father to whom we attribute power. The preserving of these three aright makes for well-ordered society,

---

[85] *Works*, V, Occasional Sermon X, 207-10.
[86] *Works*, V, Occasional Sermon X, 212-20.
[87] *Works*, III, Pentecost Sermon XV, 377-401.

government, and Church.[88] Our duty requires "everyone to find himself with a gift, in a calling, about a work. Not having the gift, not to affect to enter the calling; nor having the calling, not to venture upon the work."[89] Christ appoints everyone to his calling as teacher, helper, or governor; all are to be ministers either of the Church or of the state and commonwealth—each according to his gift.[90] Threaded through the strained confusion of this piece as a theme is Andrewes' sense of the necessity for order and authority in society.

The Gowry sermon of 1622 repeats in slightly different dress the bishop's thesis of the inviolability of kings. David, once again having Saul at his mercy, merely cuts the lap of the king's garment, quickly repents of his act as an offense, and prays God not to let him touch the Lord's anointed. From this example we are to learn, kings their danger, and subjects their duty.[91] The last of the political sermons, prepared for 1623, argues against regicide but does not advance Andrewes' general doctrine.

In all his long preaching on divine-right monarchy Andrewes merely asserted and attempted to prove the king's authority in religion; he never fully stated in what features of religious life the power was to be exercised. Perhaps, as was often the case in his sermons, he deliberately elected not to be specific. That he had definite convictions, however, he showed clearly in the *Tortura Torti* and the *Responsio ad Bellarminum;* controversy smoked him out into the open. As Macleane points out, Andrewes did not proclaim a "regal papacy"; we do not contend, he wrote in the *Responsio ad Bellarminum,* that the king is supreme head the way you Catholics claim supremacy for the

---

[88] *Works,* III, Pentecost Sermon XV, 379-81.
[89] *Works,* III, Pentecost Sermon XV, 383.
[90] *Works,* III, Pentecost Sermon XV, 386-89.
[91] *Works,* IV, Gowry Sermon VII, 153-82. The scriptural incident is related in 1 Samuel 24:5-8.

pope; the king was not "transubstantiated" into a pope: "quod vos Papae, Regi non tribuimus"; nor is the primacy of the king de fide.[92] James was not defending a new article in defending "summa Regis ad Ecclesiasticas res [potestas]"; Henry VIII was not its author, for Moses had the power over Aaron.[93] Together with this declaration of royal authority over the Church, another from the sermons summarizes Andrewes' basic contention in this matter. The Easter sermon of March 24, 1611, discoursed upon the text, "The Stone Which the builders refused, the same Stone is become . . . the Head of the corner" (Psalm 118:22). Andrewes proclaims the union of civil and ecclesiastical authority in the king; God has severed the two estates, civil and ecclesiastical which make the "main angle in every government," and has made

> these two but to meet in one; not one to malign and consume the other. And the happy combining of these two is the strength of the head, and the strength of the whole building. If it bear but upon one of them, it will certainly decay. It did so in Saul's time: he little regarded the Ark, and less the Priests. David saw Saul's error, and in his Psalm, where he singeth *Ne perdas* to a commonwealth [Psalm 75:3], promiseth to have equal care of both pillars, and to uphold them both.
>
> The first Book of Chronicles is sufficient to prove and persuade any, he dealt in both as chief over both. Not by right of priesthood, for none he had; and that of his prophecy is as cold.[94]

In the *Tortura Torti* Andrewes specified that the king's primacy gave him no power to establish new articles or to perform sacred and sacerdotal functions, but that it did give him the right to handle matters of external policy. By royal authority he may make laws respecting blasphemy, fasting, feast days;

---

92 Macleane, *Andrewes and the Reaction*, 224; *Works*, VIII, *Responsio ad Bellarminum*, 36, 38.

93 *Works*, VIII, *Responsio ad Bellarminum*, 26-27.

94 *Works*, II, Easter Sermon VI, 270-89; quotation from 283-84.

and may do whatever Constantine, Theodosius, Justinian, and Charlemagne did before him regarding religion. Judges may be delegated to judge by these laws; subjects may be bound by oath to observe them. Royal authority is to take notice of violations, such as crimes of pseudo prophecy, idolatry, blasphemy, pollution of sacred things; the king may call assemblies to lead people back to the worship of God, to deal with dedicating, rebuilding, or purifying churches. When making laws touching things of this nature, however, the king should consult persons learned and skilled in them. He has the right to declare law *(jus dicendi)* for all people of all orders, for he is king no less of the clergy than of the laity. By his authority he may abolish an alien *cultus*, and may determine matters relative to the appointments of churches. He may suppress futile and useless disputations which are wont to lead to schism.[95] Andrewes had made himself abundantly clear! Bishop Frere has nicely concentrated this teaching, which was not peculiar to Andrewes of course, in a brief passage:

> According to the theory which then held the field, the king, being the person in whom the ecclesiastical and temporal jurisdictions were united, could order the performance of spiritual acts though he could not himself perform them: he could punish an offender just as he could appoint a bishop, by ordering excommunication in the one case and consecration in the other.[96]

In the numerous preceding summaries the reader will have noticed how consistently Bishop Andrewes rejects any right of rebellion against the king, for the sermons contain an unqualified doctrine of nonresistance. In the two or three pages of the *Catechism* devoted to the problem of the obedience due wicked

---

[95] *Works*, VII, *Tortura Torti*, 466-69.
[96] Frere, *The English Church in the Reigns of Elizabeth and James I.*, 354. Andrewes' teaching as outlined above may be compared with Frere's summary of Elizabeth's *Declaration of the Queen's Proceedings since Her Reign, ibid.*, 146-47.

superiors he declares that even they are to be honored. In this
the honor is done not to the man, he explains, but to God
Himself out of reverence for His ordinance of obedience to
superiors. We owe none but God absolute obedience, and therefore need obey kings only insofar as their commandments are
not repugnant to God's. However, if it is in our power, we
should obey in things doubtful; and even in the case of an
unjust command, if it is not directly contrary to God's will,
"there may be just obedience unto it."[97]

Between Richard Hooker and Thomas Hobbes there were
few outstanding writers on political theory in England, but a
flood of political preaching poured from the pulpits of the land.
Against the pressure of the Puritans, or of a parliamentarian
like Sir Edward Coke, Andrewes raised his voice in defense of
a "high" doctrine of the origin, rights, and inviolability of
kings. Though in moments of stress his actions, and occasionally
in more neutral circumstances (as in the perorations of the
Gowry and Gunpowder sermons), his words outran the limits
of an "obsequium rationabile," he did have the courage to
confess that "we beneath are too ready . . . to deify those that
are on high, and give that belongs to 'God on high' to gods
below"; and in the *Preces Privatae* he humbly prayed to be
delivered "[ab] Apotheosi principum."[98]

---

[97] *Works*, VI, *Catechism*, 182-84.
[98] *Works*, I, Nativity Sermon XIII, 226; *Works*, X, *Preces Privatae*, 205. The index
in *Works*, XI, offers an excellent breakdown of Bishop Andrewes' teaching on
kingship, 431-32.

CHAPTER IX

Conclusion

Beyond his broad and frequent use of Holy Scripture, beyond his appeal to the fathers, the scholastics, ecclesiastical history, and the light of natural reason, there is little to remark in Bishop Andrewes' theological methodology. Like so much of early seventeenth-century scholarship, his learning was broader than it was deep, more extensive than precise; and when he assembled it for controversy it tended to overwhelm rather than to penetrate an opponent's defenses. In general, he preferred to assert, to explain, and to illustrate his theological positions through the techniques and tools of rhetoric (of which he controlled not a few) for purposes of devotion. Far less readily did he undertake formal argumentative proof of particular doctrines or religious practices. When he did, however, he showed a sound sense of the value and necessity of a critical approach to his material. For example, in a sermon delivered in 1618 he carefully elaborates a formal defense of the custom of keeping Easter as a great Christian feast.[1] His detailed study of custom, his definition of its limits, his clear separation of the essential from the incidental in determining its authenticity and in establishing its binding power; his inference from a prohibition ("non habemus talem") to the existence of the opposite practice,

---

[1] *Works*, II, Easter Sermon XIII, 404-28.

his attention to matters of fact, his appeal not only to direct statements of his authorities, but also to hymns and to liturgical practices relating to the custom which is his main concern; his rejection of favorable testimony of doubtful authenticity, and finally, his careful qualification of witnesses—all these, particularly in a man who generally tended to rely heavily on authority, mark Bishop Andrewes as a writer who knew the importance of a critical methodology. One leaves a reading of this sermon with confidence in the intellectual integrity of its author.

Andrewes once said that there was no call for the intricate weaving of argument and dispute. Consequently, he shied away from that "false conceit" which had

> crept into the minds of men, to think the points of religion that be manifest to be certain petty points, scarce worth the hearing. Those —yea those be great, and none but those, that have great disputes about them. It is not so. . . . Those that are necessary He hath made plain; those that [are] not plain not necessary.[2]

This observation admits of, but scarcely justifies, a fundamentalist interpretation. Andrewes did not consciously teach a fundamentalism such as may be found in Falkland, Chillingworth, Hales, or Jeremy Taylor.[3] While the circumstances which evoked such teaching were operative during his lifetime, intolerance, bitter recrimination, and the violent persecution of "unorthodox" or divergent religious views, Andrewes never proposed to himself—or better, perhaps, never publicly suggested—compromise in doctrine as the solution to the religious

---

[2] *Works*, I, Nativity Sermon III, 35. Dr. Wilbur K. Jordan sees in this passage a contribution to the development of toleration. He feels that the contribution of the Anglican divines toward toleration consisted in their attempts to define the fundamentals of faith. See W. K. Jordan, *The Development of Religious Toleration in England from the Accession of James I to the Convention of the Long Parliament (1603-1640)* (Cambridge, Massachusetts, 1936), 148, 147.

[3] See Tulloch, *Rational Theology and Christian Philosophy*, I, *passim*.

dissension which tore so devastatingly at European unity and peace. Fundamentalism was but a step on the road to rationalism, and Andrewes was not a rationalist. Yet here and there in his writings one comes across statements, which, if taken together (as they were probably never intended to be taken), or pushed to strictly logical conclusions, would inevitably issue into rationalism. They must be set, therefore, against his more usual practice of depending on revelation and of relegating reason to a subordinate but by no means negligible role in the explanation and defense of religious truth. Thus the quotation given above, or his more startling proclamation that "experimental knowledge is the true *comperi in veritate* when all is done,"[4] must be read in the full context of his thought or in the light of so firm and uncompromising a declaration as this:

> There is no star or beam of it; there is no truth at all in human learning or philosophy that thwarteth any truth in Divinity, but sorteth well with it and serveth it, and all to honour Him who saith of Himself *Ego sum Veritas*, "I am the Truth." None that will hinder this *venerunt* [the coming of the Wise Men], keep back any wise man, or make him less fit for coming to Christ.[5]

Indeed, in the *Catechism* he declares that reason is the worst way to try to come to God.[6]

John Hunt contends that in appealing to the Scriptures the English Church was essentially appealing to reason, and that from the Protestant principle which made the Scriptures the rule of faith rationalism developed. While it would be extremely difficult to prove that the early English reformers intended by their appeal to Scripture actually to appeal to reason, it is undoubtedly true that the rejection of the old Church as the interpreter of Scripture did lead ultimately to rationalism,

---

[4] *Works*, III, Pentecost Sermon XII, 330.
[5] *Works*, I, Nativity Sermon XIV, 245.
[6] *Works*, VI, *Catechism*, 19.

and precisely for the reason which Hunt assigns; namely, the necessity of finally settling on some norm for interpretation.[7] Andrewes was not unaware of the difficulty. While he remained loyal to the English Reformation, he was of that second generation of English reformers who were far enough removed from the heat and confusion of the early days of the Establishment, as were both Hooker and Laud, to claim for the new Church nearly the whole Catholic heritage of the past. In recognizing the defects and needs of the English Church and in broadening their conception of the Church, they dared to retain far more of the structure, liturgy, and doctrine of ancient Catholicism than did their predecessors or the continental reformers. Nor did they scruple to say that the new Church was the old historic Church purified, or to admit that the Roman Church was still the Church of Christ, though stained and fouled with accretions and innovations.[8] Consequently they appealed with confidence, especially in Andrewes' case, to the fathers and the Church, and not to reason alone (and that is reductively private interpretation) for the interpretation of the Scriptures, which, after all, in the early seventeenth century were still acknowledged as revealed and divine in their authorship. Andrewes, then, was neither a rationalist, nor rationalistic in his theology; nor, on the other hand, was he so authoritarian as to deny reason a place, for he recognized the legitimacy of theological reasoning, and in this respect remained orthodox in the traditional Catholic sense.

Though traditional and Catholic inclinations are everywhere manifest in Bishop Andrewes' thought, its distinctive characteristics were not, obviously could not be, Roman Catholic. Neither were they Calvinist; but in one important respect, his doctrine on justification, they have a definite Lutheran tone. In the last

---

[7] Hunt, *Religious Thought in England*, III, 373, 374.
[8] See *supra*, 93 (Andrewes' discussion with Toby Mathew).

analysis his thought is eclectic, and in the circumstances in which we are engaged at the moment, that means simply that his teaching is Anglican, for it was of the essence of Anglicanism in his day that it chose to retain enough of the full Roman Catholic doctrine to resemble the old Church, yet rejected enough to distinguish itself therefrom; and in addition, particularly as a result of mid-sixteenth-century influence (Cranmer, the Marian exiles, and so forth), it nourished in its bosom two doctrinal strains of which one, the German, moderately affected its teaching, whereas the other, the French or the Genevan, nearly destroyed it altogether and did leave upon it the permanent mark which is the division between the High and the Low Church.

Andrewes' dislike for Calvinist predestination broke through in his writings occasionally. He taught that we are to adore, and not to inquire curiously into the divine secret of reprobation and election.[9] No man should "peremptorily" presume himself predestined. No man is predestined to do evil.[10] We should think well of God, accept whatever He is pleased to send us, thankfully if it be good, patiently, if it be otherwise. But in no case should we entertain of Him "that opinion, for which they cannot but love Him the worse, if as of a tyrant sentencing men to death only for his pleasure, before they have offended him at all."[11] One last instance seems to show how keenly Bishop Andrewes realized the implications of the Calvinist theory of

---

[9] *Works*, V, Sermon on Prayer XI, 398. See *Works*, III, Easter Sermon XV, 32: "Yet are there in the world that make but a shallow of this great deep, they have sounded it to the bottom. God's secret decrees they have them at their fingers' ends, and can tell you the number and the order of them just, with 1, 2, 3, 4, 5. Men that sure must have been in God's cabinet, above the third heaven, where St. Paul never came."

[10] *Works*, XI, *Two Answers to Cardinall Perron*, 30. "Give me any religion," he once declared, than one which makes God the author of sin (*Works*, II, Easter Sermon X, 353).

[11] *Works*, I, Nativity Sermon XIII, 230.

predestination as it gradually came to be taught; we see, he says in a lenten sermon,

> that these "good things" which after the tax of the world are counted, and in a manner styled, the only good things, and in the deceitful balance of this world weigh down "Abraham's bosom," be not ever demonstrative signs of God's special liking; nor they, *ipso facto*, highest in His favour that receive them in greatest measure; nor peradventure, as Christ saith, so highly accounted of in Heaven as they be on earth.[12]

If Andrewes adopted the idea of the imputation of Christ's merits in the process of justification, he drew a line between his own doctrine and Lutheranism when he spoke of good works. He denied them any meritorious value, yet, he insisted on their necessity for salvation.

From Andrewes' comments on the Lambeth Articles and in the *Censura censurae D. Barreti de certitudine salutis,* from his constant emphasis on good works, as well as from specific pronouncements in the sermons regarding predestination, it is quite clear that he rejected a principal Calvinist dogma; from his devotion to the episcopacy and the liturgy it is equally clear that he rejected Calvinist Church structure; and in his balanced and very sensible asceticism one recognizes a rejection of Calvinist discipline. Coupled with the large amount of doctrine and liturgical practice he retained from traditional Christianity, and the minimal Lutheran influence on his work, such rejections leave us with no other choice than to call Bishop Andrewes an Anglo-Catholic. It would be unfair to demand of Andrewes perfect consistency in all his teaching: first, because Anglican thought was then in a fluid state, and secondly, because of the

---

12 *Works,* II, Lenten Sermon V, 86. This sermon was preached March 5, 1595. The passage deals with a false admiration of earthly riches, and Andrewes may not have had Calvinism in mind, but the position he adopts is quite antithetical to the teaching that God favors the elect with temporal blessings which was associated with Calvinism.

impossibility of constructing a thoroughly consistent doctrine out of elements which were so contradictory as Roman Catholicism, Lutheranism, and Calvinism. Elizabeth had sought a not-too-definite and an embracive theology. Her theologians had to comply; and while Lancelot Andrewes did not admire compromise, the very bases upon which he had to construct his theological teaching, the Thirty-nine Articles, are not entirely free of its elements.

In four ways Bishop Andrewes contributed to the formation of Anglican thought: he enriched and clarified its theology with his solid scriptural and homiletic preaching, he strove to establish within it a moral basis for society and the solution of its problems, he steered it into more traditional courses than those it might ultimately have followed had Puritanism established itself successfully in the formative days of Anglicanism, and by the holiness and integrity of his own life he demonstrated that it had a vitality of high spiritual worth. He failed, however, to make an important, effective, or even convincing contribution to political thought. Neither a profound theorist like Hooker nor a man of action like Laud, in his strengths and in his weaknesses Lancelot Andrewes personified perhaps better than either the new phenomenon that was Anglicanism.

Lancelot Andrewes has not lived in his sermons. They died almost with the man himself. Their style, atrocious by modern standards, has entombed a great body of edifying doctrine so deeply in a "dreary cemetery of literature" that it remains, not a vital force in religious thought, but a cold memorial to the early struggles and growth of the Anglican Church. If men will not read him today for inspiration, they can yet discover in Bishop Andrewes a splendid witness to the tremendous spiritual and intellectual struggle through which the English Church labored to establish itself with a personality and character entirely its own, in separation from Rome.

The following bibliography is somewhat limited for two reasons: the expository nature of the study necessitated concentration on the writings of Andrewes himself, and very little work has ever been done on the substance of Andrewes' thought. The likely repositories of Andrean material, Pembroke College and the University Library, Cambridge; the Bodleian Library, Oxford; the British Museum; the episcopal archives of Chichester, Ely, and Winchester, for one reason or another proved disappointing. What manuscript material did come to light was scattered and generally irrelevant to the main problem of the study. It was, in fact, the dearth of Andrean studies which determined the writer first to investigate Andrewes and then to limit this paper to the exposition of his thought as it is contained in the sermons.

Except for the controversial works Andrewes himself set scarcely anything into print. Most of the published works appeared shortly after his death, some of which were edited more than once during the seventeenth century. For the men of the rationalistic eighteenth century Andrewes apparently had little appeal, but the temper which stirred the Oxford Movement of the nineteenth discovered in him a kindred spirit, as the Anglo-Catholic edition of the *Works* and numerous editions and translations of the *Preces Privatae* testify. As late as the mid-twentieth century these fine devotional writings continue to appear in reprints or in translation.

1. Guides

Attwood, R. *Custodes.*
A manuscript catalogue in the Treasure Room of Pembroke College, Cambridge. The first item is a brief biographical sketch of Andrewes.

[Bernard, Edward.] *Catalogi librorum manuscriptorum Angliae et Hiberniae in unum collecti, cum indice alphabetico.* Oxoniae, 1697.

Bickley, Francis, editor. *Guide to the Reports of the Royal Commission on Historical Manuscripts, 1870-1911.* Part II, Index of Persons, First Section: A-Lever. London, 1935.

Biographica Pembrochiana (A-D).
A filing box in the library of Pembroke College, Cambridge; contains an envelope with several miscellany on Andrewes.

Coxe, Henricus O. *Catalogus codicum mss. qui in collegiis aulisque Oxoniensibus hodie adservantur.* 2 vols. Oxonii, 1852.

Davies, Godfrey, editor. *Bibliography of British History, Stuart Period, 1603-1714.* Oxford, 1928.

Deeds, Cecil, compiler. *Report on the Muniments of the Bishopric of Winchester Preserved in the Consistory Court in Winchester Cathedral: Including a Subject-Index to Bishop John de Pontissaro's Register.* Winchester, 1912.

Gibbons, A. *Ely Episcopal Records. A Calendar and Concise View of the Episcopal Records Preserved in the Muniment Room of the Palace at Ely.* Lincoln, 1891.

James, Montague Rhodes. *A Descriptive Catalogue of the Manuscripts in the Library of Pembroke College, Cambridge.* Cambridge, 1905.
The searcher for manuscript material in England will rely heavily on the numerous catalogues drawn up by James.

Read, Conyers, editor. *Bibliography of British History, Tudor Period, 1485-1603.* Oxford, 1933.

2. Primary Sources

A. MANUSCRIPTS

British Museum:

Additional MSS., [12, 222]. Original accounts of the churchwardens of the parish of St. Giles, Cripplegate, from 11 May, 1570, to 18 May, 1580, and from 27 May, 1596, to 2 June, 1608.

Additional MSS., 28, 571. Extracts from the Fathers on the sign of the Cross, 1605, f. 201.

Harleian MSS., 6616, art. 1. Libellus in 8vo. scriptus et continens Expositionem Evangelii S. Lucae a cap. nono. Ab. Episc. Andrewes, et propriâ manu descriptus, ut videtur.

Harleian MSS., 6617-6619. In 8° Tres Tomi eadem manu scripti, in
Anni 1608, 1612, et 1619.

Harleian MSS., 6620. Libellus eadem manu scriptus, et continens,
1. Fragmentum notarum in Psalmos; novem foliis. 2. Notas in
Epistolam ad Hebraeos inceptas, A.D. 1586, Apr. 10.

The five items listed above were noticed in the Preface of *Works*,
XI, iii. They total some seventeen or eighteen hundred pages of
closely packed writing. A comparison of Andrewes' development
of several Scripture texts in the sermons with his development of
the same texts in these notes revealed no dependence of one upon
the other, nor any similarity in treatment.

Lansdowne MSS., ccxxii, art. 2, f. 4. Bishop Andrewes's method observed in his sermons.

Sloane MSS., 118. Collection of his [Andrewes'] letters and papers.

This collection consists chiefly of letters of thanks or petition addressed to Andrewes when he was bishop of Winchester.

Stowe MSS., 76. [Ley, Roger.] Gesta Britannica praesertim Anglorum
adjectis aliquot observationibus maxime in ijs quae ad Ecclesiam
a temporibus retroactis ad A.D. MDCXLVIII spectant, 1664, ff.
246v-248.

A sympathetic biographical notice of Andrewes.

Bodleian Library, Oxford:

Additional MSS., C, 279, f. 95. Autograph letter of Nicholas Fuller to
the Bishop of Winchester [Andrewes], from Allington, August 17,
1622.

Rawlinson MSS., B, 158, ff. 144-45. [Story of Andrewes' meeting with
Nicholas Fuller.]

B. PRINTED WORKS—A SELECTED LIST

*An Answer to the XX. Chapter of the Fifth Booke of Cardinall
Perron's Reply.* London, 1629.

'Αποσπασμάτια *Sacra; or a Collection of Posthumous and Orphan
Lectures, Delivered at St. Paul's and St. Giles His Church.* London.
1657.

*Articles To Be Enquired of by the Church-Wardens and Sworne-Men in
the Primary Visitation of . . . Lancelot, Lord Bishop of Wintor
. . . Anno 1619.* London, 1619.

Articles To Be Enquired of by the Churchwardens and Sworne-Men, in the Triennial Visitation of . . . Lancelot Lord Bishop of Winton . . . Anno 1625. London, 1625.

Concio ad clerum in synodo provinciali Cantuariensis provinciae ad D. Pauli. Die XX° Februarij. A.D. *MDXCIII.* Londini, 1629.

De decimis, theologica determinatio . . . Londini, 1629.
This appeared in translation: *Of the Right of Tithes . . .* London, 1647.

Of Episcopacy. Three Epistles of Peter Moulin Doctor and Professor of Divinity. Answered by . . . Lancelot Andrews, Late Lord Bishop of Winchester. Translated for the Benefit of the Publike. no place, 1647.

The Form of Consecration of a Church or Chappel, and of the Place of Christian Buriall. London, 1659.

A Learned Discourse of Ceremonies Retained and Used in Christian Churches. [Edward Leigh, editor.] London, 1653.

A Manual of Directions for the Sick. With Many Sweet Meditations and Devotions of . . . Lancelot Andrewes . . . To Which Are Added Praiers for the Morning, Evening, and H. Communion. R[ichard] D[rake], translator. London, 1648.

A Manual of the Private Devotions and Meditations of . . . Lancelot Andrews . . . R[ichard] D[rake], translator. London, 1648.

XCVI. Sermons by the Right Honorable and Reverend Father in God, Lancelot Andrewes, Late Lord Bishop of Winchester. London, 1629.

A Pattern of Catechistical Doctrine. Wherein Many Profitable Questions Touching Christian Religion Are Handled, and the Whole Decalogue Succinctly and Judiciously Expounded. London, 1641.
First published in 1630.

The Private Devotions of . . . Lancelot Andrewes. London, 1647.

Quaestionis, nunquid per ius divinum, magistratui liceat a reo iusiurandum exigere? Et id, quatenus ac quousque liceat? Theologica determinatio . . . Londini, 1629.

Responsio ad apologiam cardinalis Bellarmini, quam nuper edidit contra praefationem monitoriam . . . Iacobi . . . regis . . . omnibus Christianis monarchis, principibus, atque ordinibus inscriptam. Londini, 1610.

Reverendi in Christo patris, Lanceloti, episcopi Wintoniensis, opuscula quaedam posthuma. Londini, 1629.

Reverendi in Christo patris Lanceloti episcopi Wintoniensis responsiones ad Petri Molinaei epistolas tres, una cum Molinaei epistolis. Londini, 1629.

Rev. patris Lanc. Andrews episc. Winton, preces privatae Graecè & Latinè. Oxonii, 1675.

Sacrilege a Snare . . . [Concio ad clerum pro gradu doctoris, &c.]. London, 1646.

Scala Coeli. Nineteene Sermons Concerning Prayer. London, 1611.

Seven Sermons on, the Wonderfull Combate (for Gods Glorie, and Mans Salvation) betweene Christ and Sathan . . . London, 1627.

A Speech Delivered in the Starr-Chamber against the Two Iudaicall Opinions of Mr. Traske . . . London, 1629.

A Speech Delivered in the Starr-Chamber, Concerning Vowes, in the Countesse of Shrewsburies Case . . . London, 1629.

Stricturae: or, A Briefe Answer to the XVIII Chapter of the First Booke of Cardinall Perron's Reply . . . London, 1629.

A Summarie View of the Government Both of the Old and New Testament: Whereby the Episcopall Government of Christ's Church Is Vindicated: Out of the Rude Draughts of Lancelot Andrewes . . . Oxford, 1641.

Tortura Torti: sive; ad Matthaei Torti librum responsio, qui nuper editus contra apologiam . . . Jacobi . . . regis, pro iuramento fidelitatis. Londini, 1609.

Two Answers to Cardinall Perron . . . London, 1629.

De usuris, theologica determinatio . . . Londini, 1629.

The Wonderfull Combate betweene Christ and Satan in Seven Sermons. London, 1592.

The Works of Lancelot Andrewes, Sometime Bishop of Winchester. [J. P. Wilson and James Bliss, editors.] 11 vols., in *Library of Anglo-Catholic Theology.* Oxford, 1841-1854.

All quotations from Andrewes' writings are taken from this edition except where otherwise noted. The *Works* include the following titles which are not listed above:

Bishop Andrewes' Form of Consecration of a Church and Churchyard. Works, VI, 307-33.

Bishop Andrewes' Judgment of the Lambeth Articles. Works, VI, 287-300.

Censura censurae D. Barreti de certitudine salutis. Works, VI, 301-05.

A Coppie of the Forme Used by the Lo: Bishop of Elye in Consecrating the Newe Church Plate of the Cathedrall Church of Worcʳ. Works, XI, 159-63.

A Discourse Written . . . against Second Marriage, after Sentence of Divorce with a Former Match, the Party Then Living. In Anno 1601. Works, XI, 106-10.

The Manner of Induction Prescribed by . . . Lancelot Andrewes . . . Works, XI, 164.

Notes on the Book of Common Prayer. Works, XI, 141-58.

3. Secondary Works

Allen, J. W. *English Political Thought 1603-1660. I, 1603-1664.* London, 1938. ·

Andrewes, Gerrard Thomas. *Bishop Lancelot Andrewes and His Influence on the Church.* Winchester, 1906.

Arnott, Felix R. "Anglicanism in the Seventeenth Century." In Paul Elmer More and Frank Leslie Cross, editors, *Anglicanism, the Thought and Practice of the Church of England, Illustrated from the Religious Literature of the Seventeenth Century.* London, 1935. One of two introductory essays to the above volume; a very satisfactory survey.

Attwater, Aubrey. *Pembroke College, Cambridge: A Short History.* S. C. Roberts, editor. Cambridge, 1936. Attwater gathered a great deal of material for a substantial history of the college, but died before completing the work. His notes are in the keeping of Sir Ellis H. Minns, president of Pembroke, and are not available for consultation. Judging from the references to Andrewes in the volume listed, these notes probably contain a fair amount of Andrean material. Attwater included no critical apparatus in the *Short History.*

Blunt, J. H. *The Reformation of the Church of England, Its History, Principles, and Results,* new edition. London, 1896, II (1547-1662).

Bray, William, editor. *Memoirs Illustrative of the Life and Writings of John Evelyn. . . . Comprising His Diary, from the Year 1641 to 1705-6 . . .* New York, 1870.

Brightman, F. E., translator. *The Preces Privatae of Lancelot Andrewes* . . . London, 1903.

   Definitive on the *Preces.*

Brodrick, James, S.J., *The Life and Work of Blessed Robert Francis Cardinal Bellarmine, S.J. 1541-1621.* 2 vols., New York, 1928.

   Volume II contains a good discussion of the controversy on the Oath of Allegiance.

Church, Richard W. "Lancelot Andrewes." In Alfred Barry, editor, *Masters in English Theology.* New York, 1877.

   A rhetorical and enthusiastic eulogy of Anglicanism with very little of Andrewes in it.

Davies, Godfrey. *The Early Stuarts 1603-1660.* In G. N. Clark, editor, *The Oxford History of England.* Oxford, 1937.

Dix, Dom Gregory. *The Shape of the Liturgy,* second edition. Westminster, 1947.

   A first-class study.

Dugmore, C. W. *Eucharistic Doctrine in England from Hooker to Waterland.* London, 1942.

Eliot, T. S. *For Lancelot Andrewes, Essays on Style and Order.* New York, 1929.

Figgis, John Neville. *The Divine Right of Kings,* second edition. Cambridge, 1922.

Frere, Walter Howard. *The English Church in the Reigns of Elizabeth and James I. (1558-1625).* In W. R. W. Stephens and William Hunt, editors, *A History of the English Church.* 8 vols., London, 1901-1910.

———— *Lancelot Andrewes as a Representative of Anglican Principles.* London, 1899.

Gardiner, Samuel R. *History of England from the Accession of James I. to the Outbreak of the Civil War 1603-1642.* 10 vols., London, 1899.

Harwood, Gina and Hopkinson, Arthur W., editors. *The Mantle of Prayer, A Book of English Devotions,* new edition. London, 1931.

Higham, Florence. *Lancelot Andrewes.* New York, [1952].

Hook, Walter and Stephens, W. R. W., editors. *A Church Dictionary: a Practical Manual of Reference for Clergymen and Students,* fifteenth edition. London, 1896.

Hunt, John. *Religious Thought in England from the Reformation to the End of Last Century. A Contribution to the History of Theology.* 3 vols., London, 1870-1873.

Hunt's treatment of Andrewes is inspired by a too-strongly Low Church viewpoint.

Isaacson, Henry. *An Exact Narration of the Life and Death of . . . Lancelot Andrewes, Late Bishop of Winchester . . .* London, 1650.

Jordan, W. K. *The Development of Religious Toleration in England from the Accession of James I to the Convention of the Long Parliament (1603-1640).* Cambridge, Massachusetts, 1936.

Judson, Margaret Atwood. *The Crisis of the Constitution: An Essay in Constitutional and Political Thought in England, 1603-1645.* New Brunswick, 1949.

Keble, John, editor. *The Works of That Learned and Judicious Divine, Mr. Richard Hooker: with an Account of His Life and Death, by Isaac Walton,* second edition. 3 vols., Oxford, 1841.

Leslie, Shane. *The Oxford Movement 1833 to 1933.* London, 1933.

Macleane, Douglas. *Lancelot Andrewes and the Reaction.* London, 1910.

Mathew, A. H., editor. *A True Historical Relation of the Conversion of Sir Tobie Matthew to the Holy Catholic Faith; with the Antecedents and Consequences Thereof. Edited, and now published for the first time, with a preface, by his kinsman, A. H. Mathew.* London, 1904.

Mathew, David. *The Jacobean Age.* London, 1938.

Messenger, Ernest C. *The Reformation, the Mass, and the Priesthood.* 2 vols., London, 1937.

Mitchell, W. Fraser. *English Pulpit Oratory from Andrewes to Tillotson, a Study of Its Literary Aspects.* London, 1932.

More, Paul Elmer. "The Spirit of Anglicanism." In Paul Elmer More and Frank Leslie Cross, editors, *Anglicanism, the Thought and Practice of the Church of England . . . of the Seventeenth Century.* London, 1935.

More, Paul Elmer and Cross, Frank Leslie, editors. *Anglicanism, the Thought and Practice of the Church of England, Illustrated from the Religious Literature of the Seventeenth Century.* London, 1935.

Mullinger, James Bass. *The University of Cambridge from the Royal Injunctions of 1535 to the Accession of Charles the First*. Cambridge, 1884.

North, J. H. *The Classic Preachers of the English Church*. London, 1878.

Ottley, Robert L. *Lancelot Andrewes*. Boston, 1894.

Overton, John Henry. "Lancelot Andrewes." In Leslie Stephen and Sidney Lee, editors, *Dictionary of National Biography* (Oxford, 1921-1922), I, 401-05.

Pastor, Ludwig von. *The History of the Popes from the Close of the Middle Ages*. Ralph Francis Kerr, editor. London, 1930.

The Political Works of James I. Reprinted from the Edition of 1616 with an Introduction by Charles Howard McIlwain (*Harvard Political Classics*, I). Cambridge, Massachusetts, 1918.

Pollen, John Hungerford, S.J. *The English Catholics in the Reign of Queen Elizabeth: A Study of Their Politics, Civil Life and Government* . . . London, 1920.

Ross Williamson, Hugh. *Four Stuart Portraits*. London, 1949.

Russell, Arthur T. *Memoirs of the Life and Works of the Right Honorable and Right Rev. Father in God Lancelot Andrewes, D.D., Lord Bishop of Winchester*. London, 1863.

Ryan, John K. *The Reputation of St. Thomas Aquinas among English Protestant Thinkers of the Seventeenth Century*. Washington, 1948.

Swete, H. B. *Two Cambridge Divines of the Seventeenth Century*. London, 1913.

Trevor-Roper, H. R. *Archbishop Laud 1573-1645*. London, 1940.

Tulloch, John. *Rational Theology and Christian Philosophy in England in the Seventeenth Century*. 2 vols., Edinburgh, 1872.

Usher, Roland G. *The Reconstruction of the English Church*. 2 vols., New York, 1910.

Venables, Edmund, editor. *The Private Devotions of Lancelot Andrewes, D.D., Successively Lord Bishop of Chichester, Ely, and Winchester*, revised and new edition. London, 1883.

Whyte, Alexander. *Lancelot Andrewes and His Private Devotions; a Biography, a Transcript, and an Interpretation*. Edinburgh, 1896.

Wood, Lady Mary. *The Story of a Saintly Bishop's Life; Lancelot Andrewes, Bishop of Winchester, 1555-1626*. London, 1898.

4. Periodical Literature

Bayfield-Roberts, G. "Lancelot Andrewes." *Revue Anglo-Romaine*, III (1896), 677-88; 731-45.

Both articles are sympathetic studies of Andrewes' work.

Coats, R. H. "Lancelot Andrewes and John Bunyan. A Study in Devotion." *Hibbert Journal* (1910-1911), 838-50.

Andrewes and Bunyan compared as examples of two types of piety in the Anglican Church, Andrewes representing the quiet and restrained, Bunyan the intense and tumultuous.

Davies, Godfrey. "English Political Sermons." *Huntington Library Quarterly*, III (1939-1940), 1-22.

A good essay on the use of the pulpit for the expression of political ideas, but fails to mention Andrewes.

[Mozley, J. B.] "Sermons of Launcelot Andrewes, Sometime Lord Bishop of Winchester." *British Critic, and Quarterly Theological Review*, XXXI (1842), 169-205.

Very sympathetic; a good study of Andrewes' sermon style.

Nairne, A. "Lancelot Andrewes." *Revue Internationale de Théologie*, XXVIᵉ Livraison (Avril-Juin, 1899), 327-47.

A study of Andrewes' contribution to the Anglican Church: the ordering of the "firm, broad principles of Anglican theology," 330.

"Russell's Life of Bishop Andrewes." *Christian Observer*, new series LX (1860), 846-56.

Critical of Russell's *Life* and at the same time of Andrewes' theology, which the reviewer considered too traditional.

"Some Brief Notices Respecting Bishop Andrewes." *Christian Observer*, XV (1816), 133-38.

Depends heavily on Isaacson.

Willson, David Harris. "James I and His Literary Assistants." *Huntington Library Quarterly*, VIII (1944-1945), 35-37.

DATE

N

Jews 1?
35-
Reaction. 45-
Aegean Sea. 48